AMERICAN CULTURE

AMERICAN CULTURE

Myth and Reality
of a Culture of Diversity

Larry L. Naylor

BERGIN & GARVEY
Westport, Connecticut • London

Library of Congress Cataloging-in-Publication Data

Naylor, Larry L.
   American culture : myth and reality of a culture of diversity /
Larry L. Naylor.
      p.   cm.
   Includes bibliographical references and index.
   ISBN 0–89789–541–X (alk. paper).—ISBN 0–89789–542–8 (pbk. :
alk. paper)
   1. United States—Civilization—1970–   2. Pluralism (Social
sciences)—United States—History—20th century.   3. United States—
Ethnic relations.   4. United States—Race relations.   I. Title.
E169.12.N387   1998
306′.0973—dc21   97–31519

British Library Cataloguing in Publication Data is available.

Library of Congress Catalog Card Number: 97–31519
ISBN: 0–89789–541–X
      0–89789–542–8 (pbk).

First published in 1998

Bergin & Garvey, 88 Post Road West, Westport, CT 06881
An imprint of Greenwood Publishing Group, Inc.

Printed in the United States of America

The paper used in this book complies with the
Permanent Paper Standard issued by the National
Information Standards Organization (Z39.48–1984).

10 9 8 7 6 5 4 3 2 1

CONTENTS

PREFACE

This volume concentrates on the study, analysis, and discussion of the United States and its culture. It is primarily designed for people seeking a greater awareness and understanding of this culture and its people. The culture of the United States is as rich and deep as any other, in some cases just as bizarre and irrational as other cultures may appear to many Americans. In actual fact, American culture is filled with the same ritual and magic, family and kinship, reciprocity and gift-giving customs, curing rituals, myths and legends, supernaturalism and ghosts, and many other behaviors and beliefs common to other cultures in the world. While such topics might seem strange to most Americans, the validity of looking at American culture cannot be questioned. For most people, including Americans, culture is an unconscious, yet very significant thing in their lives. It lies at the heart of everything they are, think and do. But, the magnitude of examining the American culture is staggering, for this society is an extremely complex one, perhaps the most complex in the modern world. The United States is a heavily populated, nation-state cultural group, and diversity is perhaps its chief characteristic. Traditionally, anthropologists have focused on other types of societies and cultures, the "traditional" small-scale ones that often appear exotic in the eyes of Americans. Focusing on such groups, anthropologists have provided numerous case materials on the many different culture patterns humans have created. Part of this effort was designed to identify the differences and similarities among them, and part of it was based on the belief that in looking at others, people are lead to a little better understanding of themselves. This ethnographic look at Americans, albeit a brief one, is directed specifically at American culture using the same categories and understandings that have been used so fruitfully in the study of other cultures. It is primarily designed to help Americans develop a more conscious understanding of themselves. But it can be of immense value to others attempting to gain some better understanding of this culture as well. The measure of success in achieving this goal will be reflected in the knowledge the reader gains about Americans and American culture, in the dialogue generated, and in what people learn about being human in the process—the American variety.

The term *American* is the common designation for citizens of the United States, and *America* is a well established and utilized synonym for the United States (Naylor 1997). Both terms go far back in U. S. history. Although others would also stake some claim to that identification, in this volume the term is used strictly with reference to those holding citizenship in the United States. Many people in South America, Central America, and the Caribbean Islands, as well as immigrants to the United States from these areas, also use the term *American* to identify themselves and are sensitive to its use with only citizens of the United States. This particular tendency appears to be related to the geographical designations used in the New World (North America, Central America, and South America). On the other hand, other peoples of the New World, for example, Canada, generally do not refer to themselves as *Americans*. They refer to themselves by virtue of their country of origin—Canadians. The same can be said for people of South American, Central America, and the Caribbean. People from these areas identify themselves with reference to their country of origin, as the Canadians prefer to do. The people of Mexico traditionally identify themselves as Mexicans. The people of Colombia identify themselves as Colombians. The people of Peru identify themselves as Peruvians. The same can be said for people of every nation throughout South and Central America as well as the Caribbean. It is rare that a person from any of these particular areas will first identify themselves as an *American*. It is in this same sense that *America* and *American* are used throughout this volume. Were this not done, we would be left with no particular referent or identifier for the people of the United States. *United Statesians* is not likely to ever make it in popular usage. The world has come to know Americans and America. The people of the United States refer to themselves as Americans and their country is known to them as both the United States and America.

Americans today face a multitude of questions and problems associated with culture, cultural diversity, multiculturalism, racism, cultural sensitivity, and political correctness. More than this, Americans are really having to think about who they are, what they are doing, want to do or should be doing—comparing what they believe and do with what others believe and do, both at home and abroad. As an anthropologist, I have taught many courses aimed at introducing college students to anthropology as a discipline and what it has to teach them about the human experience and condition. Because culture is such an important part of what it means to be human, I have always spent a considerable amount of time on the concept. The many ethnographies (cultural descriptions) compiled by countless anthropologists over a century and a half prove invaluable in conveying to students just what culture means to humans and the role it plays in the human experience. Using descriptions of other cultures, frequently very different from what students are familiar, is an effective teaching technique. Americans, as with people in other cultural groupings, tend to be quite unaware of others, but they are also largely unaware (unconscious) about their own culture—a reflection of the fact that most people do not have to think about their cultures. They simply live it as they have been taught. Using descriptions of other cultures in anthropology courses forces students to think consciously about their own way of believing or doing things in an attempt to make sense out of what they see others doing. It does not take long to recognize the limited and sometimes skewed understanding most American students have about their own culture. Most times, this does not necessarily bother me, for my goal is to further the development of some understanding of culture and its role in human life. I do not especially dwell on the fact that the students do not have a good working knowledge of their own culture. I merely think it interesting and use that reality to being the subject matter into their everyday lives—make it relevant and real for them by comparing what they do and think with what others do and think. That I brought them somewhat closer to what they unconsciously knew seemed to suffice—my goal was not to teach them about American culture, but about culture in general or aspects of it, and this did not change until I undertook a course specifically focused on American culture and society. It was during that time that I first began to suspect the use of norms (what applies to most Americans) to characterize Americans and the real role of diversity in that culture.

The increased attention to culture, cultural diversity, and multiculturalism in recent years and creating a course for beginning college students on the subject of diversity changed my focus substantially. Finding no comprehensive text I could use to teach about the real American diversity led me to edit a collection of readings on the different aspects of diversity in the United States (Naylor 1997). Most texts on the diversity topic focus on general categories of diversity (ethnic, gender, racial) that overgeneralize and stereotype people, a practice which obscures more than it clarifies. When asked about diversity, most American students (and probably most everyone else) immediately conjure up the racial (black and white predominantly) and ethnic (Asian and Hispanic) cultural groups. Social categories such as these seemed to ignore a great many other groups that also contribute to the diversity of America. Beyond these generally recognized groupings (obvious ones for most Americans), the actual cultural groups of America are either lost or relegated to a low level of importance. While there is little doubt that social categories contribute significantly to the problems of diversity, it is with cultural groupings that the problems really generate. This led me to consider the real cultural diversity that forms that pattern we understand as American culture. But this activity forced me to once again consider the problem of cultural awareness among American students and others who seemingly have some strange notions about America. After an extensive search for materials on the topic of American culture, the need for a generally understandable and readable volume on the topic seemed apparent. This kind of volume would be quite different from that designed for the scholar or those who are just trying to intellectually understand that culture. On the one hand, it had to be one devoid of the discipline jargon that to the nonacademic simply makes the obscure even more obscure and largely boring. On the other hand, any volume I created had to be more than generalizations that in reality apply to no individual or group. We have had about all we can stand of the average this and that and the proliferation of the "norms." The use of averages is not unlike the case of Standard Average American English—taught to everyone, actually spoken by no one. I had set the trap and as could be expected, I got caught. If there was going to be such a text, I would have to give it a try. It had to be clear to on-the-street Americans, short enough that it did not risk boredom, but not so abbreviated as to oversimplify to uselessness. Based on my review of the literature, this would be no small task.

After reviewing a substantial number of outstanding works on American culture (from my viewpoint as an anthropologist), the task seemed even more imposing. Most studies of American culture have focused on small segments of it, on groups that for some reason might be considered marginal, unique or perhaps exotic. The exercise did provide me with a more complete understanding of the real cultural diversity in America, but not much on the *American culture*. What I had learned about the real cultural diversity of the United States caused me to suspect that the culture concept as traditionally applied by anthropologists might not be so well suited to the evolving complex cultures of modern civilizations or nation-states (even the developing global culture that some scholars now suggest). I even began to question the scholarly treatments of the American culture based on values or shared ideas that have become so popular in recent years. The focus of such studies has always revolved around the "norms," or what most Americans tend to believe and to do. After looking at previous attempts to undertake the task of describing American culture, attempts that made some real contributions to the anthropological study of American culture, I was even more unsure. After all, despite my extensive training and experience as an anthropologist, who am I to suggest that American culture is this or that. But therein was my answer—because I am an American and versed in what culture is and the role it plays in people's lives, who better to give it a try. Not that what I have to say is "truth" or even "accurate" by everyone's standards. I am a native and therefore already biased in my views. In many ways, this has to be viewed as a "no win" kind of circumstance. But what I can say, based on my own experiences and those of others who have added to my understanding and awareness of American culture, can add to better understanding and perhaps help people build an increased awareness as to what America and Americans are all about. Perhaps it will do no more than stimulate debate or get people to think (if only to respond to what they might disagree), but there is great value in that alone. Brevity alone will mean the volume is to serve to generate discussion, to instigate interest, and generate the drive to learn more. In the final analysis of what I do, the question will be whether or not people have a little better idea of American culture, the cultural groups to which they affiliate and from which they get most of their ideas and behaviors, and those things they share with every other American.

Life patterns of a complex society can probably not be covered in a single volume. The complexity introduced to human culture (particularly nation-states) by civilizations with their fragmentations, specializations, stratifications, and large populations has made this so. In the case of the United States, a shared culture is hard to find, let alone describe, for this nation-state spans a continent with virtually every type of natural environments and a population that reflects, to some degree, people from the entire world. At the very least, American culture becomes like the puzzle. Fitting together the bits and pieces will ultimately produce a picture. But in this picture, the American population displays a remarkable diversity. In some areas the American people are alike, and even its groups resemble each other. In other areas, groups and individuals are unique. While it is apparently true that United States is a culture of diversity, it is equally true that U.S. citizens do feel a bond with each other, despite any other differences they may well recognize, and they do display an amazing degree of actual conformity. In discussing the diversity or the conformity of Americans, a certain amount of generalizing must occur and I must be guilty of this to some degree. There are exceptions to all generalizations. Within such a diverse group as found in America, idiosyncratic beliefs and behaviors abound. Another difficulty comes with trying to see the culture as others (non-Americans) see it and maintaining an objectivity that is most difficult anytime someone looks at their own culture. Earlier studies focused on relatively exotic nooks and crannies, emphasizing the differences as opposed to similarities of different groups. Americans are just like most other people, they see themselves and their culture as "natural"—simply the way things are. The challenge is to convey "the way things are" in an easily understandable form and separate the myth from the reality.

I am convinced that an *American culture* does exist. Americans are certainly convinced that it does, and most other people throughout the world also believe that it exists. It is evidenced in the pride the people of the United States take in being Americans, it draws immigrants to America in droves, and it is presented as a standard by which other nations and peoples judge themselves. The core of that culture is probably best represented in what we nominally call *mainstream culture*, itself more of an ideal than a reality, but the American mainstream culture reflects certain orienting ideas shared by all Americans, is reflected in the behavior of these people, is reflected in their material culture, and in the social and organizational systems they have created and within which all the people of the United States are expected to function. *Mainstream American culture* is what all the members of the culture believe exists (except the truly idiosyncratic) and strive to become part of, irrespective of their origins or other cultures with which they might identify. It represents the standard by which they will judge themselves and be judged by others. It is the core of *America* and *American*—the ideal that provides the order, unity, and cohesiveness essential for survival, irrespective of the cultural diversity that also characterizes the United States. Gaining a better understanding of culture theoretically is not the same thing as gaining a better understanding of it on an everyday basis. Awareness means a better grasp of its everyday workings and how the pieces of that American culture fit together, for indeed they do. This leads to behavioral consequences that contribute to its continuing to operate and survive, despite the extensive diversity that can also threaten to tear it apart and bring it down.

Chapter 1 introduces the reader to the concept of culture as it applies to the United States, a complex nation-state. It discusses the complex nature of culture and the cultures that make up the complex nation-state and makes for its diversity—the multiculturalism that characterizes such societies and their cultures. This chapter also discusses the important distinctions between ideal, real, and construct versions of culture that must be understood if one is going to gain any real understanding of a people and their culture—the many culture(s) in the case of a complex society such as the United States. This chapter is foundational and absolutely necessary given the fact that most Americans do not have a good grasp of what culture is, how it relates to them, or the role culture or culture(s) play in their lives. In Chapter 2 the context and setting of America is discussed, and a statistical profile, based on the census data, of the American people is presented. As both geography and history have combined together to produce the diversity and the conformity that has come to characterize the United States and its culture(s), these are briefly discussed in this chapter as well. In Chapter 3 American culture is characterized using its orienting ideas and values, along with some other ideas and assumptions Americans live by. The observations of Americans by Americans and those made by members of other cultures are also discussed. An argument is put forth that an American culture does indeed exist in the shared ideas of all Americans and in their shared behavior patterns. Chapter 4 focuses on American social structure, on its social groupings that establish the social relations among Americans. In this chapter are presented discussions of such things as the sex, mating and marriage practices of Americans, the family structure, and the stratification with which they live. These discussions will provide the reader with a basic understanding social claims and obligations (social relations and interactions) among Americans. The chapter will also introduce the reader to additional kinds of social groups that have made social structure more complicated in the context of the modern nation-state and difficult to understand. Chapter 5 provides a selective discussion of some of the organization of American culture, or how it is organized to get the things done that must be done as part of its survival: how the culture is transmitted and acquired from one generation to another (socialization and education); its system for establishing and maintaining social order; how it manages with its resources to meet the people's needs and wants; its religious system(s); ceremonial cycle; and, its focus on leisure activities. Chapter 6 focuses on the main theme of American culture—its cultural diversity, particularly with regard to the constituent groupings (culture groups) that come together to help make up and define the complex society and culture of the United States (America). The chapter outlines important distinctions between the social groups or categories and the real cultural groups (constituent cultural groups) of Americans that must be understood if one hopes to understand this complex society. Specific attention is directed at the different types of social and cultural groupings of America, the things that created and impacted them, what guides or determines their interactions with each other, what helps form their perceptions of their circumstances, and what has laid the foundations for the conflicts and competition among them.

ONE
THE IDEA OF CULTURE

When Americans are asked about their culture or culture in general, they generally do not have very solid responses. To be sure, they almost always have a response, but responses, more often than not, suggest that there is little real understanding of culture or the role it plays in their lives—or the lives of anyone else. Nearly all of them readily admit they rarely give it much thought. In the eyes of some, culture simply refers to the place where one is born or is that which makes us human. Most Americans in fact see culture as related to tradition, heritage, nationality, or a way of life. For still other Americans, it is what characterizes those "other" people "out there" somewhere else in the world. It is common to hear culture associated with family or some racial grouping people recognize or to which they are assigned. Fortunately, only a few Americans continue to suggest that it is a biological term or something associated with the performing arts as might be reported in their Sunday papers. In almost every case, when Americans are asked what they mean by their responses, they have considerable difficulty explaining what they mean. When asked where culture comes from, there is rarely any agreement. Their responses range from history, tradition, memory, and generations, to environment, family, and inventions—even God and nature. That it might come from the many groups with which they associate is not generally recognized, except for perhaps their family. In fact, many Americans believe that culture does come from their families where they learned their family traditions and their heritage. They know what culture is, but have difficulty in verbalizing what they know. Too many people are basically unsure of what it means. This is not so very surprising when considering that they have been deluged with the suggestion that perhaps there is no American culture, or the idea that if there is one for the United States, it is a melting pot culture. It is also not surprising when you consider that Americans in general tend to see themselves first and primarily as individuals. They tend to respond rather negatively to any suggestion that they are part of a collective, or larger group, with whom they might share the ideas and practices they perceive as unique to themselves. They are offended by the suggestion that their ideas and practices resulted from their being born and raised (taught) in America, or that they may share similar ideas and behaviors with others. That this would make them less unique than they have been led to believe is too offensive even to consider. Despite this individual centeredness of most Americans, they readily group people together into social categories and speak of these groups by way of gross generalizations and stereotypes. Of course, as with most people, Americans tend to see themselves as unlike anyone else and they are convinced that their country (culture) is better than that of anyone else.

Despite the lack of any real sense of culture and the role it plays in their lives, Americans are like most other people, they do not (nor do they have to) think consciously about their culture. Most people do not think about culture until there is a reason to do so. On a day-to-day basis, most people just go about the task of living; doing all those things they have been taught to do, believing all those things they have been taught to believe, and living with all those things that time has lead them simply to take for granted. They will readily defend it if it comes under attack from outside the group. They will criticize it if it does not live up to the promises they learned or if something must be changed because "times change." Americans, as with people in any other culture, especially those of the modern complex cultures, believe they "know" their own culture(s), but they know only small bits and pieces of it (them). Compounding the problem still more, Americans, just like everyone else, tend to see their culture in terms of it being natural—simply the way things are. Even scholars who have studied this uniquely human quality for a great many years continue to struggle with its understanding.

PROBLEMS WITH CULTURE

Coming to grips with the culture concept can be difficult for there are a number of problems to be overcome. First there is the problem of definition. Scholarly approaches and definitions to the culture concept are many and extremely varied. That the concept is applied to so many different things and to so many different groups of humans all at the same time also impacts its understanding. It makes all people the same and it makes groups of them different from one another. If these two problems were not enough, there are also the difficulties associated with the variety of types of culture as it comes in different forms or versions. Humans do not simply learn a culture, they learn at least three different versions of their culture(s). There is also the problem of culture being taught and learned as *truth*, as the most correct or right way to believe and behave—the basis on which people judge the beliefs and practices of other groups of people and their cultures. And lastly, culture as something that all members of all groups learn and share, does not appear to apply in the complex and diverse nation-state context. All of these things become pronounced in the complex societies characterized by cultural diversity, and they produce their own special challenges. Cultural diversity is the chief characteristic of the complex nation-state, and this presents Americans with what are sure to be the major social problems and issues of the twenty-first century.

Definition

Perhaps the most difficult problem to overcome with the concept of culture is a definitional one. A. Kroeber and C. Kluckhohn (1952) noted that culture has been defined in a great many ways, each depending on the perspective of the person defining it. According to these authors, there have been defined *topical* definitions —including everything on a list of topics that can usually fit into social structure or social organization, but not limited to just these things. There have been *historical* definitions that reference a social heritage (tradition) passed on from generation to generation. There have been the *behavioral* definitions wherein culture is seen as shared and learned human behavior—usually meaning a way of life. There have been *normative* definitions that equate culture with ideas, values, or rules for living, and *functional* definitions that see it as the way humans solve problems in adapting to the environments. Still other definitions portray culture as a *mental* construct—a complex of ideas or learned habits that inhibit impulses and distinguish humans from other animals. *Structural* definitions see culture as patterned and interrelated ideas, symbols or behaviors, while still other *symbolic* interpretations see it as based on arbitrarily assigned meanings that are shared in a society. The most recent entry into the definition quagmire comes with the postmodernist's view of culture as a *social process*, one taking into account moral, social, and political consequences (Seidman 1994). While all of these constructs have evolved out of the attempts by scholars to intellectually understand this thing called culture, the shear multitude of definitions have only made it extremely difficult for anybody else to understand it. Operationalizing culture for people who need to understand the role of culture in their lives has not been the result. It just seems to mean so many different things to so many different people all at the same time. It is applied to all humanity, and it is applied to all kinds of specific groups of them at the same time. On top of this, cultures can be distinguished according to the various types of adaptation, and there are multiple versions (forms) of these that must be distinguished.

Frederick Gamst and Edward Norbeck (1976) characterize culture as the human ways of maintaining life and perpetuating the species, a system of learned and socially transmitted pattern of ideas, sentiments, social arrangements, and objects tied to the symbols created and used to refer to them. On the level of a human characteristic, this may be so, but for groups and individuals, it may be something else—simply what they have to deal with every day as they try to live out their lives. On the group level, culture is a learned way of living shared (at least to some degree) with others. Human groups are distinguished by what they learn and practice in their everyday lives—the pattern of behavior and belief that becomes common to all the members of the group. To this can be added the products of ideas translated by or through behavior into the material culture (technology and material goods) or the social products (political, religious, economic systems) they create. Culture comes from commonality, as something taught, learned, and shared in groups (some big and some small), that helps humans adapt to both the natural environment and the sociocultural environments humans create. The sociocultural environment is a product of human culture, and it has its own physical component that overlays the natural environment, and it is patterned—the parts are integrated with one another. Human culture is also dynamic in that it continuously changes. No culture today is the same as it has always been. This means that culture, in addition to being "something," is also a process created by and for people.

In its beginnings, culture was intricately tied to the natural environment. It came about as a way for humans to compete and survive in competition as a species. With the development of food production and what is now referred to as *civilization*, came the territorially based state societies, increased complexity and fragmentation of people into groups that now comprise the diversity of such human societies and cultural groups. In the creation of the nation-state, human societies, cultures, and individuals became multicultural. Diversity and multiculturalism were born of the specialization and fragmentation that accompanied the development of civilizations and the territorially based states. Because of this, the nation-state is, and always will be, composed of many distinguishable cultural groups, and individuals will hold membership in many different cultural groupings at the same time as they live out their lives. Traditional models of culture that portray it as a set of ideas or behaviors universally shared among all the members of a society, are of limited value in such contexts. With the advent of the modern nation-state, all manner of existing human groups were to be incorporated into a new kind of cultural grouping, one highly complex and fragmented, but under a central authority. Cultures became more the creations of conscious thought and action, less the natural consequence of adapting to some limitations of a physical environment. The question of how to deal with these new kinds of cultures has become a vexing problem. In these contexts, all the members of the culture do not necessarily share the same beliefs and behaviors. In the creation of the nation-state, well-defined groups (already cultural groups) were incorporated into the newly created societies, some by conquest, some through coercion of other sorts, and some through simple migration. More recently, some cultural groups even defy national boundaries, in essence have become international or transnational cultures. But more important, people now had to respond to two different kinds of environments, and their cultures had to deal with problems that derived from their own creations.

Despite differences among the scholars on how culture is to be conceptualized, most do agree on some things. Culture is more than just beliefs or behaviors, or the "things" humans produce. Culture is something that has to be learned. It is shared within groups of humans. It is not a haphazard set of ideas, behaviors or products that simply accumulate over time. Culture is adapted to the environment(s) in which it exists, and it represents an integrated whole in which all the parts are related in order to accomplish that goal. It is something that is always in a state of change because the environments are always changing and there "always seems to be a better way." People are not born with their culture, they have to learn it, and each generation has to learn it all over again or the culture simply does not survive. Many Americans believe that being born in the United States is all that is necessary to be an American. This does give people the rights of U.S. citizenship, but to become Americans they must learn the beliefs and behaviors required of members of the American cultural grouping. In the United States, the primary means of ensuring that prospective members of the group acquire all the necessary knowledge and the behavior practices expected of them—the culture—rests with the formal and institutionalized educational system, but Americans learn their culture through a variety of informal means as well. The fact that culture must be learned, also points to it as something that is shared among people. While the complexity of the modern nation-state raises serious questions about how much must be shared, there is no question that it is still shared.

Culture is an unconscious thing for most people who simply learn the things they must know to be accepted as members of groups and then simply do as they have learned. For some people, culture is not the beliefs or ideas they learn, nor is it the behaviors they learn are expected of them. Rather, they simply see it in terms of customs, traditions, their way of life, or their heritage. A few scholars focus on it as observable behavior of people or as a set of rules that generate behavior, while others see it as a combination of these things and the products that result from them. Despite these differences, culture is used to refer to the entire human group and to the learned ways of specific groups of people. Constructions of scholars have been developed to provide for its intellectual understanding as a human phenomenon, to make sense out of this uniquely human phenomenon that seems so often to defy logic. While such constructions have certainly contributed to a better understanding of culture on the intellectual level, the existence of so many different constructs produces considerable confusion for just about everybody else. Most people simply find themselves in a quandary as to what scholars are talking about. They tend to conclude that culture is no more than an analytical creation of intellectuals without any concrete reality. They sense that it is important, yet few realize that culture lies at the heart of just about everything they will think and do throughout their lives. Even fewer people understand that it is something they have (had) to learn or, that in reality, they actually must learn (have learned) at least three versions or forms of it for every cultural group with which they are going to be (have been) associated during their lifetimes.

Culture refers to all those learned and shared ideas, the behaviors and the things they produce, that provide for human needs and concerns. It is the ideas that lie behind or produce behaviors, and the products of ideas translated by or through behavior (physical artifacts or organizational systems). All three of these aspects of culture are complementary and dependent on each other, and each plays a role in the whole of it. They are co-dependent, integrated in combinations that together serve one or another of the needs of people in relation to their basic interests and needs of social living. Some parts of culture apply to everyone in the group while others represent alternatives that allow for choices acceptable within the group. Still others apply to only particular members of the group. What is important can, and does, vary from group to group, but some things are important to nearly all cultural groups. Those things determine how the individuals and the group will live, how they and their culture will survive, and how they will cope with the circumstances in which they find (or create for) themselves. There are things that all people must address if they are to survive as individuals, as cultural groups and as a society.

These are the core areas of human concern, and they are very much related to the fact that humans tend to live together in groups, sometimes very large ones. The larger and more diversified the group, the more complex such core areas become.

CORE AREAS OF CULTURE

For a culture to survive, the people who share it in groups must survive. Among the most basic concerns of humans are food and shelter. Food is the most important of all, for if people do not have enough food to survive, they die. Shelter from the elements is perhaps next in line. If they cannot devise ways to protect themselves from the elements, they can also die. In both cases, if groups do not provide for these things, their other concerns become moot points. Both food and shelter are tied to the naturally existing resources available to satisfy all human needs, and resources lie at the heart of what we call the economic systems or patterns found in all societies. Whether called economic systems or something else, human groups must focus their attention on the natural resources available to them to meet their needs. They will opt for customs regarding who has access to them, how they will be transformed into those things people require, and how to distribute those things to the people who want or need them. Such customs together represent a crucial area of common concern for all cultural groups.

Simply because people live together in groups, the need for order is essential. This results in structured social relations and other customs aimed at establishing and maintaining the behavior deemed appropriate for members of the group. From structured social relations, individuals know what to expect from others and what is expected of them. These represent the social claims and obligations people will have to one another as they combine into distinct groups and societies. The society or group stipulates the relationships among its individual members or subgroups within the society, even creates the means by which they are established, for example, marriage, family, or socioeconomic stratification in classes, castes, etc. In the complex nation-state, the problems of social order often transcend the ability of social structure to deal with them. In these kinds of societies, sometimes with exceedingly large and fragmented populations, made so by specializations and special interests, more formal systems of control (political/legal systems) have evolved to augment what social structure alone simply cannot do. All societies must establish and maintain social order, and deal with disorder when it occurs. Some manage it quite informally, while others are highly formalized to accomplish the task. This too, represents a core area of concern for all societies and their cultures.

Because culture must be learned by each new generation, another crucial concern for every cultural group is cultural transmission and acquisition, the processes by which culture is reproduced. Individual members of the group must learn about their economic, political, or legal systems and about the claims and obligations of their cultural group(s). If the culture is not taught and learned, if it is not passed along to each new generation, culture will simply cease to exist. Cultural transmission and acquisition encompass how groups provide for the teaching and the learning of culture, and outlines what must be learned and how or through what processes. In the United States, a formal system (education) is used as the primary means by which this is accomplished, although many want to believe that it is accomplished in the context of the family where it is initiated. To be sure, cultural transmission and acquisition does begin within the household or family and from family members in virtually every culture. But in the complex ones, this task falls to other organizational groupings. In these contexts, cultural transmission and acquisition are accomplished informally as well as from the formal institutions created to undertake these tasks.

Some process of cultural transmission and acquisition must be provided for if a culture is to survive. In this context and throughout this process, the central role of language looms large, for without language, culture as we know it would simply be impossible. It is within language that all the ideas, rules, behaviors, and products of the culture are encoded. Language is also the primary means by which people acquire their culture, and it is part of what they must acquire. In the process of culture acquisition, people also acquire a perspective on the world, the universe, and their place in it. This view of the world and one's place in it provides members of the group with perceptions and attitudes about the world they live in, and this would also appear to be a core concern of all culture groups, albeit it a little less tangible than others. It helps people make sense of their world, provides the means by which they will perceive it, and defines their place in that world. It provides the foundation for many of their beliefs and it provides answers as to what is, why it is, what it should be, and what their relationship to that might be.

All of these parts or aspects of culture contribute something to the definition of the whole of any culture. When these things are adequately cared for, and where the parts integrate fairly well, the survival of the whole is fairly well assured. But this does not mean that culture must be in some kind of perfect balance or harmony to survive. No culture exists in perfect harmony or balance all of the time, for circumstances continually change. Both the natural/physical and the sociocultural environment are constantly changing and exerting new pressures on the existing cultural pattern. As they do, contradictions appear as gaps between how people think about something and how it might actually be, such as, a belief not being translated into real behavior. Because cultures are always in a state of change, there will always be some disharmony or incongruence somewhere in the culture. It is usually in such areas of imbalance or contradiction that the greatest amount of change can be seen in culture (Naylor 1996). Culture is the learned way or ways of belief, behavior, and the products of these two things shared to some degree within human groupings, which together serves to distinguish the group from other human groups. In a sense, it is a set of problem-solving solutions elected from among the alternatives available to the group given the limitations of their physical or sociocultural environments. The question is not whether culture can be defined, but how to operationalize the definition so that people can better understand its role in their lives. This comes with understanding its relationship to both the individual and various humans groupings to which culture can be applied.

CULTURAL GROUPINGS

Humans are social animals. They seem to require association with others of their own kind and tend to live in, or as groups. Human societies are made up of people who have recognized claims and obligations to one another. These social relations are part of the culture that holds them together as a group—along with other ideas, behaviors, and products directed at their core concerns. Unfortunately, this means that culture can be attributed to a wide range of different groups, regardless of its origins or specific makeup. A *culture group* is one with a relatively permanent existence, rules for acquiring membership, shared expectations, and reason to exist. Such cultural groups exist in the ideas and practices that are shared, in the claims and obligations their members have to one another, and in structures that ensure the group continues over time despite the loss or gain of individual members. All cultural groups originate for the general or specific goal of surviving given a particular set of circumstances of either the natural or sociocultural environments, or they come into being as groups pursue other common interests or purposes. While members of cultural groups are recruited through recognized rules and procedures, actual membership depends on the individual learning those things that ultimately distinguish the group from others. There is a clear sense of belonging (pride) associated with membership in such groups, and individuals gain elements of their identity as a consequence and in the process. The group is identified as a culture group by the members themselves and by the members of other groups who perceive the differences. A cultural grouping can be identified when a group of humans learn a set of beliefs and practices that distinguish it from other groups learning different beliefs and practices.

Once the members of a group learn the culture of that group, identifying *us* from *them*, the *we versus they* syndrome, quickly follows. Once a culture is learned, it becomes the measure of every other culture. Members of the group judge the ideas and actions of other groups based on what they have learned. This is because culture is learned as *truth*. No cultural group teaches its members that someone else's culture is more correct than theirs. When members of different culture groups come in contact with each other, the interaction will be based on conflict as the truths held by cultural groups come into conflict—the learned truth of one group competes with that of another group. Members of all culture groups equally believe and follow their culture—defend their culture as the "best," or "most correct" truth. As there are many culture groups, there are many *truths*. It is a product of cultural learning that members of the group will judge the cultures of others based on what they have learned and believe to be true or correct (Downs 1975). In anthropology, this is referred to as *ethnocentrism*. Members of all human groups are going to be ethnocentric, whether they have learned their culture at home, in school, at church, or anywhere else. When members of different cultures come into contact, there will nearly always be conflict among them as their truths conflict. To understand the ramifications of this, and because culture can be attributed to all manner of human groupings, it is necessary to examine the different types (kinds) of groupings to which the concept of culture can be legitimately applied.

On the most generalized level, culture is used to characterize humans as a species, as the primary means of human adaptation to the environment(s). All humans have culture, for all humans rely on it to adapt to their environments. It represents that rather unique ability of all humans to adapt to any and all kinds of environments, consciously change them to suit their own purposes, control them to a certain degree, even control significant aspects of their own biology. No other animal has exhibited such an ability. When culture is used in the most general sense, it represents this unique characteristic that separates humans from the other animals. It does not make humans better, only different from other animals in their adaptations. In this, all humans are essentially the same in that they use culture to provide for their basic and derived needs. Sufficient food, shelter, and association with others of their own kind all seem to be common basic needs of all humans regardless of where they might be found. All people are equally concerned about sufficient food, shelter from the elements, and human association. People in the United States are concerned with these same things. What this means is that people throughout the world are not all that different. People everywhere laugh when they are happy, cry when they are sad or hurt. In satisfying their basic needs, every human is the same as every other, despite how they specifically meet such needs. It is in the specific beliefs and behaviors they select to satisfy these needs that humans and groups appear different from one another. It is because humans elect different means for satisfying their needs that the concept of culture becomes so complicated, for this means that culture can be legitimately attributed and applied to all sizes and kinds of human groupings.

While all humans have culture, they tend to develop their own local varieties of it in their attempts to survive in different kinds of places and under different conditions. In this, cultures are actually little more than sets of problem-solving solutions. Because of this, it is a common practice to distinguish cultures according to type of environment (e.g., desert, arctic, or tropical, etc.). As environments differ, the individual groups inhabiting them will differ. Even groups within particular environments can differ simply because choices are made from among all the alternatives available to them, for example, environments limit the possibilities as to what will be perceived and utilized as food. As groups of humans adjust to the specific circumstances of the particular environments in which they find themselves, they create their own cultures, specific to them and distinguishing them from other groups of humans. Some cultures can be distinguished according to the size and complexity of the group and their learned adaptations, as with small-scale, tribal, traditional, or complex nation-state cultures. But culture also is used to identify people who may share characteristics that distinguish them as members of groups existing within larger cultural groupings, particularly in the complex societies (e.g., as ethnic, racial, socioeconomic, or special interest groups). This is a function of the fact that while human groups have to adapt to particular natural environments in their efforts to survive, they must also adapt to the various aspects of sociocultural environments they create with their cultures.

Each type of natural environment has its own distinct conditions, problems, or limit of possibilities. In the earliest stages of cultural development, adaptation to the natural environment clearly was the most important force in the survival of humans and cultures. In adapting to them, human groups created their cultures. But it is important to remember that physical environments do not determine culture(s), the physical environment only limits or provides the possibilities. All physical environments provide alternatives for solving human problems or needs, but choices from among those alternatives still must be made. Because of this, cultures adapting to the same type of environments can still be quite different. In choosing from among the alternatives that exist in the natural environment, humans create their own particular or specific cultures, reflective of that environment. But, the specific cultural pattern will still be determined by the actual choices the people make. The problems of culture become more complicated as humans find they also must adapt to what they create for themselves with their cultures, including sociocultural environments that have their own physical components that will overlay parts of the natural environment. This sociocultural environment, consisting of both social and physical components, then poses its own limit of possibilities and provides for even more choices. From this culturally created sociocultural environment come many more alternatives from which to choose, and thus, diversity appears among human groups. As groups become larger and the nation-state appears, the sociocultural environments become more complex as specialization and fragmentation become the norms. New cultural groupings appear reflecting that diversity. The new cultural groupings appear based on occupational specialty and on the stratifications that come to characterize complex societies, and groupings tied to economic, political, religious, race, or other special interests. Additional groupings even form out of the movement of groups from one nation-state to another.

CULTURE TYPES

Among the many kinds of specific cultures that have come to be recognized and generally accepted are those based on size and complexity, such distinguishing the *traditional* and *modern* cultures associated with the small-scale and complex societies. Traditional cultures are those generally viewed as not having achieved the level of civilization, that continue to exist as they seemingly always have. They are characterized by a relatively small population and one that lives day-to-day without the complexities of the scientifically and technologically based societies, with centralized political and economical systems—attributes usually associated with the modern nation-states. For most people in the developed or modern world, traditional culture is synonymous with the so-called "primitive groups" they read about in *National Geographic* or are exposed to via television. Americans do tend to see the aboriginals (original inhabitants) of their country as traditional, but that is somehow different from those they see in other parts of the world. Most can readily accept traditional societies as examples of specific cultures. They have more difficulty seeing their own nation-state as an example of a specific culture.

As indicated earlier, the idea of a specific culture is also associated with sociopolitical units that evolved with the advent of territorially based states, today simply seen as nations or countries, such as the United States, Germany, Russia, and so on. This practice nearly always obscures the real diversity of the people that make them up, for such nation-states will nearly always be multicultural, despite the imposition of a nationality or national culture atop those of their constituent groupings. Nation-states are societies and political entities with varying levels of sociopolitical integration and it is nearly always presupposed that all people given membership in such groups share the same set of cultural beliefs and behaviors. Whether this is or is not actually the case, people tend to believe and subscribe to it because it is what they are taught. According to some current thinking, a nation is a community of people—a society—who see themselves as one people, based on common traditions, ancestry, institutions, ideology, language, and perhaps religion (Clay 1990:28). Such representations rarely coincide with the actual diversity to be found in all nations.

The term *nation* is usually equated with the modern nation-state, and this with culture. Nations are integrated social and political entities, territorially bounded units within which someone holds the power to enforce member compliance with the rules of behavior. This definition differs little from traditional definitions of society and few nations exhibit the homogeneity implied. States are usually seen as autonomous political units encompassing many communities, with centralized government and the power to coerce (Carneiro 1970:733). As with a nation, the idea of a state must be approached with caution. State refers to a certain level of political integration (a kind of political system) that might characterize a human society and be made part of its culture. Equated with culture, it presupposes its people share the same set of beliefs and practices and, furthermore, assumes that people will, or can be forced to lay aside any beliefs and practices learned before being made part of the larger group. The use of the term nation-state is an attempt to group a complex society with a political system and attribute culture to it. But this fairs no better for it too assumes a level of sharing in belief and practice that simply may not be present. Rarely will the people of any complex society share *all* the same beliefs and practices. The more complex the society is, the less likely its members will share many of the same beliefs and behaviors.

Nation-States

The term *nation-state* is used to refer to modern societies with clearly defined and recognized territorial boundaries that are perceived to have reached the state level of political integration. A central authority exercises control over the use of force to ensure its members comply with the rules of the society. It has been equated with culture as well, for as already discussed, the centralized government is nearly always concerned with creating a national culture—a sense of nationality among its members. Thus far, attempts to create a unified sense of nationality have achieved only limited success, for no modern nation-state culture in existence is characterized by only a single set of cultural beliefs and practices shared by all of its citizens. While nation-states may achieve some success in getting its people to share some things, this does not mean they will get them to share all of the arbitrarily and consciously created culture to the exclusion of other sets of beliefs and practices. There is a tendency for most people to perceive the nation-state as a culture, for people included in such groupings do learn and share some ideas or values (at least ideally). All of a nation-state's members follow the prerequisite behaviors enforced on all of its citizens, and most of its members are forced to function within the same imposed political, economic, and in some cases, religious structures. Nation-states become cultural groupings by virtue of such things, but this does not mean that other cultural patterns will not be present within them. In fact, significant differences among constituent groups of the nation-state do exist. For the sake of national unity and conformity, recognized cultural differences will be portrayed as secondary to the beliefs and practices advocated by the state for all its citizens.

Creating a nation-state culture by fiat or legislation does not mean that all its citizens will actually comply. Groups incorporated into the state come with their own set of beliefs and practices already learned, practiced, and believed as truth. They may elect to continue their older cultural pattern in so far as they may be allowed or choose to do that. This can mean that the cultural beliefs and practices they brought with them can continue despite any recognized level of acceptance of the national culture, waiting for the right opportunity to be fully expressed once again, as seen at the heart of the ethnic conflicts of the former Yugoslavia. Because of this, and the steadfastness with which groups will hold on to their specific beliefs and practices, such groupings are usually referred to as *subcultures*. This suggests they are subservient (secondary) to the dominant national culture superimposed on them that all its citizens share—simply microcultures within the macroculture. This tendency fails to recognize that such groups frequently continue their original beliefs and practices as strongly as those prescribed by the state. In some cases, depending on circumstances, they can be stronger than those of the state, as seen in the Muslim, Croatian, and Serbian factions in the former Yugoslavia. The use of the term subculture denotes that cultural groupings identified as such are somehow less viable than the culture of the state, implies they are of secondary importance to the imposed culture of the state, and fails to recognize the legitimacy, viability, and even primacy of such cultures to the actual members of such cultural groups. The term also suggests that such groups have been absorbed (assimilated) into the culture of the state, but this is rarely the case. For example, in the United States, Native Americans have distinct heritages, ways of life—cultures. As distinct cultural groups, many continue substantial portions of their traditional ways. At the same time, they have had to adopt many of the ways, beliefs, and practices peculiar to the national culture of the whole United States in order to survive in that context. In the process, they have created a new culture, neither traditional nor American. This can be said for all ethnic groups in the United States.

Constituent culture groups would seem to be a more appropriate way to refer to all the groups that actually comprise the modern nation-state. While they help to constitute the national culture and play a role in the definition of that culture group, each is a distinct cultural group in its own right, and its members believe in it just as strongly as might be the case with a nation-state culture or any other type of culture. If there is a use for the term *subculture*, it is with the variants within identifiable constituent cultural groupings, for indeed, there are variations within each group. Even they are not homogeneous as generally supposed, constituent cultural groups should be used to identify the different ways of belief and behavior that distinguish the many cultural groupings that make up the modern, complex nation-state. Constituent cultural groups together make for the modern nation-state, contributing to its definition or characterization.

People in the United States readily associate cultural difference with ethnic and racial groups. For them, the differences can be based on physical characteristics, language, common origins, and even religion. The idea of race is based on the widespread belief in a natural and historical reality of human groupings based on physical characteristics. Despite all the evidence dispelling the idea of pure races or even a set of characteristics limited to any single group of people, the belief in the existence of races continues among most Americans. The idea of ethnicity, was originally developed to refer to people who migrated from one sociocultural context to another. It has undergone substantial change over the years. Where once its use was based on geographical or tribal (traditional culture) linkages and origins, many people now resist the idea of a distinct culture for ethnic groups within the nation-state, arguing instead that such groupings are still part of the national culture. Still others argue that it is now a combination of cultural patterns that originated out of migrations of cultural groups from one place to another, or that it is contextual, created out of a social need or circumstance favoring a combination of older traditions with new ones, in essence creating something quite unique and used primarily for group self-identification. Still others argue that ethnicity has lost all of its meaning, or that it is nothing more than another label for culture. They may be the most correct in their perception of the ethnic group, for ethnic appears to be little more than another term for culture and then simply to denote a kind of one in the complex setting. However seen, ethnic groups are part of the modern complex society.

Generally, ethnic kinds of constituent groups appear to subscribe to many of the same ideas and practices required of all people within the boundaries of the nation-state. But, this is not the same thing as saying they will share all the same beliefs and behaviors established for or expected in the state. They may adhere to many of the required behaviors prescribed for everyone living within the national borders as their survival in that context may depend upon it. But this does not mean they will adhere to all such expectations. They may choose not to adhere to all of them, or it may be that they are not allowed to share in aspects of the nation-state culture. While sharing some, maybe even a great many of the beliefs and behaviors of the larger grouping, it is apparent that they maintain their own distinct patterns of belief and behavior as well, patterns that distinguish them from other groups. For example, some cultural groups simply refuse to recognize any relationship or allegiance to the nation-state, for example some Native American cultural groups. Some groups may see themselves as part of the national state, but with unique beliefs and behaviors they believe they should be allowed to continue because of a belief in the desirability of diversity, as with the Quaker or the Hutterite. The term *constituent* means to form, compose, or make up something. Nation-states are actually composed of people with distinct ethnic traditions or cultures that combine with those of other groups produced in the social context to help constitute the complex modern society. These are tied to all manner of special interests. Both kinds of groupings are legitimate cultural groupings. Both are specific constituent groups that come together with others to make for the wide diversity of the modern nation-states. James Spradley and David McCurdy (1972) use the term *cultural scene* to differentiate the special interest group from the ethnic group. For these authors, the special interest group can be made up of varied ethnic individuals, and they come into being as part of the larger society. What is more important, they are still legitimate cultural groups within the diversity of the complex nation-state.

Cultural groups based solely on special interests are difficult to deal with, for members of these groups are drawn from other identifiable groups within the larger society, from the racial and ethnic groups that are also a part of the diversity context. They also can be created by incorporating members from throughout the world, in essence transcending national, racial, or ethnic boundaries. These cultural groupings are related to the social situation of the nation-states, the complexity of such groups, and the forms of stratification found within them. In essence, these cultural groupings are created in response to the sociocultural environment to cope with particulars of that context and the limited sharing of culture that is actually possible among people in an age of fragmentation, complexity, and specialization. As pointed out by Spradley and McCurdy (1972), it is impossible that all the people of any culture share all the beliefs and behaviors that might be attributed to it, whether traditional, modern, constituent, or otherwise.

These culture groupings become constituent groups right along with racial and ethnic groups, and they contribute to the cultural diversity that will come to be associated with them. They are created for a variety of purposes and to fit specific circumstances: to denote occupational specialization (business, professional, white collar, academic, blue collar, etc.); along regional or geographic lines (Southerners, Yankees, Westerners, Texans, New Yorkers, etc.); according to where people live and under what conditions people live (urban, metroplex, rural, small towns, farms, cities, etc.); created on the basis of sex and gender (male, female, homosexual, heterosexual); based on age (infant, teenagers, young adult, mature adult, retired, etc.); in terms of specific religious beliefs (e.g., Muslim, Christian, Catholic, Baptist); political ideology (democratic, socialistic, communistic, republican, and so on); and with a host of other special interests (environmentalism, pop culture, conservationism, physical limitation or disability, and even into leisure activities). The list is almost endless for it must go on until the full complement of cultural groupings for any complex culture is complete—depending on how specific one wishes to get. Even within these groupings, additional breakdowns are possible. For example, business culture can be broken down into distinct cultural groups or types (restaurant, industrial, shipping, service, etc.), and these provide for even more specific breakdowns. Distinct cultures can be identified for transportation and communication. The cultures of IBM and Texas Instruments, McDonald's, Burger King, and Wendy's are clearly distinguishable. The restaurant business itself, can encompass the cooks, hostesses, waitresses, waiters, management, and customers. Educational culture can be further distinguished as public or private, preschool, primary, secondary and higher education, and each of these displays their own constituent groups—the teacher, student, service staff, administration, historian, mathematician, anthropologist, and so on. The academic culture of Harvard is not the same as the culture of an Iowa State or a metropolitan community college. Virtually any special interest group can be viewed as a cultural group so long as they tend to learn beliefs and behaviors *that distinguish them from others learning something else.*

Members of constituent cultures follow the distinct beliefs and behaviors of their group, while at the same time they subscribe to some of the same ideas and follow some of the same rules of prerequisite behavior as do all those who are part of the particular nation-state. Some of these constituent groups are created and shaped out of the conditions in, and with which some groups are forced to exist, as dominant groups (holds political/economic power) over subservient groups (cultural minorities). The fact that the nation-state is made up of many constituent cultural groupings accounts for the diversity that characterizes them and the social problems that accompany that diversity. All nation-states exhibit these kinds of constituent groupings and thus are culturally diverse. The nature of modern society is reflected in the diversity of its constituent cultural groups.

America as a Nation-State Culture

Americans readily recognize different types of culture, such as traditional, primitive, or modern, with the term modern being equated with complex societies and cultures also associated with some conception of civilization. The United States is a nation (large and socially complex), and it has a state form of political system as part of its culture. Thus, the United States is best identified as a nation-state. This also means that its culture is arbitrary and consciously constructed, a culture created then superimposed over the existing cultures of its constituent populations. Nation-state culture is created as such sociopolitical units are created. Most of the nations of the modern world were born out of the incorporation of already existing cultural groups into such territorial units we now call nations or countries, which are also characterized by the state type of political organization (incorporates various communities under the control of a central authority). Incorporation came by way of coercion, conquest or in some cases even involving some choice. All the groups incorporated were established cultural groups before they were "nationalized" or made into de facto citizens of the newly created grouping. In an effort to create some sense of identity, belonging, and loyalty to the new group—essential for its existence—the nation-state has to develop or create a sense of nationality, in essence, create a new culture. To do this, someone in the new group, an individual or a selected group of individuals, has to create or design the new culture to go with the new national grouping.

In the case of the United States, a selected group (the founding fathers as it were) wrote the a Constitution containing a Bill of Rights in which they outlined what they envisioned for the newly created United States of America. With all the diversity and difference of opinion represented among these founding fathers, agreement as to what the new culture would be, or should be, was difficult. On what it should be, there was no universal agreement. Each came to the negotiating table with their own ideas on that issue. Because many ideas were placed on the table for consideration, they found they had to compromise—create a culture that was not exactly what any one of them really wanted. Compromises do not reflect what people want, only for what they must settle. But even in compromise, the arbitrarily created culture was presented in ideal terms—it reflected what the culture ought to be, how they envisioned it, or hoped it could be. It reflected how they wanted to be seen in the world of nations (other arbitrarily created cultural groupings). As with other such nation-state creations, it was essentially based on a group process that produced a compromise culture in its most idealized form. The compromise was then given to all the people within its arbitrarily created borders to live and practice. For people who suddenly found themselves citizens of this new country, society and culture, there was still the reality of everyday living with which to contend. What was created through the group and compromise process was the culture in its most idealized form. The individual members of the newly created group were then left alone to bring it to life, operationalize it and live up to its stated ideals on a day-to-day basis, despite whatever limitations with which they might have to contend. This forces us to consider the various forms of culture that people actually have to learn.

FORMS (VERSIONS) OF CULTURE

Individuals are taught one form of culture, live in another, and produce a third culture that provides them the means to do it. Simply saying humans have culture is not enough. Even being able to say that culture is simply this or that may not be enough either, for people learn many cultures in their lifetimes. While this can help in easing some of the confusion with the concept, it does not eliminate all of it. Culture also comes in a variety of forms, and this needs to be understood as well. Not only do people learn a number of cultures in their lifetimes, there are different versions of these cultures they will learn for each of them. Ask anyone to tell you about their culture, explain some idea, belief, or action, and they will tell you, for they were taught such things as they acquired membership in culture groups. The answers provided in response to such questions represent *ideal culture*, but there is also a *real culture* that can be quite different from the ideal one, and there is a *culture construct*, which attempts to bridge these two for specific purposes. These different forms of culture must be understood if one expects to understand the role of culture in the lives of humans and their responses under certain circumstances. People know what they learn, learn how much of this is possible in their actual day-to-day living, and they learn how they may have to adjust to deal with it based on their own set of limiting circumstances.

Ideal Culture

Ideal culture is that version that is taught, both formally and informally, to every aspiring member of a cultural group. It is taught by those who already know about the culture and are members of the group. It is transmitted as the required (and "right") beliefs and behavioral expectations of the group that must be learned. Ideal culture relates to how people think of themselves, and may reflect what they want to believe they are all about, the way they ought to be, or how they want others to perceive them. It is the form of culture passed on from generation to generation as the culture is basically reproduced. In the nation-state, it is reflected in the things new or aspiring members of the group must learn to be accepted as they attempt to achieve full membership in the group. This form of culture is a reflection of how people see themselves and how they want others to see them, but it is no more than a belief in what their culture is all about, and it is always presented in the most perfect form. Ideal culture represents the values, ideas, and behaviors that have been established for the cultural group, what the members want the culture to be, or as they think it ought to be about.

For example, asking an American if the United States is the land of freedom and equal opportunity, or whether Americans believe in the worth of the individual, in free enterprise, in honest competition, and in providing an honest day's labor for an honest day's pay, their answers will inevitably be "yes." Americans learn about the importance of the individual, about the equality of people, to be responsible, honest, truthful, law-abiding citizens. The cultural learning simply does not provide that Americans should be dishonest or that they should lie, cheat, steal, or that they are better than anyone else. When asked about such things, Americans have the responses right on the tip of their tongues. They learned these things from parents, teachers, religious leaders, peer groups, orientation sessions, and their television sets. All Americans know what to believe and what is expected of them—their culture. In the United States, the ideal culture is best reflected in the documents that brought the culture into being and in the curriculum that must be learned by all aspiring members of the group. It was the result of compromise, and it was a group creation. It was a statement of how the founding fathers envisioned it and how they wanted the world to come to know the United States and its people. In the process, it determined what needed to be taught (conveyed) to its citizens. What needed to be taught and acquired by the members of the culture reflected the beliefs and behaviors that the founding fathers had agreed upon as most appropriate for all Americans—reflecting the culture they had created through compromise.

Real Culture

On the other hand, when asked about their culture, people will provide qualified responses. Actually, it is rare that the real thoughts and actions of people live up to the stated ideals of their cultures. There are acceptable ranges of behavior in all societies and these are learned right along with the idealized ones. Individuals learned how far they may deviate from the stated norms or expectations and still be accepted by the group, and this may be a consequence of the compromises that brought nation-state cultures into existence, or the realization that to live up to ideals is always hard. This is certainly the case in the United States. While the national culture resulted from a group compromise effort, individuals are still left to live it to the best of their abilities. But it may be impossible for any individual to live up to the stated ideals established for any nation-state as a whole. Despite ideals to the contrary, in actual practice the United States is a stratified society, with inequality actually structured into the society (institutionalized). Socioeconomic classes, racial, ethnic and other specific groupings simply do not have equal access to economic resources, status positions, prestige, and so on. It would appear that American society and culture could never be a land of true equality or even equal opportunity because of this stratification. If equal opportunity exists, it is according to class or by virtue of other group affiliations. Americans resist admitting this reality for they learn their country is supposed to be the land of equality and equal opportunity. That inequality actually exists is only grudgingly recognized.

While individualism is highly valued in American society, it is simply not possible within any large social group. A person's individuality has to be sacrificed for the common good, the stability and order of the group. In short, allowing individuality would threaten the unity, harmony, and even the continued existence of the larger group and its culture. America is the land of the free—more accurately a land or place where individual freedom is greater than anywhere else—but no nation could actually exist where individuals were free to do anything they might like. Americans enjoy many freedoms, but only up to the point where individual actions might impinge on the rights of others or as it might threaten the continued survival of the nation-state group. What Americans say they believe and do rarely correlates with what they actually may think and do as individuals or as a group. Sometimes people do things with the conscious thought that they are not exactly following the rules. People learn what their fellow group members expect, but they also learn what they will accept. Sometimes only a small deviation is acceptable (as with the small "white lie" to protect the feelings of friends) and at other times the latitude can be great (okay if you can get away with it—whatever it may be). People learn how far they can go in stretching, bending or even violating the rules. For Americans, they learn through trial and error, where it might be acceptable to "cut corners just a little" or "cheat just a little." Americans learn what they can get away with and yet remain an acceptable member of the group.

Sometimes there is only a small difference and sometimes there is a substantial difference between the ideal and the real cultures, between what people have been taught to think and do and what they actually think and do. Recognizing this difference between the culture forms is an essential step in understanding culture and its influence on the lives of people, their behavior, and beliefs as individuals or as groups. Regardless of what kind of group(s) that can be credited with having culture, members must learn ideal culture, but they must also function in the real world and with their real cultures. On the one hand, every member of every group learns the rules and the ideals, but on the other hand, they also learn just how far they can or *must* deviate from those rules and ideals. There are many areas in which a substantial difference can be noted between the ideal and real cultures of American society—where contradictions or paradoxes exist. The same can be said for any culture at any level of human grouping. Given the development of the modern nation-state, the difference between these forms of cultures can be extreme because of the arbitrary and somewhat artificial nature of such societies which frequently necessitates compromises as to what will be, or how they wish the rest of the world to see them. The fact that most people in culture groups recognize the difference between their stated ideals and the realities of everyday living leads us to consider yet another type of culture.

Culture Constructs

In a very real sense, all cultures are creations and thus, all cultures are constructs. People create (construct) their actual cultures as they respond to the limitations or problems of their environments. In some cases, this is an unconscious process and in others it is a conscious and arbitrary process, as in the nation-state context. Culture constructs are also the result of people attempting to make some sense out of the beliefs and behaviors of others, to describe the culture of others in an attempt to understand them. People create cultural descriptions for other people with different beliefs and behaviors. The resulting constructs then stand as descriptions for groups, and they, in turn, guide the interactions of the groups. Creating cultural descriptions for others is a process aimed at helping people make sense out of the differences they see. The generated constructs then become the basis for interacting with them. Both individuals and groups produce culture constructs as they attempt to live on a day-to-day basis within the experiences and constraints of their sociocultural environments. Individuals and groups in the complex social structure of the modern nation-states must accommodate the realities of living in their national cultures. The realities of actually existing day to day determine whether or not they will, or can, live by the ideals as they have been taught, as they have been given them. This, and learning the beliefs and behaviors of a wide variety of cultural groups with which individuals might also affiliate, together produce the individual cultural construct—the culture of the individual, as it were.

The idea of a cultural construct has been used in anthropology for a long time to refer to the cultural descriptions (ethnographies) that anthropologists produce. Anthropologists have always been involved with cultural constructs as they have attempted to describe cultures using the norms of belief and behavior as exhibited by a group. The ethnography of an anthropologist is a construct culture based on what people say they are all about (ideal culture) and what they are actually seen doing. This combination is then presented in terms of norms—that which applies to most of the people. Ethnographies are cultural descriptions with interpretation, created for people based on systematic observations, interviews, and the direct , experience of the ethnographer. For anthropologists, these cultural descriptions are, in fact, no more than selected representations of the cultures they are produced to describe—designed to provide only sufficient information to convey the level of understanding for which they are presented. They are very much like the road map that provides only the necessary information to get the person where they might wish to go. As road maps do not show all the details of the actual route from a starting point to a destination (number of houses, bridges, potholes, rivers to be passed, etc.), ethnographies provide only that detail sufficient to provide the reader with some better understanding of the culture described or the way of life of the people for whom it is created. They are not total descriptions of the cultures nor will they be replications of reality. They are selective descriptions presented as only representations. These ethnographies are based on the systematic analysis (putting together) of what the people think, believe or say their culture is all about and what they really think and do in their everyday lives. Then these cultural descriptions only represent what applies to the majority of the people or as might appear in the majority of cases in the culture or some aspect(s) of it. Anthropologists are not the only ones to produce cultural constructs that are then left to stand as descriptions for some group's way of life—its culture.

All people do this on a fairly regular basis, whenever they see someone behaving in a way different from what they know. It is a way of trying to make sense of what other people, not members of your cultural group, think and do. When members of one cultural group see others doing something quite different from themselves, hear something different from what they think, they have to make sense of it. To do this, they will refer to their own experiences, their own beliefs and practices, to interpret what they see or hear, and to put the differences in perspective. They will draw conclusions, make judgments, and characterize the ideas or practices of those others based on what they have learned as the most correct or best way to think and behave. The conclusions drawn are then allowed to represent or stand as part of the description of that other culture. The descriptive statement that is produced about that "other" group is allowed to stand as part of their definition—wrong or right as it may be. The ethnocentrism of the observer provides that such interpretations are quite likely to be incorrect. Misinterpretations and misconceptions abound when people do this for other cultural groups. The interactions between the members of the different groups are made much more difficult in that many of these generated perceptions can be quite faulty. For example, Americans hold very different views on such things as time and the role of women in society than might be the case in other cultures. Americans, Mexicans, and some Middle Eastern groups do not value time in the same way. This will almost always ensure some misunderstanding. An American's interpretation of the value of time or its use in those other cultures might be that they are unmotivated, waste a lot of valuable time, even that members of such groups are lazy. In actual practice, the importance of time to people in those cultures may not reflect any of these conclusions or characterizations. The misconception will underlie the American's approach to members of these groups, however. The same situation can come from culture's interpretation of the role of women. In parts of the world where only "loose" women or prostitutes display aggressive behavior, or appear in public thinly clad, the attitudes and behaviors of liberalized American women, including their public dress, will quite likely be misunderstood.

Producing cultural constructs is undertaken by people when there is a need to understand what others believe or do that is different from what you might believe and do. They are created by people as they try to make sense of the beliefs and behaviors of people from cultural groupings other than their own. In other words, cultural constructs are created for people to account for the differences they think they see—cultural differences. For example, if an individual from the Dani culture of the highlands of New Guinea was invited into an American corporate boardroom and he appeared in a feathered headdress, wearing a penis gourd, and carrying a sixteen-foot spear, the Americans in the room would immediately sense a difference between him and themselves. Their explanation would be a culture difference—they obviously do that (dress like that) in his culture. In essence, they create part of his cultural description for him. People rarely describe their own culture(s) for there is simply no need to do that. They just go about living their lives as they have been taught and as they have learned it. But when someone is confronted by behaviors or beliefs that are different from those they know and understand—when they meet someone from another culture—they have to make sense of that. The culture construct is the result, and this is then allowed to stand as part of the description of that culture. This is not all that different from what is done by anthropologists, just less systematic and more prone to perceptual misinterpretation.

Cultural constructs are also created by individuals as they must accommodate or attempt to bridge the gap between the ideals they are taught and the realities of their own circumstances. All people in nation-state groupings are taught the ideas and expected behaviors of their cultures. What they are taught is ideal culture—the way the people want their culture to be seen or what it ought to be about. In reality, as individuals attempt to live out their culture, members of the culture group may find it impossible to live up to the ideals of the group. In the case of Americans, the creation of the nation-state society and its culture was a group compromise effort. Individuals may find it exceedingly difficult to live up to the ideals and behavior set out for them. It might be because of an individual's physical or mental limitations, or it may be that limitations may be imposed upon them as members of social groups within the society, as in the placement of groups in the stratified social structure. It just might not be possible for the individual or group of individuals to live their lives as they learned. Given the limitations imposed on them by others or given any individual limitations they might be born with or are assigned, the individual and group produce their own cultural constructs for day-to-day living. In this sense, cultural constructs are ultimately unique to each human being, much like the fingerprints of humans are different. The individual's construct will be based on the individual's limitations and his or her own unique assemblage of experiences that cannot be duplicated by any other person. But in creating their own constructs, individuals have only the ideas and behaviors of the many cultural groups with which they associate from which to choose. Americans generally do not like to hear that they are not unique, that they are the product of the cultural groups that have provided them with the ideas and behaviors they put together in creating their own cultural constructs.

Ideal culture represents the standard by which they wish to be identified, the standard by which they want to see themselves or want to be seen. The real culture represents actual conditions, the ability of the group to live up to its ideals, and the result of the limitations and differences among the individual members of the group. The construct culture provides the basis for action for individuals and for categories of people within the larger group. They are generated to adapt to the peculiar social context and allow individuals and groups to confront those circumstances created by the gap(s) between the ideal and real. Individuals may not be able to adhere or live up to the stated ideals of the culture because of their own personal limitations or the particular circumstances in which they might find themselves through no fault of their own. Categories or groups within the larger society may find themselves in similar circumstances, and culture constructs help them account for the contradictions and paradoxes and devise ways to respond to them. In the complex nation-state, individuals and groups create their own cultural constructs in order to adapt to the reality they perceive.

Individuals who find that they simply cannot live up to the ideals of the nation, or who are not permitted to do so, or those who might choose not to subscribe to all of the ideals established for them, create individualized constructs. Each individual creates his or her own set of beliefs and practices based on perceived reality, and this will be constructed from many different sets of beliefs and practices from which they choose. No two of these constructs will be alike. Groups do much the same thing as they respond to the circumstances in which they find themselves, and they create their own cultures in the process. For example, Mexican-Americans are not groups of people that put together the Mexican culture and the American culture, rather they create a unique culture all their own out of common origins, shared characteristics, and common treatment in the context of the United States. In the case of both individuals and categorized groupings of people, the culture constructs they create in the process are designed to help them survive given the conditions they might face. Construct cultures are created for others for the same operational purposes of understanding and action.

Groups of people that share a culture develop their own particular set of skills (responses) for dealing with the economic and social necessities of life. They choose their own set of values (in some cases prioritize their values), as to the higher or less important purposes in life. Emigrants and conquerors carried their own cultural patterns (ideas, skills, and behaviors—their cultures) across the planet and into their sociopolitical environments or creations. These patterns persist over time, sometimes for generations or centuries. But these patterns do not remain unchanged, for their circumstances differ from place to place and time to time. Such groups find themselves in circumstances where some of their beliefs and behaviors are clearly unacceptable, out of place, or are acting against their best interests. They alter their patterns and become neither what they were nor what they are now supposed to be. They create a new pattern, unique to themselves and their particular circumstances. Cultures are not erased as people cross borders or are suddenly included within the borders of some nation-state, nor do they always disappear in later generations as members of the group adopt the language, dress, or any other outward manifestations of the lifestyle in their "new" country. Cultural borrowing and influences between the groups are inevitable, but they remain quite distinct. These differences represent the normal state of affairs in the complex society, not the exception, whether their destiny is within their own hands, or those of other groups or institutions.

CULTURE AS TRUTH

In addition to the fact that people tend to learn a variety of culture forms, what they learn in all three incidences is perceived as truth. In its ideal form, the set of ideals, correct behaviors, and the products of those are taught as the most correct, or the best form. It has already been noted that Americans tend to see their cultural beliefs and practices as the best, considered or compared to any and all other ways of believing and practice. Americans are not alone in this view of their culture. All cultural groups learn their cultures as *the* way to believe and behave, the *most correct* way, as the *true* way. It is a natural consequence of being taught what one has to know to be a member of the group. No culture group teaches new or aspiring members that someone else or some other cultural beliefs or practices are more correct than the ones they are being taught. The transmission and acquisition of culture are necessary activities if a culture is to survive. But, the consequence of this activity is to create culturally bounded individuals who are biased and ethnocentric, convinced of the truth of their culture. With this as their standard, they will naturally judge everyone else's culture based on what they learned. Because they were provided with the truth, everyone else's truth (their culture) is going to be judged as somehow less correct than the culture they have learned. This is *ethnocentric behavior*—judging another culture by the standards of one's own learned culture. As one might expect, no other culture will measure up to the truth of one's own pattern of beliefs and behaviors. People of all cultural groups tend to be biased or ethnocentric. It is part of the process of learning a cultural pattern and obviously the way someone learns is the most correct way.

When people representing different cultures come into contact, the result is more than simply cultural contact. It will also be more than just the possibility of some misunderstandings. Cultures in contact really mean cultures in conflict—one truth against another truth—and who is to determine which of these is the more correct. Sometimes the conflict is not too terribly dramatic. Other times, it can and does lead to violent conflict, particularly when one culture assumes a dominant position over others and attempts to impose its truth on the others. As can be readily seen in the recent events of Europe, Africa, and the Middle East, this can lead to a belief that the only way to resolve a dispute is to eradicate those others—genocide. On a large of small scale, this is murder, the sincerest form of criticism. Winning the argument is guaranteed by eliminating those with whom one disagrees. On a more limited scale, such cultural conflicts result in many of the social problems faced by the complex nation-states made up of so many different constituent groups, themselves a result of the development of civilization with its fragmentations, complexity, and specializations. Given the particular circumstances under which the constituent groups may have to exist, the many perceptions of the truth can vary dramatically and become a steady source of conflict. It can be made more so as some constituent groups find themselves precluded from full participation in the nation-state culture or find themselves on an unequal footing with other groups.

DIVERSITY AND MULTICULTURALISM

With the development of nation-states, the incorporation of many already established cultural groups into the state and the movement of people from one nation to another, questions of diversity, multiculturalism, and cultural pluralism, social problems, and cultural conflicts also develop to become the normal state of affairs. The term diversity is quite appropriate for any nation-state. There is no nation-state that is not characterized by a diversity of cultural groups that together make them up. It is natural for nation-states to exhibit such diversity that was a consequence of their creation that brought together groups of people who already had culture. The attempt to overlay a *national culture* on such groupings has been only marginally successful as history can attest. In the case of the newly created nations out of the former Soviet Union and in the former Yugoslavia, imposed artificial nation-state cultures simply do not replace those cultures people brought with them into these nation-states. While they may not have been able to practice them for many years, with the breakup of the Soviet Union and Yugoslavia, their continuing presence was aptly demonstrated. The original cultures of the people incorporated into these states, cultures that might have seemed to have disappeared or had laid dormant for many years, exerted themselves and the competition among them resulted in deadly violence.

Multiculturalism is a term that is frequently used synonymously with cultural diversity. It is generally used whenever a multitude of cultures can be identified in the context of any human society. The world is multicultural, for it contains many cultures. The United States is multicultural, for it too, contains many distinct cultures. All people must learn culture(s), and once learned, it (they) becomes part of their identity, their reality and a driving force in their lives. Often overlooked is the fact that most individuals in the context of a complex society, out of necessity, are multicultural as well. As people learn many cultures in their lifetimes, it is also true that they will identify with a number of them simultaneously at any given point in time. An individual might be an American, a Mexican-American, a female, an anthropologist, a Southern Baptist Christian, environmentalist, a republican or socialist, an antiabortionist, and more, all at the same time. A worker carries to the job and into the workplace, all those cultural beliefs and behaviors obtained from all their cultural memberships. The workplace itself represents still another cultural context and each employee must learn the culture of that workplace in addition to all the others cultures that might characterize them. The other cultural beliefs and practices obtained as members of other groupings that characterize them are not left at the door as they enter their work setting and culture. This frequently can produce great conflicts for the individual who must choose which culture set (beliefs or behaviors) to follow in particular circumstances.

The different and multiple cultures with which any individual may affiliate can actually be in direct contradiction or conflict with others with which they also identify, such as a conflict that can easily develop between one's political, national, or religious cultures. The business culture can conflict with one's religious or political cultures. The demands of occupational culture can easily conflict with religious, political, or even social cultures. In such cases, individuals are forced to choose which culture set will influence their decisions and guide their actions. Most people separate aspects of their lives into distinct categories of activity, then use the cultural set that is most appropriate in each. But, it may also be that one of the cultures becomes the dominant or the primary cultural force in an individual's life, that particular culture becoming the sole or primary determinant of the choices made in all circumstances, even to the exclusion of all other culture groups with which they may choose to affiliate. For example, some religious groups disavow any allegiance the state, to nationality or national culture. This would be in direct contradiction to the interests, goals, and beliefs of the nation-state. Fortunately, no single cultural pattern will guide the choices of everyone all of the time, except perhaps in the totalitarian state where, superficially at least, everyone is guided by the same things. Some people are more influenced by politics and political groups, others by economics and economic groups. Still others are influenced more by their religious beliefs and religious group than anything else. Normally when individuals are perceived as oriented and focused to the beliefs and practices of a single group, they are judged to be shortsighted, narrow in view, perhaps even fanatical in their steadfastness. Sometimes the choice of culture set will be determined by its fit to the circumstances of the moment. Most humans are not influenced or motivated by a culture, rather, most are motivated by any number of cultures, any one of which can exert the greater influence on their actions at any given point in time or given a particular set of circumstances. Unfortunately, the multiculturalism of individuals has not yet been given any significant attention.

CONCLUSION

Every society, regardless of size, has a distinct culture that distinguishes it from all others. It is an integrated, adaptive, and always changing complex of learned ideas, behaviors, and products suited to the particular environments in which people find themselves. Culture is created in response to the problems posed in environments. It is a set of problem-solving solutions learned as truth. People will judge all others based on it. What they learn are actually different forms of that culture and each will play a role in the culture change process. Any one of its forms can guide, determine, or impact a person's or a group's response to particular situations and actions.

Humans group with others for all kinds of different reasons. They group together in response to problems or interests that arise in the natural or sociocultural environments created out of their actions in responding to the natural environment. But not everyone chooses the same solution to the same problem. When all the needs are satisfied, we end up with a system of solutions to problems that together we call culture. All of these solutions are related to one another and form an identifiable whole. The system is an integrated one that is then passed down from generation to generation as *the* way of thinking, believing, and doing. It has been created by them, and it becomes their reality. Culture becomes life's blueprint for thinking, acting, and believing. It becomes the road map that gets them from one day to the next. Putting together all the learned ways that an individual accumulates over the course of a lifetime, the individual's own culture construct provides the individual with all he or she needs to know, the prescriptions for what to think and do. It represents truth, their truth as they have learned it. They operate as if it is the only truth, or at the very least, the more correct one.

In the final analysis, given culture can be applied to all manner and kinds of human groupings within something as complex as a nation-state, it is not surprising that the concept is a difficult one for people to understand and apply. While it can make sense to those who intellectually study it as a human phenomenon, for others it is simply not meaningful. While culture is something that can be credited to all kinds of human groups, more important is the realization that culture is something that characterizes any relatively permanent human group that learns a specific way of belief or behavior that serves to distinguish it from other groups. Viewed in this manner, a cultural group becomes any distinguishable group of people who learn their own way of thinking and behaving, use this to distinguish themselves as a group (used by others to distinguish them as a group), and then pass the pattern on from generation to generation.

SUGGESTED READINGS

Barrett, R. A. 1984. *Culture and Conduct,* 2nd edition. Belmont, CA: Wadsworth. This volume is a well-written and concise discussion of the culture concept, the adaptiveness of culture, the symbolic nature of it, and its persistence over time.

Gamst, F. C. and Norbeck, E. 1976. *Ideas of Culture: Sources and Uses.* New York: Holt, Rinehart and Winston. This is a collection of readings on culture in which the authors examine the development of the culture concept and all the ways it has been looked at and used. This book should be considered basic reading on the culture concept.

Haviland, W. A. 1997. *Anthropology,* 8th edition. Fort Worth, TX: Harcourt Brace College Publishers. This is a basic introductory textbook for the discipline of anthropology, useful for anyone who desires an understanding of this discipline devoted solely to the study of humans and the human experience. This particular book is a straightforward and thorough presentation of the who, what, how, and substantive materials of the major subfields of anthropology.

Nash, D. 1993. *A Little Anthropology*, 2nd edition. Englewood Cliffs, NJ: Prentice-Hall. This volume is an abbreviated, yet insightful presentation on anthropology, its goals, perspectives, and methods. It serves as a suitable substitute for the more comprehensive introductory type book for gaining an understanding of this field.

Spradley, J. P. and McCurdy, D. 1972. *The Cultural Experience.* Prospect Heights, IL: Waveland. While primarily an introduction to ethnographic fieldwork, this volume is one of the few volumes to examine the concept of culture in the complex settings of nation-states. It also presents a number of ethnographies (cultural descriptions) for various cultural groups in America.

——— Two ———
America and Americans

PHYSICAL SETTING

The United States, setting for the American culture, is a huge nation by comparison to others throughout the world—the fourth largest—spread across some 3,615,123 square miles. The bulk of this nation-state (country) lies primarily within the temperate zone above the Tropic of Cancer and below the frigid zone, but parts of it lie outside this area, with Alaska bordering on the frigid zone to the north and Hawaii actually located in the Torrid Zone of the Pacific. Within this vast territory, one can find virtually every type of physical environment found on this planet. The human adaptations to this physical diversity have contributed to the diversity that now characterizes the nation. Virtually every type of human adaptation can be found within the borders of the United States, and its original inhabitants developed lives and cultures based on hunting and gathering, agriculture, or a combination of both kinds of activities. With the coming of the Europeans to the shores of this land, the existing diversity among cultural groups across America was only increased. The cultures of all those groups of Europe were added to the already wide variety of aboriginal cultural groups (Native American cultures) in America. Many of these were the malcontents and leavings of the Old World, who came to the New World to escape persecution, to find religious freedom, or to practice the cultural beliefs not tolerated where they originated. Some of them came simply to start a new life unhampered by the social conventions of the Old World. The ideas held by many of these immigrant groups and their reasons for coming to the new world combined with the values and ideas of the aboriginal peoples to provide the foundation for the American culture and society that developed. That culture would begin to develop almost immediately, continued to develop during the early colonial period, and would eventually lead to the revolution that resulted in the independence of America from England—the creation of the United States of America. Even before their independence from the English, the original inhabitants of the land that was to become the United States, were identified as *Americans*, basically to distinguish them as colonials of the British Empire in the New World. Over time, the term American became the common designation for citizens of the United States, well established and used both at home and abroad, and the term America has become synonymous with the United States.

Most scholars maintain that the new world was first occupied some 12,000 years ago by big-game hunters following the big herd animals across the Bering Land Bridge. Some recent research now suggests that the original occupation of the Americas may be as old as 35,000 to 40,000 years ago. It may also be the case that the original inhabitants were not simply the "big game hunters" as has been widely accepted, but were accompanied by others who practiced of a variety of lifestyles. Whatever the final resolution to the questions of occupation for the New World and by whom, it is clear that people entered what is now the United States well before the Europeans who took credit for its "discovery" in the 1400s. This means that a large number of cultural groups were already well-established in the area before the onset of the European invasion(s) that would substantially change the area that ultimately would become known as the United States. All of this diversity simply added to the diversity that already existed. While this may not be the place for an extensive discussion of the prehistory of America, there are some significant stages in the development of the original cultures of some significance. By 8000 B.C., most of the earliest inhabitants could be generally grouped into what has been referred to as the Clovis and post-Clovis (Paleo-Indian) cultures (Fagan 1991). By 2500 B.C., these earliest peoples evolved into what archaeologists term the Eastern Archaic (e.g., Lamoka, Dustin, Indian Knoll, late Plano, etc.), and the various desert culture groups (Carson, Pinto, San Jose, Grove, etc.). By the beginning of the first century, these highly generalized groups had evolved into more easily identifiable cultural groupings that spread across the breadth of the country. By A.D. 1000 these evolved into other groups more easily identified by their environmental adaptations, for example, southwestern farmers, desert, early Mississippian, and late Woodland groups. From this point on, until the coming of the Europeans, they continued to evolve into the specific cultural groups with which most American school children are quite familiar, albeit with a rather distorted picture based on the painted warrior of the plains.

By the time of the European invasion, there were already many distinct American Indian cultures in that part of the New World that would become America (Leacock & Lurie 1971). In the American Southeast, Indian cultures reached a sophisticated level of developed town life with elaborate ceremonial centers. In the Northeast, village life was based primarily on horticulture, augmented by the nomadic lifestyle of the hunter. On the plains, Indian cultures combined hunting and gathering with some of the Eastern agricultural adaptations. The hunting lifestyle focused primarily on the exploitation of the vast buffalo herds that filled and spread across the plains. This would become the adaptation that would lead to the culture of horsemen of the plains (what many Americans generally think of as the "typical Indian"). In the Southwest, groups of hunters and farmers also evolved, while in the Great Basin, the cultural groups could primarily be characterized as hunters and gatherers of nuts and other wild vegetables. On the Northwest coast, where food resources were quite plentiful, the people developed cultural patterns focused on fish and the other resources of the sea. In the Arctic and Subarctic regions, people lived in particularly harsh environments, but they also were able to create ingenious adaptations that enabled them to exploit both large herd animals and the mammals of the sea. In the far West, despite the absence of agriculture, people would develop an adaptation that included a fairly stable village life. It was into this array of quite diverse, yet well-established and well-adapted cultural patterns that reflected the many different physical environments of America, that European settlers arrived to change the face of the land and the peoples occupying it. Diversity was added to the already existing diversity.

In the interaction of the first immigrants and original inhabitants, the indigenous experience (more often than not simply the Indian experience) was almost as varied as the cultures that came in contact with it. Despite what Americans have learned through television and movies, no single theme characterizes the contacts between European immigrants and the aboriginal inhabitants. Some believed them to be civil and mannerly, others saw them as savages to be "saved." In the area that was to become Maryland, both Catholic and Anglican groups integrated quite well with the native cultures, oftentimes protecting the rights of local Indians and purchasing rather than simply taking land from them as occurred elsewhere. The Quakers of Pennsylvania made no distinctions between themselves and local Indians. All three of these groups believed the Indians to be well mannered and even civil (at least when compared to European standards). The Pilgrims and Puritans of the Northeast, saw the Indians as the "fallen people," or in the grip of Satan. This perception was to dictate their treatment of them. Where the Spanish influence was greatest, the Indian was perceived as a *primitive savage* or *barbarian* that needed to be civilized, meaning they were to be given the Christian religion. In Northern territories where English, French, and Russian influences collided and competed in the fur trade, economic ties and interactions between the aboriginal inhabitants and the colonials were frequent, strong, and in most cases, beneficial for both parties and the merging American culture. In nearly every area, the earliest immigrants to the New World had to rely on the local people for the knowledge essential to surviving in their new environment, a fact frequently forgotten or overlooked in the history of European American and Native American interactions. In many ways, the earliest relations were mutually beneficial to all the cultural groups who came in contact with one another, and in many parts of the nation, the early contact period is still referred to by Native Americans as the "Golden Age" or the "Shining Times."

From these varied experiences of contact, overall relations between the Indians and the immigrants rapidly deteriorated into something else as more and more immigrants came and the need for places for them grew. During the period from the 1700s to late 1800s, relations between the original inhabitants and the ever growing group known as the "white man" became a competitive one. Natives were largely viewed as savages and therefore enemies, but at the same time the idea of the "noble savage" was also becoming quite popular. American Indians were seen as a noble race, well formed, active, and intelligent. Despite this, the dominant perception among most Americans was that the Indians represented a military obstacle to be overcome (conquered). From this point on, the native groups were to experience a continuing loss of their sovereignty, constant conflicts with the white man whose appetite for land seems to be endless, and the severe disruption of their lives that continues up to the present time. Indians were pushed from their lands to make room for white settlers. The never-ending need for land simply fueled a steady expansion of the country and the spread of its influence into the remotest parts of the land. From the point of view of the new immigrants and dominant government, Indians simply had to "move over or die" to accommodate the steadily growing numbers of people making their way to the newly established United States. Overpowered by the sheer numbers of white people, many Native American groups and their cultures stood no chance at all. From the late 1800s to the 1930s, relations between the American government and the Indian groups were characterized by conquest and policies designed to destroy the Native communities. Relocations of Native groups from their traditional territories coveted by the growing number of Europeans became quite commonplace. Reservations, forced assimilation (loss of traditional culture and adoption of many of the new ways introduced by the outsiders), and the destruction of native religions also became commonplace. In essence, indigenous groups were forced to abandon traditional cultures, or significant aspects of them, and become *white Indians*. Treaties were ignored and treaty rights were terminated when it served the purposes of the white government. In their place came the discrimination, apathy, prejudice, and the inequality that seem to accompany such orientations.

More recently, an Indian consciousness has developed that serves to unite the otherwise very diverse Native American cultural groups. This loose, but identifiable Indian unity is based on common concerns and purposes that all such groups recognize. A corporate Native American now focuses on self-determination and full participation in the American sociocultural system. While many Native American cultures were able to (still do) maintain much of their traditional culture, there is little doubt that they were changed, and they have become part of the American culture as it exists today—part of the diversity that makes it up. Most Americans categorize all the Native Americans into a highly stereotyped and overgeneralized category they refer to as the "Indian culture." There is actually no such thing as an "American Indian culture," but there are many Native American Indian cultures across the United States, each reflecting its own historical heritage, unique beliefs, and practices. While in recent years they have come together to fight for their rights as citizens of the United States and as groups with treaty rights, they remain as culturally distinct as the many people who came to take away their lands.

AMERICAN HISTORY

Most people have a fair grasp of American history beginning with what they perceive as its "discovery" by the Europeans and their first heavy colonization, albeit skewed somewhat as history seems to be so constantly rewritten. Up until recently, the colonial history of the United States focused almost exclusively on the Eastern coast colonies—not surprising in view of the fact it was with these groups that the movement for independence was initiated. While there is little dispute that the primary heritage of America is an Anglo one, it is important to point out that different regions of this land were under other influences that left their historical legacies as well, for example, the Spanish in the Southwest, French in the Midwest, and Russians in the northern most part of the United States. Understanding the history of the United States is important, for understanding what is the American culture is in a large measure understanding how it got to be that way. Knowing what combined to produce what exists now, helps in the understanding of it and perhaps provides some hints as to where it may be going. To be sure, understanding the regional differences that have contributed to the diversity of the United States is going to be tied to each region's historical development. Learning about major events in the history of the United States is an important part of the cultural learning that all new or aspiring members of this culture must go through. But it is the issues and aspects of life that led up to and followed such events that are far more significant, for they combined to help create and sustain the culture as it now exists. The diversity that is American culture comes, in part, from the historical forces that have shaped its development.

In heritage, the American culture started with European traditions, primarily Anglo. With this as a foundation, what developed was distinctly American as this Anglo heritage combined with other traditions, particularly those of the aboriginal inhabitants. Many of the ideas originally held by the earliest immigrants, or those that they generated very soon after their coming to the shores of the United States, combined with many of the existing ideas of the Native Americans. Religion, environment, ethnicity, regional adaptations, and the idea of the individual were all to come out of this combination. All of these things are simultaneously involved with whatever historical period one might want to consider. The very diversity that today characterizes the culture is a common theme of its history. For example, the period of settlement and birth of the nation was not simply focused around an industrial (commercial) North and an agricultural South as it has been portrayed in the history book. The North actually consisted of both the commercial New England and a very agricultural New York, New Jersey, and Pennsylvania. The Chesapeake area (now Maryland, Virginia, and West Virginia), the Carolinas (with plantation agriculture) and the back country South (Kentucky and Tennessee) were all part of the South. There simply was not one North, but two; not one South, but three. Each of these environments were different, contained different resources, and were settled by different people, from different backgrounds, traditions, and religions. Vastly different adaptations were necessary. The specific adaptations made by those settling into these areas remain the basis for the regional differences that are still used to distinguish them. The same elements that serve to distinguish the earliest European Americans can be seen through the history of the United States as new areas were added to the nation. Evidenced by their presence throughout history, one can only conclude that the history of America is not simply the story of a single people coming out of a colonial past, but a history that is as complex as the diversity that frequently obscures its understanding. But it was from this varied history, as it combined many traditions, ideas, and behaviors that the American culture was forged.

AMERICAN PORTRAIT

In creating a demographic portrait of Americans, the usual place to begin is with the statistics provided by the United States Census. The United States Bureau of the Census (1992a) listed the population of the United States at 248,709,873, but later revised this number to 264,755,000 (1996). Other agencies of the U.S. government present other figures, for example, the U.S. Department of Commerce (1995), carries a population figure of 260,651,000 people for the United States. Whatever the exact figure might be, it is clear that the population of the United States is even more varied than the territory it collectively occupies. Within this population number are people from many parts of the world that have come to take up residence in America. There are few of the world's groups not represented in the United States. This fact is underemphasized in the population reports of the United States Bureau of the Census which is responsible for the national census every ten years. Started in 1790, the census numbers are supposed to reflect growth and shifts in living patterns, and in a most general way, they do provide a picture of where and how Americans live. But such reports are far too generalized, tend to group distinct populations together indiscriminately, and are subject to serious limitations, as evidenced in the need to "correct" them periodically. The ultimate faith most people have in the census is probably misplaced except on the level of statistical probability—meaning theoretically.

Everyone who has ever worked with the numbers provided by the Bureau of the Census knows about the questionable validity of them—most Americans do not. The figures of the bureau are always subject to correction, and many of these can be based on no more than someone's arguments (mostly political) rather than actual headcounts. This is not to say that the census does not provide some statistical understanding (profile) of the population of the United States. But it does suggest that the results should not be taken as the absolute truth or its results unquestionably accepted as facts. At the very best, statistical study only provides estimates, and then only because they are "close enough for government work," which after all, is an estimate's major purpose. They are widely used by government at all levels as the basis of policy decisions. Census statistics are used for urban planning, market projections, spotting trends, but more importantly, as the basis for government representation, the allocation of resources (budget allocations) for education, public transportation, housing, and any number of poverty programs. Given the numbers of actual Americans (leaving out for the moment any undocumented or illegal aliens within its borders that always go uncounted), a really accurate number could only come from an actual headcount and no one would want to undertake that.

A new strategy for taking the census strictly by statistical sampling is in the works. Whether or not this is done, the failings of the census will remain. For example, it is well known that the urban poor are the most likely to go uncounted, followed by the undocumented, and then those who simply refuse to respond. Be that as it may, the numbers provided by the Bureau of the Census, based on its sample surveys every ten years, do provide us with some data that can help us paint a telling picture of America and Americans, which can add to a better understanding of such things. But, there are some additional cautions that must be noted with regard to using census information.

Notwithstanding the limitations of the numbers given out and used for a variety of purposes, census categories perpetuate long-standing misconceptions of such things as race and culture. They provide numbers for social groups they have identified as races and numbers for races they identify as cultures, as if either one (as they have identified them) really exists. The categories used are arbitrary and artificial, but policy decisions are made based on them as if they are real. The categories and numbers reported tend to reinforce long-held stereotypes and over generalizations that even the government says it wants to eliminate. One can only wonder at the overgeneralized categories of dubious value used by the bureau to break down the population into various groupings, for example, African-Americans (meaning blacks in general), Asians (meaning anyone who comes from the East, Far East, or Southeast Asia), Hispanics (the term used for anyone, or their ancestors, who might speak Spanish), or American Indian/Pacific Islander/Others (a category created for people the government does not know how else to characterize). All of these are listed and understood as "racial groupings." The categories actually reflect either an artificial (and arbitrary) physical basis for a grouping (some kind of physical similarity), or it is based on artificially created cultural similarities where there are none (there is neither an Asian nor a Pacific Islander cultural group in the world). Native American is obviously intended to address aboriginal (native) people of the United States, while at the same time two very specific cultural groups from among the vast number of them are singled out, the Eskimo and Aleut.

At first glance, the distinction made by the bureau between black and white seems clear enough until one sees Hispanic—a cultural designation as a race, but then one is told this category includes all races! "Other" as a category, is obviously used to include all those others (races and cultures?) not specifically identified by the bureau as numerically significant to be identified separately. That bureau "racial" categories are little understood is obvious when an American is asked to identify, define or number the "races" in the United States. The very act of grossly grouping cultures into "races" and interchanging "racial" groups (as established by someone) with what are clearly cultural designations just leads to people equating culture and race—seeing them as basically the same thing when clearly they are not. Most Americans pay little attention to the census numbers until they are used by somebody arguing for something knowing that Americans have ultimate faith in the factual nature of a number. Of course, Americans accept them without question if it confirms what they already want to believe.

The consequence of census numbers and the established categories is to confuse and confound all but the scholars who take the time to look a little beyond the numbers that are released or discussed in the media. For example, the use of racial categories usually revolves around knowing how to combat obvious inequities and imbalances in the system. But if one looks closely at the categories, Hispanic includes all races, but this is separate from the black racial category. Just what is the "real" percentage of blacks that make up the general population? If the numbers lead to policy decisions, it would seem to be reasonable to count all blacks together rather than to divide them based on whether they speak Spanish or not, or is culture the desired distinction? One might expect that in a culture of diversity, but then races and cultures are much confused on a regular basis. To be sure, the numbers are made smaller and this means you may not have to do as much as if you included all those who would in real life simply be viewed as part of the black racial group. Then of course there are those of "mixed" descent and where do they get placed in the count? Clearly there are government motives that the average American will never really understand. More important is the tendency of Americans to accept the numbers—fallacious as they may be—that are then assumed as "reality." Americans "know" that numbers do not lie.

When contemplating the inclusion of demographic information on Americans, it is generally based on the idea that Americans need to have a better understanding of this kind of information. It is clear they have a somewhat skewed idea of the population of which they are a part and that where population trends are headed in the future will dramatically alter the American profile. The usual practice is to provide some graphs and charts for the numbers germaine to greater awareness. Upon reflection, doing this only reinforces the misconceptions of "reality" and "fact" already based on such things. While Americans in general have an unfaltering faith in quantification (the use of numbers as facts), some scholars have a bias against using numbers to represent actual humans. In the 1990 census material, the bureau reports 2.63 people per American household. While this simply extends what can be termed the ever popular "average," "norm" or "common man (person) mentality," it is difficult to envision the numbers representing reality. Two people perhaps, but a .63 person is a little more difficult to picture in one's mind. Some of the things reported in the census, albeit in statistical estimates, do provide some useful information as to this cultural group we call as a whole Americans. Even the most current population count may have over counted some, undercounted others, and maybe left some people out all together. Because of the manner in which such population numbers are generated, this could hardly represent the exact number of all Americans, but would probably be "in the ball park" or "be close enough for government work." Basically this tells us that there are a lot of these so-called Americans, with about 7.5 of them per square mile of land (here comes a partial person again). For the sake of keeping people intact, let us say seven to eight per square mile. Of this number, approximately 121,239,418 are males and 127,470,455 are females. For most people who see numbers determining minority status, clearly females should not be considered a minority.

While the census data do not really address the actual diversity of America, breaking the total number of people down into subgroupings as devised by the government, even on the fallacious racial/cultural basis the government uses, does allow that some information of value can be abstracted. For example, the total number of people who are categorized in the white racial group (anyone not stipulated as black or Asian [Oriental?]) clearly outnumber all other categories: 199,686,070 or 73.6 percent of the population (revised to 219,377,000 in 1995). Of course, as Americans can readily see, being included in the "white" racial group only applies in the census game, not as it exists in real life. For example, people with an origin in India are classified as white for the census, but for all other intents and purposes, they are categorized as part of the "black" category. The Bureau of the Census gives us a figure of 29,986,060 for the "black" racial group (roughly 11.1% of the total population, revised to 33,536,000 in 1995), but almost casually point out that a number of blacks (who knows how many) will also be found speaking Spanish and therefore are included in the Hispanic racial category, actually bringing down the numbers of "blacks" in the United States. Hispanics number 22,343,059 or 8.2 percent of the population (later revised to 27,774,000 in 1995), and the only requirement for inclusion in this group appears to be based on one's ability to speak Spanish, or one's ancestors spoke some version of that language, or they come from an area of the world where Spanish is the predominate spoken language. The Bureau of the Census also tells us there is an Indian, Eskimo, Aleut race that numbers 1,959,234 or some 0.7 percent of the total population—an interesting construction based on race and culture, with some casually overlooked built-in contradictions. There is no Indian race or culture. There are many Native cultures. Eskimo unfairly overgeneralizes three distinct groups of Eskimo, and Aleut is only one of the many cultures that actually can be identified for Native Americans. It reports an Asian/Pacific Islander race (simply collapsing a very large number of distinct groups, both physically and culturally, into a single one) that equals 7,273,662 people or 2.7 percent of the total population in the United States, revised to 9,572,000 in 1995.

If over generalizations surrounding the categories of race used by the government are not confusing enough, they also provide an "other" racial category and simply drop everyone else into this one, suggesting its numbers to be around 9,804,847 people or 3.6 percent of the totals (later revised to 2,210,000 in 1995). In another part of the census, the government reports the following races: White (83.1%), Black (11.7%), Eskimo/Aleut (0.6%), American Indian (0.6%), Asian/Pacific Islander (1.5%), Chinese (0.4%), Filipino (0.3%), Japanese (0.3%), Asian Indian (0.2%), Korean (0.2%), and Vietnamese (0.1%). It breaks down Hispanics (6.4%) into Mexican (3.9%), Puerto Ricans (0.9%), Cuban (0.4%), and others (1.3%). This probably provides a little better conception of the actual population makeup of the United States. Of course, other government offices (e.g., U.S. Department of Commerce) provides somewhat different numbers, listing 216,470,000 Caucasians, 32,672,000 African-Americans, 22,354,059 people of Hispanic origins, 7,273,662 Asian-Americans, and some 9,804,847 "others" in the United States (1995). Simple mathematics demonstrates that even the government agencies are not together on the "official" numbers.

With still more numbers, the census tells us that in terms of income levels; 9.8 percent of the whites live below the poverty level, while 29.5 percent of the blacks, 28.2 percent of the Hispanics, 14.1 percent of the Asia/Pacific Islanders, 30.9

percent of the American Indians (Native Americans), and 25.3 percent of the "others" live below the poverty level. In translation, the numbers suggest whites have more opportunities than other "racial groups." The category or group in this worst state is the American Indian, often overlooked with so much attention paid to the "blacks" and "Hispanics" in the political arena. These statistics translate into an average income of $30,056 per household, $35,225 for families, and $17,240 for nonfamilies (interesting concept). In 1995, the figures were revised to $32,264 as an average income level for Americans, with 31,742,846 people living below the poverty line ($12,674). The average middle income was set at $45,041—$31,241 by the Department of Commerce. Whichever figure is closest must still be viewed with caution as such numbers represent averages in which a few making absurd incomes (e.g., athletes, entertainers, corporate executives) skew the numbers of what more normal American will earn.

Attempting to use these census categories for some portrait of the American population makeup is thus, risky at the very least. What the government means by race is certainly contradictory, perhaps politically motivated. But the generalized groupings represented in the categories and numbers reported for them over time does provide us with a sense of history and developing trends. The significance of the newest numbers being reported speaks of a majority group that will soon outnumber the "whites," even if we do not know exactly what that might mean. Comparing the latest numbers to those of previous census efforts also points to a long developing trend that foreshadows the future makeup of America. Clearly, by the year 2030, minority groups will numerically overtake the group with the largest numbers at present (unless the government can come up with more ingenious means of including them in the white race later on). Overlooking the obvious limitations of the figures, the census provides other bits of information that can help us understand the United States and its people.

For example, the average family size in the United States has been set at 2.63 (U.S. Department of Commerce has set this at 3.2) and this is apparently still dropping. Family size is relatively small compared to other nation-states in the world. Nuclear families are found in one-quarter of the population, while childless and single-parent families are obviously on the increase. In translation, this simply means the American family grouping tends to be small. The average age of the males is 31.7 years and 34.1 years for females. This means that females tend to live longer than males do. Of the combined total, about 25 percent of the population is under the age of 18 and about 13 percent is over age 65. The larger numbers of people between these two age groupings fall much closer to 65 than 18. What this means is that, overall, the population is aging. The focus of most decision making and commercialization in the country is on the younger Americans. The median age for all American is 32.9 years. This means half the population is older than that. Most Americans seem to prefer living as married couples without children, in "nontraditional" arrangements, or as single parents with children. Men and women living alone seem to be on the increase. It also appears that most Americans are waiting longer to get married, the average marriage age now some 26.1 years. The number of divorced Americans continues to rise, and one child in four lives with only one parent. Most Americans (75% of the population) are urban dwellers, rural inhabitants comprising up to one-quarter of the population. Of course, among the numbers of rural dwellers are those who work and play in the urban environment and simply return to the rural areas for bedroom purposes. What this means is that most Americans are urbanites, live in the cities, and the earlier agrarian settlement pattern of the United States has been usurped. According to George and Louise Spindler (1993), the American hinterlands (rural areas) look very much alike, small populations, materially organized around houses, yards, main streets, and so forth. The people found there tend to value competence, noninterference, independence, earning a living, separation of sexes, local loyalty, and the importance of family, kin and friends. Urban (suburban and metropolitan) inhabitants tend to focus on career and success, are oriented to the future, are self-disciplined, highly competitive, hold rather low regard for kin and family, are unisex in social relations and ideology, and understand little neighborliness. For them, the workplace is the neighborhood.

Based on the statistics, it would seem that most Americans live in three or four different kinds of household types, with an unspecified number (there was no attempt to determine how many) living in no household at all—the homeless. The Bureau of the Census cannot count them, but Americans need only to look out the window to know of their existence. At any rate, based on what was counted, 55.5 percent of the population lives as couples in a household, 29.8 percent lives by themselves, and others live in what is referred to as group quarters. About two to three people occupy the household on average, such numbers also pointing to the rise in individual households. The bureau reports that some 64.2 percent of the population owns their own homes with an average value of $79,100. Because of the wide gap in the cost of home ownership, this average quite likely skews reality as already noted with income levels. Compared to other nations and areas of the world, the stated average income probably creates the perception of Americans as "rich" people, while the majority of Americans are clearly not "rich." It probably does contribute to the idea of the American Dream, which also is tied to home ownership. But while the numbers reflect a continually declining number of Americans who own their homes, the reality is that nearly half of the American population do not own their own homes.

According to the census data, some 67.1 percent of Americans still live in the state where they were born. This would seem to contradict the characterization of Americans as a highly mobile population, perhaps the most mobile population in the world. That Americans are a highly mobile population has been around for a great many years. Perhaps the mobility being spoken of is mobility within one's birth state.

The spoken languages of Americans is another questionable category of the Census. According to the census reports, the primary languages of the United States are English, Spanish, Asian, and Pacific, but this downplays the real numbers of different languages spoken within the country. Based on responses to the census survey, the ancestry of Americans is heavily English and German, with thirty-four other ancestries left unspecified. Given the vagueness of the population figures, the assertion is obviously misleading and questionable.

The latest statistics also show that most immigrants to the United States continue to flock to select states and urban or metropolitan areas. In these areas, their ethnicity, racial categorization, and skill levels tend to differentiate them from already established resident populations. Existing inhabitants are moving out to those areas where the immigrants are not attracted. This even more sharply isolates and segregates people. People with low levels of skill are being pressured by the continuing influx of immigrants. What was a pattern of segregation throughout history is simply getting worse. Whereas in the past, ethnic or racial segregation was limited to neighborhoods in the same cities, now the pattern is moving toward entire cities becoming segregated, distinguished by their race occupation or ethnic occupation. This can only lead to more difficulties and conflicts.

So what is the actual demographic profile for Americans? Notwithstanding the multitude of other statistics and numbers provided in the most current census, there seems to be some things that can be said even if they are based on questionable numbers out of questionable practices by the Bureau of the Census. First, it seems readily apparent that the United States as a nation enjoys a favorable ratio of population to land mass. As compared to Indonesia, with a ratio of 134 people per square mile (at least on the major islands and minus Irian Jaya), the United States is not densely populated. As the country encompasses a vast variety of different kinds of landscape, it is hard to determine the exact ratio of population to useable land. In terms of the population at large, it appears to encompass a wide range of people from different racial/cultural groupings (as determined by someone in the government at least), with whites (presumably mostly European American) as numerically dominate, with blacks and Hispanics following with the next largest numbers. That there are a great many other groups also seems apparent. Coming as no real surprise to anyone, the United States is populated by a very diverse group of people representing nearly all the "so-called" races and cultures represented in the rest of the world. As one might also expect, based on the numbers alone, it would appear that some groups do better than others. Most of this population tends to be centered in the cities, or more precisely the major metropolitan areas. This suggests a different lifestyle and adaptation for those inhibiting the urban areas as compared to those found in nonurban areas. Because of the tendency to accept numbers as facts, it is surprising how much of the census is generally accepted as the way things really are, although many people question the conclusions that relate to the dramatic increases of minority group populations, increases that threaten the current power structure. At the very least, the statistics get us moving in terms of defining this American culture and its people. Based on some of these statistics, perhaps in spite of them, certain perceptions about this society continue to survive relatively intact.

PERCEPTIONS OF AMERICAN CULTURE

Asking Americans to define or characterize their culture generates an interesting array of responses. A great many of them are clearly based on the census materials they are provided, but others base their perceptions on what they have learned over the years, or discovered for themselves. Some people even suggest the notion that there is no single American culture and no "true" Americans, but an amalgam or conglomerate of many cultures, a fusing of the many groups that combine to make it up. This is based on their understanding of the history of immigration that has lead to the presence of people representing so many different cultures of the world in the United States. This kind of perception is tied to the belief that immigrants who come to America tend to keep their traditions intact, simply adding their contribution to that of others to produce whatever American culture might be. Other Americans suggest that this compilation has resulted in an America that is different from any other culture by virtue of the very diversity that has produced such a varying population—diversity added up as it were. Despite everything else said, Americans generally recognize that diversity is a major characteristic of the United States and its culture. This generally means regional, racial, and ethnic differences, all of which are usually referred to as something akin to *subcultural* differences.

Many Americans see their culture as defined by some ideas tied to freedom, politics, economics, change, and its countless contradictions. The United States as "the land of the free" is certainly one of the main themes (characteristics) that members of this cultural group will relate to the outsider. The idea of freedom is intricately tied to their beliefs in the individual and the freedom of the individual, which presupposes Americans as tolerant and nonconformist, as well. These things underlie many other things they tend to believe about themselves. Certainly, the ideal of democracy is another of the first things Americans will use to characterize their culture and many of them see this as creating the capitalist government and an extremely cumbersome legal system. America also is perceived as a constantly changing culture, a peaceful one, a culture centered around the nuclear family and socioeconomic classes organized around wealth. This usually sets off a listing of other things that are American; an economically driven system with a materialistic orientation, a capitalist system, the worship of money for its own sake, the credit card economy, and so forth. Many hold that America is a Christian nation (society) that believes in God, while at the same time they will also note the religious diversity that is part of America. Other people focus on the culture differences that focus on race and ethnicity, as they cite the racism, sexism, discrimination, and prejudice that accompany them. Having characterized their America using these kinds of comments, Americans are also very quick to point out the contradictions or paradoxes of their society and its culture. Generally, while pointing out that their culture is one of peace, Americans recognize the apparent contradiction generated by the amount of violence in their world. They recognize their own tolerance for difference is contradicted by the continuation of cultural bias (that of their very own cultural groups), tied to racism, sexism, and the realities of multiple social classes. While Americans see their world as one of nonconformity, the need for conformity, meaning a need for social order, is not lost on them. They also freely admit that the much-touted work ethic is counterbalanced by the laziness displayed by many of their fellow Americans and the seemingly overemphasized leisure activities that consume considerable amounts of their time and wealth.

Non-Americans have significantly different views of Americans and their culture (DeVita & Armstrong 1993; Spindler & Spindler 1993). American culture is seen as an individually centered society, with an emphasis on self-reliance. Depending on what part of the world the perception comes from, the character of American culture will change. In the view of many, given the immigrant makeup of the United States, there is a widespread belief that there is no American culture at all, only a society that is a patchwork of the "leavings" of many other nations of the world. In some quarters, the central focus of the culture is solely an economic one wherein Americans are portrayed as skillful merchants with a "healthy" respect for fiscal achievement. This is generally a positive characteristic given the patterns of the industrial world—a world of merchants and mechanics. But it also means they are perceived as having no morals, but operate from rules in their stead. There is no honor or dishonor, but only winning and losing. This gives them a shallowness and insensitivity. Americans are seen as loud, bold, brash, clumsy, good-hearted, and generous to a fault. They appear eager to share, in fact insist on sharing, their wealth and ideology with all the world, particularly their political or democratic ideology, which they huckster to the entire world. Their government is seen as nothing more than a series of social contracts. They sell their education on a per hour basis. Their marriages are shallow and easily broken. Most outsiders see no work ethic among Americans, but readily recognize Americans as racist, with superiority/inferiority tied to cultural characteristics or physical difference and origins.

Based on interviews of university students in an American culture class, and based on their talks with fellow Americans and international students attending classes on American campuses, it would appear that the perceptions of what makes for an American or American culture by both Americans and other nationals have not varied much since the onset of the 1990s. Most internationals point to the freedom and diversity of America. Many continue to point to family structure, treatment of the elderly, education, self-righteousness, a fast pace, and impersonal attitude as the greatest weaknesses of the culture. Among the other observations they have made: (1) Americans are trusting, liberal, open-minded, yet prejudiced; (2) they are conformist; (3) oriented to change; (4) quantify everything; (5) lacking in religion; (6) live isolated lives; and (7) are generally viewed as "rich." Many internationals find dealing with Americans very difficult. When Americans are pressed for descriptive adjectives for their culture, they still tend to use money, status, power, sex, freedom, success, entertainment, material wealth, and physical appearance to describe it. Many of their descriptions are also seen as the greatest threats to the culture (perhaps better seen as weaknesses). Among the threats to American culture elicited from interviews, Americans see themselves and their culture threatened by such things as the closed-mindedness of Americans, the erosion of their manufacturing base, rampant prejudice and ignorance, television, poverty, crime, technology, continuing immigration, religion and science. Many of these same observations have been made by non-American scholars who have commented on America and Americans.

Francisco Ramos notes that Americans generally take their language use, social life, body ritual, leisure, and a great many other customs for granted, rarely, if ever, thinking about them on a conscious level (1993:1–10). Harriet Marineau in the 1830s remarked that Americans worship opinion, that the will of the majority rules, and the need to belong produces the conformity that characterizes the United States (Spindler & Spindler 1993). According to Alexis de Toqueville, Americans are independent, resistant of authority, committed to equal justice, and preoccupied with making money in order to obtain the material. He also notes Americans are lonely people, consumed by the constant drive to improve themselves, and focused on equality, which he saw as conformity as well (Spindler & Spindler 1993:47). According to the Spindlers, Baron J. A. Graf von Hubner (1870s) also recognized individuality as significant to Americans but saw this as meaning self-centered and preoccupied with self-grandizement (1993:47). They also suggested that Frederick Turner in the 1890s formulated the "frontier hypothesis" for Americans, an idea that has stuck right through the 1990s. This was also based on individuality, conformity, and resistance to authority. The Spindlers also report that David Riesman in 1951, characterized Americans as inner-directed, something tied to a society preoccupied with production, discovery, and science. And lastly, they credit David Potter as trying to configure American attributes based on the notion that to be American meant that all Americans had something in common—individuality and conformity at the same time. It would appear that all the writers on American culture agree that individuality is very important to Americans.

Cultural Metaphors

Because of the diversity of its habitat and people, diversity has become a major defining characteristic for the culture. On the most general level, characterizing the people of the United States and its American culture, while hardly informative, has been a much loved pastime for people within the United States and throughout the world. For many people in other parts of the world, particularly those with long histories to their own nation-states (countries), civilizations, or heritages, the United States has no culture of its own simply because as a nation-state it is just too new, too young to have developed one, or because it consists of people from throughout the world. To many, the United States is simply a place where many cultures will be found, and Americans are people who live in the United States. Beyond those who would suggest the United States has no culture, because of the diversity of natural environments within its borders and its people who have come from every corner of the world, the United States culture has been likened to many things. Perhaps the most widely used characterization of the United States (and its culture), even among Americans themselves, is the perception of it as a *melting pot*. This particular idea (metaphor) of American culture that is shared by a large number of Americans, as well as those from other parts of the world, is a reflection of the diversity that is immediately recognized for the United States, a diversity born out of so many different people coming to the United States to live, work, mix, and blend together into what is perceived as one big assimilated culture. From the point of view of the Americans who hold such a notion of America, the resulting culture is stronger than the sum of the parts and better than the unique cultures that blend together to make it up. The main idea conveyed in this metaphor to describe American culture is assimilation. People come to the United States with their cultures, but ultimately become assimilated (disappear) into the mainstream of America, much as two metals are melted together to produce a new one, both losing their original character in the process. While this is clearly the most prevalent and popular metaphor in use with regard to American culture, there are other metaphors that are popular as well.

Another metaphor used to characterize the culture of the United States is that which likens it to a tributary system or watershed. In the image engendered in this metaphor, the United States provides numerous paths for the many cultures (much like the waters or rivers making up a watershed) to maintain their unique identities while they all move in the same basic direction to a common destination. Another metaphor portrays American culture as a tapestry or decorative cloth. As with a tapestry, which consists of a variety of threads, some thick, some thin, with different textures, strength, and exhibiting a panorama of color, the culture groups of the United States are like groups of these threads and colors—they vary, but when woven together make for the American culture. The Garden Salad Metaphor sees American culture much as one sees a salad, made up of many different ingredients that when tossed together result in a unique salad mix or blend.

Given the difficulty in coming up with a characterization of the culture with the great diversity of cultures contained within the Unites States, the Puzzle Metaphor is probably as good as any. This perceives American culture consisting of a finite number of pieces that when fitted together form a picture. Trying to fit the pieces together is certainly a challenge in view of the fact that pieces can share attributes (color and shape) while they remain separate and different. Combining the pieces produces various parts of the picture, or in the case of the United States, combine to form different aspects of the culture. If one believes there is something called American culture, the coming together of the picture is accomplished by matching geometric shapes that fit just right to produce the picture. Of course, the entire effort to understand a culture is not unlike trying to make sense out of the pile of puzzle pieces with which you begin the process. In the case of the puzzle, the effort is made eminently easier when a representation of the end produce (the picture) is provided that can serve as a guide in putting it together.

All of these metaphors used to characterize American culture can be and are strongly criticized by the scholar and nonscholar alike. The Melting Pot Metaphor assumes the assimilation of people, the laying aside of the cultures they had or brought with them, and the wholesale acceptance of the lifestyle associated with living in the United States. As in the combination of metals to produce a new one, the original metals used in the process lose their original properties. In terms of people, an amount of assimilation must certainly occur if the group is going to survive in the new environment (foods, ideas, and behaviors might have to be changed), but the total assimilation assumed in the "melting process" simply does not occur. Some immigrant groups and many Native Americans steadfastly resist total assimilation, preferring instead to continue many of the beliefs and practices that characterized them before becoming citizens of the United States. Such groups have to assimilate to a degree, but rarely do they lose all of what they were before. If the Melting Pot Metaphor has any validity at all, it is in association with each individual group, where the old and the new is melted together to produce a whole new culture that is unique (e.g., Mexican-American, Japanese-American, Irish-American, etc.). People must change some of their beliefs and behaviors in order just to survive in this context.

While the Tributaries Metaphor is intriguing, the separateness of the cultures (tributaries) is illusionary in that they could not remain that separate and survive intact, despite the commonality of any objectives or goals. As with the Melting Pot Metaphor, some traditional practices simply may not fit into the pattern of the new culture (e.g., the practice of female circumcision of many African cultures would not be tolerated in the United States). The same can be said of the Tapestry and Garden Salad Metaphors, with their emphasis on maintaining separate identities, although the Tapestry idea does probably fit the circumstances of the United States to a greater degree. Even the Puzzle Metaphor seems somehow to miss the real point of American culture. Each of these attempts is alike in the main—they all try to capture the whole of what the culture is about given the diversity that is readily recognized by everyone. They all suggest that there is something called American culture. They all suggest that the something is a result of the combination of the diversity of cultures that somehow contributed to a uniqueness that differentiates Americans and their culture from others.

MAINSTREAM AMERICAN CULTURE

If there is an American culture, it will be found in the learned beliefs, behaviors, and the products of these that are shared by all (or nearly all) Americans. Joseph G. Jorgenson and Marcello Truzzi (1974) suggest that on the level of learned and shared beliefs, American culture is probably best reflected in what has been called the *American mainstream*. This mainstream culture is outlined in the Declaration of Independence, United States Constitution, and the Bill of Rights. It also is reflected in the many laws passed by the American government throughout the history of the country. There are those who would suggest that an American culture exists only on this ideal level, in the ideas and values reflected in these founding documents. But, there exists a significant gap between these stated ideals and the realities of actually living in America—real beliefs and behaviors rarely living up to the stated ideals of any culture grouping. Mainstream American culture does pinpoint the idealized beliefs or ideas that are shared by individual Americans. They identify the ideas behind how the people think of themselves, about who they are, what they stand for, where they want to go in their lives, and the way they believe things ought to be. The ideas of the American mainstream generate individual and group behaviors in the direction of achieving the American Dream, the shared goal of all Americans. It represents that goal to which every American strives, and it is the standard by which the success or failure of the individual American or group will be measured. But, as pointed out by Lucy Garretson (1976), the portrait of the American mainstream is closely intertwined with what has become known as the middle class, and there is a great difference between the American Dream and the reality of actually achieving it. Despite this, the fact remains that nearly every American, irrespective of his or her origins, other cultural affiliations, assignments, or identities, shares the goal of achieving the American Dream and becoming a part of the American mainstream.

It is important to remember that nation-state cultures are arbitrary creations, they come into being as new nations are created. A sense of identity and affiliation—a sense of nationality—has to be developed among the members of the new cultural grouping if it is going to survive. Before that can be accomplished, some effort must be devoted to defining the new nation-state, how it wants to see itself or as it wishes others to see it, what it will stand for, and defining the basic rights and obligations of its members. How this is done will vary from nation to nation, group to group. In the specific case of the United States, it was accomplished by a group of people representing the different areas and interests represented in the country at the time it was created. By compromise, these representatives came to an agreement as to what the United States would be about and they presented this to all those who suddenly found themselves a part of a new nation. It was a group effort, and it presented their collective and compromised ideas of what the new country should be and how they wanted the rest of the world to see it. This was presented in its most ideal form and the ideal American culture was born. This is what is reflected in the American mainstream and embodied in the American Dream, both of which underscore the thinking of all Americans. It is what brings immigrants to the country and what becomes the goal (ideally) of all Americans.

George and Louise Spindler (1993) discuss the American mainstream at some length, while at the same time they disavow the existence of American culture because it is too diverse. According to these authors, the American mainstream includes anyone who acts like a member of it (the true mainstream), acts like anyone else in the dominant population, and has the income to support it. As with most other treatments of the mainstream, the focus is on the shared values or value orientations. While the authors list five major orientations (freedom of speech, rights of the individual, achievement, social mobility, and equality), all can be reduced to individualism. According to the Spindlers, mainstream value orientations emphasize the individual and individuality. Interestingly enough, while identifying the mainstream values, the authors only attribute them to some Americans, citing diversity as precluding it from being used to identify American culture. While not all Americans meet the criteria for mainstream identification, this does not mean that they do not share the ideas or are not striving to become a member of it. In point of fact, people immigrate to the United States for what it promises, and they constantly work toward being identified with this ideal. Once attaining the markers of it, they make it part of their identification. The Spindlers also suggest that a biculturalism is created for a group, one that is quite workable in the larger context. This would suggest that the diversity of approaches used by the various groups to achieve mainstream success in the United States is quite valid. As pointed out by

David M. Potter (1993:51–52), a configuration of attributes can be posited for Americans, only after accepting that all people have an obligation to "be American." This suggests a commonality among Americans, while at the same time provides for individualism. The usual difficulty comes with discussing minorities in America in relation to the mainstream culture profile. But in this, the mainstream remains a viable standard for the culture. While the expected use of English may be added to the characteristics normally provided for it, there remains little doubt that minorities have internalized, at least ideally, the main value orientations of America. They participate in the institutions that are part of it, and if they are successful, they accept the affiliation as part of their identity.

As already suggested, the mainstream is frequently used synonymously with "middle America," or more precisely, the white middle class of America, which encompasses the vast majority of Americans. W. Arens and Susan Montague (1976) see the culture of the middle class as embodied in symbols, and the measure of participation in the mainstream and the middle class associated with the symbols that mark it—material well-being relative to the acquisition of things of comfort. Even Dennison Nash (1993) would agree that the middle class comes with shared ideals. While it does establish a dominant tone or theme for the culture, it cannot be ascribed to only the predominant whites of America, for all other groups are striving for the very same things associated with it. Nash associates it with the power elite—being on the boards of large corporations, owning an expensive home, and so on. While this does characterize more "whites" than others, the "others" are clearly going after the same things. They obviously share the values, the question comes with the struggles to come to grips with them when they are frequently denied access to those areas of the society where they can obtain them.

If one accepts the notion that culture exists in ideas that then generate behavior, they have to conclude that the American culture does exist in this suggestion of a mainstream culture in America, that body of ideas usually associated with the middle class. There is little doubt that the ideas that are inherent in the notion of the mainstream do generate the behaviors that then characterize Americans in their striving to reach the level of being identified with it. But American culture is more than just the ideas of the mainstream that generate behaviors. While the ideas certainly generate behaviors deemed essential to attaining the level of success implied, the actual behaviors may not be the same for everyone, are not, perhaps cannot be, shared among those calling themselves Americans. In fact, the behaviors can be quite different, given whatever circumstances of equality and opportunity they may experience as part of other constituent groups. But there are other behaviors that all Americans share, and this too, suggests the existence of American culture.

There are the prerequisite behaviors that all Americans are expected to adhere to, irrespective of where they may have come from or what other cultural affiliations that tend to identify them (ethnic identities, economic class, special interests, or whatever). Members of all the constituent groups making up the population of the United States must live up to certain rules laid down for all. All societies require social order and in the nation-state this means the development of rules by which everyone will live. Social order is a core concern of all culture groups, essential for the continued survival of the society and its culture. In the case of the United States, there is federal law and that applies to every citizen. The national curriculum is mandated to produce fully functioning adult Americans. The same core is to be taught in all public schools (a uniform curriculum) and these same things must be mastered by immigrants seeking citizenship. Wearing clothes in public is requisite for everyone. No one can advocate the violent overthrow of the government. Everyone enjoys the freedom of speech, but only so long as it does not cause injury to anyone else. Individuals are not supposed to go around killing people, stealing their property, or violating any of the other laws written down in codified law to establish and maintain social order. In this sense, American culture does exist in these shared behaviors required of all American citizens. The same goes for many of the cultural products of the American society and culture. All Americans share the same enculturation system, the same political and economic systems.

Ideas translated by or through behavior produce physical or social products. Once again, with the products of culture, all Americans do share some things, irrespective of any other cultural affiliations or identities with which they are associated. Americans share the organizational systems created to take care of the things all cultural groups must make provisions or they simply do not survive. Much of the prerequisite behavior noted above is part of the political and legal systems that characterize all human groups—in essence provide for the social order necessary for large groups of humans to live together. As noted on several occasions, in the larger populated nation-states, the problem is a bit more complicated than in a small-scale society. All American citizens are forced to function within the same political process or legal process. All Americans participate (more or less) in the same money dominated market-exchange economic system. While this could go on indefinitely, the point is that an American culture, dependent on the shared products of culture does exist. Those who would suggest that there is no American culture because of the very diversity that characterizes it simply do not understand culture. It is easy to document the learned ideas, behaviors and products shared by all those calling themselves Americans. They share the "idea" of America (as reflected in the white middle class and mainstream), the prerequisite behavior established for all Americans (the law of the land), and the social products or organizational systems that are created to determine how the group has to organize itself to get things done that must be done if they, their society, and culture are to survive.

SUGGESTED READINGS

Crunden, R. M. 1994. *A Brief History of American Culture*. New York: Paragon House. Rather than present another dry history of the United States, the author of this volume discusses the historical developments of American culture from its beginning to the 1990s, focusing on Christianity, capitalism, and democracy. While this might be seen as a bit peculiar in emphasis, the author does provide a rather interesting look at the culture of the United States and is a good source for obtaining a historical understanding of some of the forces that have shaped this culture from its beginning.

DeVita, P. R. and Armstrong, J. D. (eds.). 1993. *Distant Mirrors: America as a Foreign Culture*. Belmont, CA: Wadsworth Publishing. The authors of this collection of essays look at American cultures as strangers might do, using the perceptions and interpretations of foreign scholars looking at America. This book is not highly theoretical or jargon-filled, but it does offer a fresh perspective on American culture—as outsiders see it. The authors present a challenge for Americans to look at their own culture. Of special note, is the contribution of Francis K. Hsu in which he characterizes Americans as individually centered and having a core value of self-reliance.

Drechsel, E. J. 1993. A European anthropologist's impression of the United States. In *Distant Mirrors: America as a Foreign Culture*. DeVita, P. R. and Armstrong, J. D. (eds.). Belmont: Wadsworth, pp. 120–145. This author argues for a unique American culture, one based on European influence but also influenced by aboriginal cultures and non-Europeans.

Fagan, B. M. 1991. *Ancient North America: The Archaeology of a Continent*. New York: Thames and Hudson. This particular volume focuses on the prehistory of the United States, or that period before the coming of European immigrants. Based on archaeological data, the author reconstructs the various cultures and lifestyles of America's aboriginal inhabitants.

Leacock, E. and Lurie, N. 1971. *North American Indians in Historical Perspective*. New York: Random House. Organized around the idea of cultural areas within which people share cultural similarity, the authors present characterizations of Native Americans across the country prior to European contact.

Roberts, S. 1995. *Who We Are: A Portrait of America Today Based on the Latest U.S. Census*. New York: Random House. This excellent volume looks at the information of the latest census to create a demographic profile of the United States and its people, cutting to the most relevant information as contained within the census. The author goes well beyond just relating the numbers, providing insightful interpretations and conclusions that can be drawn from a statistical look at this society and its people.

Spindler, G. and Spindler, L. 1993. *The American Cultural Dialogue and Its Transmission*. Bristol, PA: Falmer Press. This volume is organized around the theme of a cultural dialogue in which all Americans participate, They emphasize values of individuality, freedom, community, equality, and success. It also addresses the differences in America between the urban and rural areas, and the viewpoints of black and Chicano racial groups. A good treatment of how groups not part of the dominant cultural group scene attempt to adapt to it.

Three
Ideas Americans Live By

Many attempts have been made to identify just what values, assumptions, and other ideas Americans share. Of course, up to now, the question as to how much needs to be shared has gone unanswered. In the last chapter, it was suggested that there are some basic or core ideas that all Americans do share. These are presented quite eloquently in the various documents creating the United States (Declaration of Independence, United States Constitution, and the Bill of Rights). These basic or orienting ideas on which the country was based are reflected in what is known as the mainstream culture, usually equated with the predominant white middle class. Mainstream culture represents the idealized standard for many Americans, both a short-term or long-term goal for most of them. The ideas of individualism, freedom, diversity, and conformity on which the founding documents and the mainstream culture are based are the dominant orienting ideas of Americans—ideas on which those things most desired or deemed most valuable are based. Not only do these lie at the heart of American culture, they generate most of the other ideas, values, and assumptions by which Americans live, along with the behavior they elicit and by which Americans function on a daily basis. While these orienting ideas generate many other ideas and behaviors for Americans, what they generate is not the same for all individuals or groups. There are even variations on them within all groups. Because of this, identifying the other shared ideas and values of Americans has always been a major problem. They generate different ideas for different individuals and groups depending on their circumstances. In terms of behaviors, the problems are even greater, for while values may influence behavior (sometimes even direct it), given cultural differences based on class, religion, ethnicity, special interests, they have generated so many different behaviors that it would be impossible to list them all, even for a well-delineated or specific cultural group wherein significant diversity can be documented. On top of this comes the realization that some behaviors have no relationship to the values of the group. The simple fact is that most Americans do not associate value orientations with self or any of their actual cultural affiliations. The most that can be expected is to identify those values that all share, those that are widely shared, those that many tend to share, or relate specific ideas or combination of ideas to the specific constituent culture groups within which they are predominant. Even here, generalization is necessary, but risky. There will always be exceptions to generalizations that might be suggested. Some of these differences are consequences of the multitude of social and cultural groupings that exist in America, the diversity even within the identified constituent culture groups, the differing perceptions of individuals and groups as to what is valuable to them and how to obtain that, and the different conditions within which individuals and groups have to live in the context of a complex nation-state.

Most studies of American culture focus on shared ideas or values, and they all reach the same basic conclusions. Beyond the dominant, major, or orienting ideas of individualism and freedom, Americans seemed to share very little. Because of this, there has always been a great deal of generalization and discussion of certain ideas as American norms—what *most* Americans *seem to share* or to which they *seem to subscribe*. Just how far one could or should generalize across all Americans has always occasioned considerable debate among those undertaking the study of American culture or some aspect of it. There always seem to be some individuals or groups that do not share whatever is identified. In the complex social makeup of the nation-state, individual inequalities, group stratifications, specializations, and fragmentations all seem to preclude any widespread sharing of much of anything among its members. Coupled with the widely differing individual experiences and resulting individualized cultural constructs for living on a day-to-day basis, the conclusion that all Americans are simply not the same seems inescapable (Garretson 1976).

The cause of the difficulties rests with the nation-state culture itself, a cultural creation of people that is quite different from that which naturally evolves as a group simply elects from among alternatives to solve problems and needs posed by the physical environment or adapts to the problems of the environment for survival. The nation-state culture came about with a conscious effort to create a culture, one based on the past experiences of those creating it, the wants and interests of those creating it, and one that reflects how the group wanted to see themselves or have others see them. The effort was one that was to represent the interests of the many groups that were to be integrated into the new nation. The culture they were to create then was to stand for everyone. The result, a compromise of special interests, was then given out to be voted upon by the newly created citizens of the nation-state culture. The vote was hardly unanimous. But with ratification (the approval of the majority), the United States came into existence with a culture all laid out for its members, one that everybody was expected to share. Besides being arbitrary and artificial in many respects, this new culture, altogether, was something no one actually wanted. A compromise always results in something that nobody exactly wants. It represents the best they can get when there are widely differing views. Even at the beginning, the creators (founding fathers) recognized what they were creating was a compromise culture, as they wanted it to be (at least what they could agree to), as it ought to be, and not necessarily as it already existed at the time.

Those who came together to undertake the task of creating the American culture were the representatives of the varied and competing interests (already established groups) that were present in the colonies, excepting, of course, Native Americans. The American culture ultimately created was the result of this group effort that actually produced an ideal culture for the United States and people. It was a group effort, but living up to the ideal America as they constructed it was still left up to the individual and already recognized groups. Given different experiences, histories, and the conditions within which people found themselves, the lack of shared values and ideas was apparent right at the start. The founding fathers of the United States were already a part and product of the complex and fragmented stage of cultural evolution known as civilization. The diversity of human society was already a fact of life. The culture they were to create was already conditioned by those things that had come to characterize all such human societies and groups. They could agree on freedom and the individualism, but little else.

ORIENTING IDEAS

The idea of freedom, which was to become the foundation for American culture as the preeminent orienting idea, was a product of what brought the earliest settlers, both individuals and groups to the shores of America: the freedom to practice their religion or other cultural ways; the freedom to begin anew; and freedom from the social constraints of the old world from which they came. That the individual should be free to do this was enhanced and reinforced by the lifestyles of the indigenous cultural groups already inhabiting the land, appearing to live a lifestyle oriented around freedom, and who equated individualism with groups as well as persons. Freedom and individualism go hand in hand, and these two ideas very quickly became the orienting ideas and dominant values of the new arrivals, and the even set the stage for the revolt from colonial domination. Values of a group become a significant part of the worldview of that group, explicit but not always in the open, even though they prescribe actions. While on the one hand they serve to integrate, on the other, they can create much conflict. Ideals can be identified as valuable, but how they relate to everyday life can produce much conflict. There was much conflict among groups of earlier settlers because of the diverse cultures from which they came, their reasons for coming, and their local adaptations. Even with these differences and conflicts, perhaps because of them, the ideas of individualism and freedom were reinforced. Individuals and groups can believe in an idea, even deem it valuable, but find in their own lives that it is nearly impossible to live up to given whatever circumstances in which they find themselves. It is even more difficult when a degree of conformity to a national standard is essential if a nation-state is to survive as a whole. Thus, in America, individualism, freedom, conformity, and an accompanying belief or acceptance of diversity have always gone hand in hand.

If the individual or any particular group is to be free to follow its own dictates or lifestyles, then differences are not only expected but the resulting diversity must also be valued. While there is a relationship between the values a culture group may hold and the ideas or assumptions they then make regarding aspects of their lives, this does not mean a direct correlation to their everyday life. Additional values can be created out of their individual or group experiences that then go along with the ideals enhancing (at least they believe this to be true) their efforts to meet the standard or attain the ultimate goal—the American Dream. But one's perspective on the American Dream can constantly change. Values can change over time as conditions change, and priorities can shift or alter as the gap between ideals and realities widens or narrows.

THE AMERICAN DREAM

The basic themes of the American Dream emanate from the highly valued individualism of Americans, and this is tied to their belief in equal opportunities to attain the abundance of America, freedom to pursue the wealth (the measure of attainment), and all the rest that goes together to make for the American Dream (home ownership, expensive cars, lots of material goods, etc.). Most people tend to see this as tied to freedom and wealth or material well-being from the "plenty for everyone" idea associated with it. This idea of material well-being has shifted over the years to an American "right" to the things that have come to be associated with it. The specifics of the American Dream vary from individual to individual, group to group, year to year. For example, the American Dream almost always includes home ownership, but it can range from the mobile home or manufactured home (the lower income person's home ownership), to the modest three or four bedroom home in suburbia, to the mansion located in the expensive surroundings of a large estate. As one's ability to achieve this piece of the dream improves, just what constitutes home ownership also changes. As one's ability to obtain a better home increases, the individual's level of aspiration changes—one never reaches the ultimate nor acquires enough. Regardless of the differences in what constitutes the home, owning one is part of the American Dream, visual proof that one has succeeded in obtaining some of the dream. Of course there are other visual markers that one is achieving the dream. For example, the automobile has assumed a very special place in the American Dream. As with the residence or home ownership, it will also change as one's ability to purchase one improves. From the purchase of a used car, one might graduate to the Chevrolet or Ford (the common person's autos), to the higher priced Buick, Lincoln, or Cadillac. Ultimately, the car that becomes part of the dream can be the BMW, Mercedes, or the Rolls Royce, automobiles that are outside the range of all but the financially well-off. The point to all of this is simply that the American Dream is not the same for everyone, and its specifics constantly change as the individual's circumstances change.

It is also true that attaining the American Dream is easier for some, more difficult for others. Class stratification produces the circumstance wherein those who "have" will nearly always get more, while those who "have not" (very little) will not get much of anything. This probably accounts for the growing popularity of lotteries, gambling and various sweepstakes in the America of today. Such things represent a means, sometimes the only means, for people to achieve the American Dream. The dream exists in the minds of most Americans, but so too, does the realistic possibility of not attaining it, as poverty and racism, the limits of individualism and equality come into daily conflict with its realization.

AMERICAN VALUES

Perhaps the place to begin the search for the patterns of values that Americans tend to share is with the particular idea that generates or underlies most of them—individualism. While the main idea of the earliest settlers who came to the United States (then the colonies) revolved around freedom, this idea was already closely tied to the idea of individualism, which then became synonymous with the freedom being sought. Nearly every American now believes first and foremost in individual freedom with a self-centered focus on life and their independence (freedom) to "pursue for oneself"—directly related to the many other ideas they also hold on equality, social success, privacy, fairness, assumptions and the other ideas tied to these. Individualism also was applied to individual groups seeking freedom to practice their religions or other cultural traditions, and this led to ideas concerning the separation of church and state, minority groups rights not being dictated to by any majority group, to being unique and still fitting into the culture. Individualism and freedom are the major orienting ideas of all Americans, but they also have become the dominant values of America, irrespective of the other cultural affiliations or the origins of individual Americans. In this, all Americans share a belief in freedom and individualism. Above all else, Americans see themselves as individuals (Althen 1988) and they are easily offended by the notion that they are influenced by the culture of any group with which they affiliate, including the American one. This is probably the one thing on which nearly every American can agree.

Individualism (which also assumes freedom as part of its definition), is the clear dominant value of all Americans, then generating most of their ideas concerning freedom, which means more than just more freedom to live their lives than might be possible in other nation-states. It is tied to their ideas of free speech, the freedom of the individual "to do," "to succeed," "to become whatever they might wish," irrespective of where they came from or whatever else they might be. As a dominant theme of American culture, it both creates individual freedom and produces the very diversity that characterizes the country at the same time. Americans see themselves first as individuals, unique ones, and this leads to valuing diversity—the only place where this individualism can exist and survive. While clearly a dominant theme of long historical standing, diversity has also meant constant conflict because of it. This theme of diversity and conflict is easily documented with ethnic and racial groups, and religious, political, economic, social, and ideological diversities that have come to characterize the United States and the American culture.

Nash (1993) suggests that in American culture, individualism runs so rampant that the entire culture has become a culture of therapy. He bases this conclusion on problems of self-identification that accompany such an emphasis. This "therapy culture" consists of psychiatrists, counselors, psychologists, religious practitioners, social workers, and the like who adhere to a variety of therapeutic systems, some focusing on psychotics, drug use, or hospitalization for treatment. While there is little doubt that given the focus on the individual or "self," and the struggle coming to grips with the mainstream values, the temptation to see American culture as one of therapy is a strong one. Given the possibilities of attaining the mainstream, there is no wonder Americans get frustrated and experience severe anxiety. If they do not attain it, they are failures, in their own eyes and those of others. On the other hand, Nash seems to be describing the upper class as opposed to the middle class in which most Americans like to see themselves, and this is the striving group as reflected in the values tied to individualism and social success. One could just as easily argue that individualism is not what has led to an over dependence on therapy, but that the individual's inability to actually achieve the American Dream, or a significant part of it for whatever reason—a major difference between ideal and real culture—has led to anxiety and stress, and this has necessitated the growth of therapy.

Francis Hsu (1972) concludes that individualism permeates all other American values and gives Americans that particular flavor of self-reliance that he suggests characterizes them. In the eyes of other scholars of American culture, this is directly related to the value Americans place on fairness and freedom of speech (Spindler & Spindler 1993). Individualism seems to go hand in hand with the general idea Americans have regarding equality. For most Americans, equality means equal participation in the political, educational, and economic systems, and these, in turn, become highly valued things. Equality does not necessarily mean that all people have the same talents or skills. Americans know they are not equal in such things. Equality means equal access or participation in these systems, thus, translates into *equal opportunities* for all people and bringing it back to its roots in individuality. Individualism is even tied to their ideas on space and privacy, how they determine who their "heroes" will be, and most everything else in their lives. Even the value placed on change is grounded in this individualism where the individual can be whatever they might want, inhibited only by their individual efforts, which speaks of change. Change has become another dominant theme and value of the American culture, along with an unswerving faith in the idea that all change is for the better. In this society, it is believed that individuals can achieve a better life or success through hard work and their own effort. Recognizing that individuals can and do change, members of this culture seem to accept that change of any kind is basically a desired thing. Even change for the sake of change is okay, for example, clothes, cars, technology, and so forth.

When the idea of the American mainstream culture is considered, the usual image is that of the "WASP" or white, Anglo-Saxon Protestant male, with roots in Europe (primarily Anglo-Saxon), but also augmented by Native American and immigrant traditions. The American mainstream culture actually embodies all those orienting ideas Americans share, whether they do so as individuals or groups. There is no question that historically, the characterization of the mainstream culture has focused on the white, European, Protestant male who invariably was also a member of what was also recognized as the middle class (Althen 1988). Of course, the mainstream has never been this. Rather the mainstream has historically consisted (and still does), of all those people who *support* the basic ideas of its main tenets, which also serve to dominate the wider population. Members or subscribers to the mainstream culture tend to focus on freedom, the rights of the individual, equality, achievement, and mobility. The simple fact of the matter is that members of other groups who are not generally identified with the mainstream are actually striving to become part of it, for they too, internalize the values that lie at its heart, participate in the political, social, and economic institutions that reflect it. Those who have achieved affiliation, or who can function within it, readily accept it as part of their identity.

Spindler and Spindler (1993) tend to see the mainstream as essentially built around the middle class. This idea that would be shared by Nash (1993). For the Spindlers, American culture is a holistic process (all the pieces integrated with one another), defined by the continual dialogue on independence, freedom, conformity, success, community, optimism, cynicism, idealism, materialism, technology, nature, work, and other things. For most Americans, it is the middle class that establishes the dominant tone of the culture. For Nash, this group is made of people who are predominantly white, represent the power elite, are the board members of the big corporations, are owners of expensive homes, and are the big donors to charity campaigns. The Spindlers note the struggle between those who have internalized certain values and those who struggle to come to grips with them. These authors see the mainstream as encompassing a fluency in English with a native-like oral skill, the internalization of middle class values, participation in American social, political, and economic institutions, along with an acceptance of mainstream affiliation as part of that identity.

According to the Spindlers, the major orientations of the mainstream culture are seen as: (1) freedom of speech (along with other freedoms); (2) rights of the individual; (3) equality; (4) achievement; and (5) social mobility. They also point to the high value Americans place on technology, the free market, private business, independence, respect for others, and competition for place in the mainstream. They go further and suggest that there is a constant set of value orientations (tenets) that together constitute the core configuration for the mainstream culture: (1) that all [men] are created equal; (2) that honesty is the best policy; (3) that by hard work, anyone can achieve success; (4) that the individual is all important; (5) that what counts is what people do; (6) that time is precious; and (7) that there is little use in "crying over spilled milk." The emphasis is on the individual and individualism, individual achievement, individual success through hard work, equal individual opportunities, openness of the socioeconomic structure (free markets and private enterprise), and strong beliefs in honesty, progress, the future, and getting along with other people. It is interesting that such ideas are more identified with those who have already achieve a significant piece of the American Dream. While one can argue that believing does not necessarily make anything so or one can agree or disagree with what the authors are suggesting on the specifics of the mainstream culture in America, they do demonstrate the direct relationship of orientations and values to other ideas and assumptions held by many Americans.

ASSUMPTIONS AND OTHER AMERICAN IDEAS

Values are very much tied to other assumptions and ideas Americans live by. The central features of the mainstream culture together form the core values and ideas that are shared by most Americans and these same features tend then to characterize the culture. These ideas and values play a major role in determining a great many other ideas among Americans, although they will vary in terms of importance from group to group. For most Americans, or groups of them, in addition to the major orientations and ideas already eluded to, there is also a strong belief in technology and a faith that it will always be able to solve problems, even those it creates. The desirability and value of a free market are tied to the importance of the individual and the equality that permits individual achievement and mobility. Even among those whose upward mobility is severely restricted, and whose participation in the so-called "free market" is severely limited, the idea embodied in it is valued simply because of its idealized promise for everyone. The idea underlying this notion is tied to the orientations of the mainstream, emphasizing that the individual and individualism, personal achievement, and success through hard individual work, equality of opportunity, honesty, the faith in capitalism, belief in progress and the future, and getting along with others, are all tied together. From the core idea of the individual come many additional values, values focused on private business, independence, competition, the idea that all people are born equal, and so on. In the metropolitan areas of the country, these things produce people focused on careers and success, a future orientation, and self-discipline. In nonmetroplex areas, the values of competence, noninterference, independence, working to live, separation of sexes, local loyalty, and importance of family (kin) are emphasized (Spindler & Spindler 1993). Despite such settlement differences, people in both places value good manners and proper social behavior (Hall & Hall 1990). One has to be careful how far such things are taken, for it is common for each to be qualified, depending on what other cultural affiliations a person might have.

For example, while the idea that all people are created equal is widely shared among most Americans, those who subscribe to that idea actually recognize that people are not equal. Americans readily admit (albeit somewhat grudgingly) that neither individuals nor particular groups of them are equal in any sense. While it is often said that in America, honesty is the best policy, dishonesty or cheating "just a little bit" is apparently okay if it does not hurt anyone directly. While it is believed that anyone can achieve success with hard work, not everyone does, for it is not automatic. Individualism and its accompanying diversity are okay as long as the group constraints are respected. What people do is more important than what they say as long as it produces the desired results. There is no use "crying over spilled milk," but this idea seems to be contradicted on a regular basis as people seek to ignore responsibility for their own actions, attempt to find scapegoats for explaining what happens to them, or as they simply seek to place the blame for just about everything on anyone but themselves. Americans seem to believe that *it*, whatever *it* might be, is always somebody else's fault. Freedoms are important, but primarily for oneself, not necessarily for others with whom the individual might disagree.

Rights of individuals must bend to the will of the majority—as long as one is not in the minority or the one being asked to bend or change. Equality for oneself is important, but that same equality for others is not so important. The problem with all of these things comes from the fact that they are ideals, not necessarily realities with which people are faced every day.

While frequently quite abstract, values are organized into patterns that are closely interrelated. More important, they do pervade the individual's outlook and behavior, define the *real* in ideal terms as well as the actual nature of that reality, even if they are oftentimes contradictory. As noted by Althen (1988), individualism leads to the assumptions about freedom, privacy, and equality that are shared among Americans, but rarely practiced. Freedom of speech in public goes hand in hand with equality in public, but the "private" is also part of the reality with which people deal. The view that all people are of equal value and should be given the same or equal opportunity is tied to individualism and abundance, even if it is often violated in actual practice. It is an imperative as opposed to a fact of life for them. All of these assumptions lend themselves to a belief in the personal self as a separate entity and unique psychological being, and to the ideas of individuals as self-reliant, self-motivated, and resistant to any kind of systems of thought (Hsu 1972). It relates to the ideas and assumptions Americans have about hard work and self-discipline (inner direction), the most appropriate path to personal achievement and success, mobility, the lack of family ties, the idea of humans being unique among living things, measurable achievement and quantification, emphasis on "facts" and action, competition within cooperation, and a preoccupation with the future, not the past or the present.

Achievement, action, work, fairness, and materialism are all tied to the idea of individualism valued by Americans. Achievers are always admired and this serves to motivate most Americans. The ideal person is the hard worker, and this is tied to a strong belief in action or doing something most of the time, materialism (acquiring possessions), and the upward movement from one class to another as the measure of achievement. A strongly held belief in the fairness of things is closely related. Obviously, all Americans want to believe that the opportunities for this are available to them individually and no one is precluded, given special privilege, or treated differently than anyone else (Tiersky & Tiersky 1975). Achievement is something the individual can accomplish by their own actions and hard work. The value placed on work or the work ethic among members of this culture is a puritanical one, and this becomes a motivator (Hall & Hall 1990). There is little, if any sympathy or understanding for those who do not believe in hard work. Materialism—money and what it can provide—is the measure of individual achievement and the quantifiable measure of his or her success. While idealistic in its conceptualization, there is little doubt that most Americans take their measure from this and evaluate their progress according to it. For most Americans, mobility (here meaning improvement) means more than geographical mobility, it means mobility between classes (the groups with whom the individual associates) becomes part of the achievement criteria, identifies the hard worker, and becomes part of the measurement of one's success. Americans still believe they can easily move from class to class, and that education provides the major mechanism by which the above can be achieved. Education is the means, the process, by which the individual can position him- or herself for work and achievement. In the American version, it is for a changing society as well.

OTHER OBSERVATIONS OF AMERICAN CULTURE

Gary Althen (1988) makes the point that there are many other values and assumptions Americans live as well, but Americans are largely unconscious of them. Heroes are those who can overcome diversity, and this reinforces the belief the individual can succeed. Most Americans would not attribute it to their undying faith in individualism. Because they believe in the future, change as progress (upward and for the better), Americans do not place great importance on history or tradition. This has led to the conviction that they can dominate (control) the environment. Edward and Mildred Hall (1990) observe that most Americans are monochronic, their time is scheduled and compartmentalized. Individual space is jealously guarded and communication tends to be direct, informal, and a largely unconscious activity. High mobility (in residence, social class, or social standing) has lead to a lack of roots for most Americans—work or other groupings substitute for family and provide identity. This leads to indifference to community welfare and shallow personal relationships. Communication is usually direct and informal, and it is related to good manners and expected social behavior. Courage to try new things constantly is another characteristic of most Americans as they look for ways to improve their chances of being successful. Lucy Garretson (1976) points out that while Americans believe their system of government is rational and moral, they value the sanctity of established government because of it. As noted in Hall and Hall (1990), Americans tend to believe in their democracy, not just as a form of government, but as a way of life. This has contributed to a naive patriotism that holds that America is the best of all places. They also tend to take a very pragmatic approach to life—the value of knowledge is related to it usefulness. Their greatest fault comes with their competitive outlook.

Ethel and Martin Tiersky (1975) suggest that competition is America's greatest fault. It is tied to the individual's striving to achieve, move up, attain the "dream." This comes out in the high regard Americans have of winners and their low regard for losers or those who are not successful. Winning at any cost has come to be acceptable, and a belief in the proposition that the end justifies the means. This has now led to the ethical dilemmas of sports, business, education, and even into the personal relationships of individual Americans. Nearly everyone in America is introduced to the idea of competition at a very early age; at home; in the school, in their leisure activities, and even into personal relationships. The idea is constantly reinforced from then on and in nearly every aspect of life. It has made Americans aggressive and direct. It has made them quite insensitive to others, even their own relatives. The competitive nature that develops permeates their lives at home, at work, at church, and nearly everywhere else. Occupations compete for prominence. Competition determines one's movement up the company ladder. "My religion (church) is better than yours." "My team is better than yours." "My therapist is better than yours." The competition is never ending and there is no relief from it.

Althen (1988) also observes the informality of Americans, suggesting this can be observed in most of their relationships and general behavior. This also makes them superficial in friendliness. This author suggests that the ideas of future, change and progress are tied together. Progress and the promise of the future counts for more than history or tradition, and this is tied to their belief they can dominate (ultimately control) nature with their technology. Americans assume that human nature is basically good and this helps to account for their attitudes toward education being essential for everyone to make them better, and the belief that all people can be rehabilitated (mentally, convicts, physically). Democracy leads to making people better; they volunteer, believe in educational campaigns (e.g., health, crime, drugs, aids virsus, whatever) and are strongly tied to the belief in self-improvement. As with Hall and Hall, Althen also points to the use of time by Americans as a resource to be saved, spent, wasted, and so forth. He also points to the direct and assertive nature of Americans, the tendency to "lay their cards on the table," while at the same time strictly recognize certain topics to be avoided (personal, religion, and politics). Communication (mostly unconscious) consists of small talk. Argument, limited interaction (ritual or otherwise), and the personal are to be avoided. Because of these ideas, it is suggested that Americans rely on verbal communication and pay more attention to "facts" than emotions. Reasoning means to focus on the "point" and proving it with facts (they exist or can be discovered), and the most reliable facts are numbers, which do not lie. The best way for an American to prove a point is with quantification (numbers), but of course the problem is still always the same, different numbers can be used on the very same questions (e.g., demographics). Americans rely on sight, distrust theory and generalization (suspicious of these as opposed to fact), believe in cause and effect relationships, which can be discovered. As with people in other parts of the world, they believe their actions are "natural," not customary or learned. For many Americans, only it is only those "other people" that have customs. Courtesy, punctuality, treating males and females with the same respect, and standing at arm's length are terribly important.

Edward Stewart and Milton Bennett (1991) suggest that Americans see culture as natural, simply the way things are. For these authors, American perceptions are oriented around action more than thinking, held more than rational or efficient. Americans emphasize objective and valid facts which they perceive as empirical, observable and measurable (quantifiable), and this leads to the pragmatism that characterizes Americans and their focus on how to get things done. It also favors a technical approach to human behavior in which all decisions are made from alternatives, tied to probability and according to a set of criteria. Analysis focuses on identifying obstacles and the universal search for the single factor with which to explain events. This leads to an emphasis on inductive reasoning wherein they believe principles come from the analysis of data. Putting all these things together, the authors identify a number of beliefs that serve to characterize Americans. All of these beliefs are oriented to action, which they believe has a cause, and this leads them to getting things done with very little depth or considered thinking. They separate work and play and are motivated more by what one does than by what one says. Achievement is measurable and this leads to strong competition, even into their personal affiliations and relationships.

While Americans see themselves as an egalitarian middle class, social status is very important and they experience a specialization in culturally significant roles. In other social relations, they tend to see equality as intricately tied to "humanness." They avoid personal commitments and in confrontational situations prefer to "say it straight." Americans are informal to a fault. Even their friendships are based on spontaneity and rarely deep. They tend to be depersonalizing in their interactions with others. Competition is all important to them, but in the context of cooperation. Americans need to be liked.

In their perceptions of the world, Americans believe humans are unique in having souls, while other life forms are merely material or mechanistic. Both the natural and physical worlds should be controlled in the service of humans. They emphasize material things and place a very high value on private property. For them, progress means better, and this has led to a false trust in the technical to solve all their problems. They measure the future and progress on concrete things that are measurable. They quantify the world. Numbers become facts and only facts can be believed, and these lead to conformity (if the individual does not conform, they are viewed as deviant). This also accounts for the pragmatic outlook of Americans that the value of knowledge is related to its usefulness in achieving their goals.

Americans are characterized by the conformity stressed within all constituent groups—America is a nation of "sheep"—populated by those who simply follow the dictates of their group affiliations, in dress, education, actions, and even into personal matters (when to engage in sex and go to the bathroom). The common person is codified for conformity and even the "do your own thing" idea stresses the conformity that is necessary and accepted by most Americans. They are change oriented but this creates a dilemma for those who learn and feel comfortable with things the way they are. In American culture, one must conform to achieve, or be accepted as a member of a group. One is expected to conform to the national culture (nationality), and to the cultural groups with which they affiliate (e.g., sex, age, ethnic, racial, or special interest).

PARADOXES AND CONTRADICTIONS OF AMERICAN CULTURE

Earlier it was pointed out that the apparent contradictions in American culture do not go unnoticed by most Americans. As could be seen in the previous discussions, paradoxes or contradictions exist between values and actions, between ideal culture and real culture, and these can cause great difficulty for individuals and groups. When people are asked about their culture, the answers are right on the "tips of their tongues," for they will respond as they have been taught. But, most Americans recognize the difference between the way it is suppose to be (ideally or as they might have been taught that it is), and the way it might actually be (real culture). This difference or gap between the real and the ideal cultures of Americans, has occasioned many scholars to point out the contradictions or paradoxes of the culture. Nearly always, Americans will qualify their responses to questions about the nature of their culture, suggesting they, too, recognize the contradictions. For example, as noted by Garretson (1976), most Americans believe in equality, but recognize equality by class and without the mobility normally supposed. While equal opportunity suggests that anyone and everyone has the same opportunities to pursue or achieve the American Dream, the existence of poverty, racism, prejudice, discrimination, and the contradictions inherent with the emphasis on individualism and equality of any kind, precludes it for many people. Even in terms of material culture (possessions), essential parts of the American dream, the ability to acquire them is actually quite fluid and idealistic—there is never enough. Edward and Mildred Hall (1990) point out that for Americans, it is appearance that is more important than reality. The individual may be emphasized and valued, but so, too, team play is important. They also point out the contradiction of individualism and the need for the approval of others and the importance of popularity to Americans. The Tierskys (1975) suggest much of the same thing. James Spradley and Michael Rynkiewich (1975) indicate a wide range of diversity in wealth, property, education, manners, tasks, but also point to the surprising amount of conformity among Americans. This too would seem to contradict the individualism touted by most. In language, diet, dress, basic skills, land use, community settlement, and recreation, Americans are pretty much alike. Conrad Arensberg and Arthur Niehoff (1971) suggest that despite the egalitarianism spoken of and touted by most Americans, there are substantial differences based on occupation, education, and financial worth, and the very achievement sought by Americans determines one's position in the society, and these can hardly be viewed as equal. Equal opportunities exist, but with limitations based on sex, ethnic background, and social class assignment. The consequence is that people are characterized as successes or failures based on their level of achievement or success. There is a general frustration for those who have not achieved or do not achieve from those who have achieved success. Equality, egalitarianism, and equal opportunity for all are simply moral imperatives, not facts of life. America has always had groups viewed as inferior by way of socioeconomic class, ethnic inequalities, or inequality based on a loose interpretation of race. There is equality for those who embrace the major value system of the United States, not for others. There is sexual inequality, and all manner of minorities can attest to the lack of equality and opportunity. But paradoxes can also be seen as simply other possibilities or the acceptability of diversity.

Interviews of Americans produce some interesting responses as to what is most valued. Most Americans focus almost immediately on money and success as the most valued things in America. Freedom, justice, education, and honesty are also noted but usually with reservations or qualifications. Family is valued among Americans. When pressed to identify the most important values of Americans, most respondents suggest that Americans are preoccupied with money and success, both of these synonymous with status (usually said in such a way as to suggest this applies to just about everyone but themselves). It would also seem to be the case that Americans give "lip-service" to such things as freedom and honesty, when they really intend to do whatever it takes to accumulate the money and the success that go along with it. The difference between expressed values and actions become clear with such responses. Some people called these paradoxes, other referred to them as contradictions. For some, they are simply alternatives, or simply the differences between the ideals of a people and the realities—the difference between what they want to believe and the way things really are.

While there is little doubt that most Americans believe in individualism for themselves and their groups, conformity is a must for the survival of both. Groups expect conformity from its members. Some level of conformity is a must for any cultural group to survive, even more so with heavily populated complex nation-states. This provides the social order required to survive and provides the members with what to expect from other members. Individualism can only be allowed to go so far—individualism but with conformity. Total freedom of the individual would ultimately lead to conflict as the desires of one individual (or group) come into conflict with those of other individuals or groups. Conformity seems to play an important role in checking or slowing down ("putting the brakes on") rampant change. Having learned what is expected of them in cultural groups, individuals acquire a kind of comfort in knowing that. The longer one has practiced a culture, the more they resist change to it. There is freedom, but only so long as one lives up to the responsibilities that in fact restrict it. Individualism yes, but everyone is quick to recognize that they as individuals cannot do it alone—their achievement is only possible in the recognition of it by others. Individuality is touted at the same time Americans are quick to recognize and generalize subgroupings. Uniqueness is valued, but the need for conformity is the unspoken but understood expectation. There is a constant pressure for the unique to conform ("fall into line"). This pressure to conform to the will of the so-called majority is very strong. However, it should be clearly understood that in some cases the so-called majority is actually no more than a minority group with the power to influence the decision makers.

Many of the contradictions and paradoxes of American culture become evident in their emphasis on appearances over reality. For example, to obtain recognition that one is attaining, or has attained, the American Dream (is successful), superficial markers will be used. Some people will become "house poor," in that they will buy a home clearly beyond their financial ability to sustain it, even put furniture in it. This gives an appearance to the general public that they are "successful." Others will purchase cars that imply their success (e.g., the Cadillac, Lincoln, Mercedes, etc.), but then may be forced to live in substandard housing, apartments or no homes at all. Still others are pressured to participate in other of the elements of the American Dream at a substantial cost to their actual goal of achieving it, for example, giving beyond their means to political parties, churches or other charitable groups, or joining the expensive country club simply because it is the expected behavior in the groups with which they wish to be associated—the successful ones.

That such contradictions should characterize complex societies really should not surprise anyone. In such cultures, these things always tend to stand out. Americans like to see themselves as a peace loving group, but American society is filled with violence, has a history of war, hate, and so forth. Human equality may be the ideal, but if it actually exists, it comes with a "common man equality." American society is class-structured and equality becomes a relative thing—relative (common) to your class level. People within the upper class have equality, but that differs from the equality of middle or lower classes. Upper-class people have the same access to the productive resources of the economic system, legal, and political system. Individuals within the lower classes simply do not—none of them. While mass education is desired for all, viewed as a basic right of all Americans, the access to quality education is a function of one's ability to pay for it. Of course, in fiscally tight years, educational funds are among the first to be decreased. Anti-intellectual campaigns at both state and federal government levels have been rather cyclical as well. Americans also like to see themselves as humanitarians, giving regularly to such programs as the United Way and any number of special programs to feed the children of the world or those who are starving due to some natural disaster. Yet there has always been great opposition to foreign aid programs and study centers supposedly doing this kind of work. Of course, giving actually means "as long as it is convenient," not necessarily according to one's ability. This humanitarianism carries over into charity at home. But how many people really give to the poor or those with less than they have? Most Americans are totally unaware of the poor and starving within their own cities or towns. The idea of "loving one's neighbor" seems directly contradicted by the "dog-eat-dog" character of business and the "cut-throat" approach taken to competition in the business world. The great value placed on life is contradicted by what one sees on nightly news television, reads in newspapers about murder and mayhem, and the fact that this society puts millions of people into uniform whose only purpose focuses on violence (e.g., police and military).

The greatest discrepancy in what Americans want to believe and what might really be the case comes with equality. They are not equal and most want it that way. People are not mentally or physically equal. They recognize that people differ in their intellectual capabilities. They recognize that people are not equal in terms of individual skills or talents. They can readily see that people are not equal in the eyes of the law, or even in their churches. Even if one assumes that equality means equal opportunities, women, minorities, religious groups, and other special interest groups are summarily prohibited from equal participation in American society for they are restricted in their access to the political and economic systems. There is little doubt that in American society, one's ability to participate in much of anything is directly tied to his or her socioeconomic status, this many times related to their racial affiliation or other cultural affiliation. The financially well-off can participate; those who are not, cannot. That most people do not really want to be equal to others is demonstrated in their attempts to gain an advantage in job competitions, through education or some form of training. Education is sold to the average American on that basis. While Americans tend to believe that opportunities for education are open (guaranteed) to everyone, clearly they are not. All of these paradoxes, these contradictions in American culture and society, simply reflect the differences between ideal culture and real culture. The greater the gap between the ideal and real, the greater the potential for conflict.

SUGGESTED READINGS

Althen, G. 1988. *American Ways: A Guide for Foreigners in the United States.* Yarmouth, MA: Intercultural Press. This book is primarily written for non-Americans who need to understand the ways of Americans. The author describes the basic characteristics of Americans, their values, styles of communication, patterns of thinking, and customary behaviors.

DeVita, P. R. and Armstrong, J. D. (eds.). 1993. *Distant Mirrors: America as a Foreign Culture.* Belmont, CA: Wadsworth Publishing. The authors of this collection of essays look at American cultures as strangers might do, using the perceptions and interpretations of foreign scholars looking at America. Not highly theoretical or jargon-filled, it offers a fresh perspective on American culture—as outsiders see it. Represents a challenge for Americans to look at their own culture. Note the contribution of Francis K. Hsu in which he characterizes Americans as individually centered and having focused on a core value of self-reliance, an idea that can also be found in his paper on American core values and national character in *Psychological Anthropology.*

Spindler, G. and Spindler, L. 1993. *The American Cultural Dialogue and Its Transmission.* Bristol, PA: Falmer Press. While focusing on a constant dialogue between competing interests in America, the authors provide some insightful discussion of the dominant values of the culture. These authors believe that the basic elements of the American culture can be seen in this dialogue.

Stewart, E. C. and Bennett, M. J. 1991. *American Cultural Patterns: A Cross-Cultural Perspective* (revised edition). Yarmouth, MA: Intercultural Press. This volume is aimed primarily at intercultural relations. The authors present some interesting cross-cultural comparisons of America's cultural patterns. Organized around the idea of cultural contacts, certain assumptions, perceptions, and values of Americans are examined and American cultural traits are isolated out, analyzed and compared with those of other cultures.

——— Four ———
American Social Structure

In the study of cultures, anthropologists generally focus their attention on the universal patterns of culture, on those things found within all human cultural groups that must be considered and managed successfully if the group is to continue and for its culture to survive—the core areas of culture. It is in the comparison of these patterns or systems that the basic similarities and differences are established in the ways humans structure their relations with one another and organize their lives. But as suggested earlier, Americans generally do not think about themselves in these terms. Most Americans tend to see what they do, their lives, and their customs as somehow just "natural." The things usually associated with the idea of culture are more readily viewed as things that apply to those other people—culture is what characterizes others. In reality, American culture is not so very different from any other culture. This suggestion reflects the fact that on one level, the needs of all humans (individually or in groups) are basically the same. All humans need food to survive, natural resources for meeting their wants and needs, shelter from the elements, human association, and explanations for their presence and role in the universe (explanations for the nature of things). People in all cultural groups throughout the world must be concerned with these same things. Even more basic, regardless of where they might be found or the kinds of lifestyles that might characterize them, people everywhere laugh when they are happy and cry when they are hurt or sad. On this level, all people are basically the same. But on another level, individuals and groups of people do differ in how they meet these concerns or needs. This means human groups will appear to be different from place to place, circumstance to circumstance. Unfortunately, this has meant a greater emphasis on the differences among humans rather than on their similarities.

American culture is structured and organized, integrated and patterned, just as any other culture, just not in the same ways. Americans recognize both a secular (ordinary) and a sacred (out of the ordinary) world. Their rituals and ceremonies reaffirm and play out American beliefs and practices, just as they do for people in every other culture. People in American society are as concerned with meeting their basic needs, just as are cultural groups anywhere else. Their major concerns are tied to the continued survival of themselves as individuals and groups, just as they are for any other culture. They have a need for, and develop ways of establishing and maintaining social order, just like everyone else. Americans recognize claims and obligations they have to one another (social relations that establish the mutual expectations among members of their group), just like people in any other cultural group. As with societies everywhere, Americans have natural resources with which to meet their needs and wants, and they develop customs as to who will have access to them, how they will be transformed by technology and labor into the products the people require, and how the finished products will be distributed or gotten out to the people who need, want, or simply desire them. They recognize that there are cause and effect relationships in their universe to explain some things (their natural law), and they have the supernatural to explain what their natural laws cannot. They have developed a means or process for ensuring that their cultural beliefs and practices will be transmitted to each new generation, just as it must be done in every culture. In this, American culture is comparable to any other, for Americans must address these essential concerns of survival, just as other cultures must be concerned with them. But assuming that American culture cares for these things in the same way as other cultural groups would be a tragic mistake. For America, as with any other nation-state culture, understanding such things and the intricate relationships among them is made far more difficult because of the complexity of them as compared to more traditional societies, even other nation-states. In small-scale societies, most of these concerns and needs can be handled quite easily within the context of the family or larger kinship group. In the modern nation-state, simply because of the numbers of people involved, the diversity of cultural groups in them, and the shear enormity of the task because of that diversity, responding to such needs and concerns is a far more difficult and complex problem.

SOCIAL STRUCTURE AND ORGANIZATION

One of the main concerns of all human societies is to establish and maintain social order, without which there is little likelihood they can survive. It is usually within the social structure that establishing this social order begins by outlining the claims and obligations (expectations) that members of the group will have to one another. Social structure is a consequence of people attempting to live together as a group, in the case of the United States, an extremely large and diversified one. In complex societies the bulk of the responsibility in meeting survival concerns has fallen to the state, its political/legal system, and groups created for this sole purpose. In these complex societies, social structure means more than just the claims and obligations among family members, it also means the claims and obligations among a multitude of social and cultural groups that actually constitute the social fabric of the country and its culture. In the perspective taken here, such groups are not simply aggregates of people who might come together for a passing moment, but represent relatively permanent groupings of people, the members of which share something that helps distinguish them as a group within the context of other groups. Most social groups are relatively permanent in that they will continue despite the loss or addition of individual members. The members derive part of their identity by virtue of membership in them. The group's members are recruited or designated through recognized rules, and there are mutual claims and obligations incurred through membership in the group. The members of such groups know what is expected from them and what they can expect from the other members of the group. In some cases, individuals obtain membership by being categorized with others into artificially created social groups where they may share no more with other members than the characteristic used to create it. Interestingly, over time, such artificially created social groups can become cultural groups, taking their place in social structure along with other constituent cultural groups in the context of complex society.

Be that as it may, in most studies of human societies and cultures, the discussion of social structure usually focuses on the family or larger kinship group, sometimes augmented by voluntary or nonvoluntary special interest groups or associations. Where these groups are treated unequally, the society is said to be stratified and this becomes part of the discussion. Stratification means group inequality is structured (institutionalized) into the basic pattern of the society. Despite the presence of other kinds of groups or some kind of stratification of the society, most of the discussion of social structure usually begins, if not ends as well, with an examination of the kinship groupings of the society, starting with the family or household. This kind of social group is considered the most minimal or basic of all the groupings found in human society, itself a social group. Even if the family group is enlarged by the inclusion of relatives established through recognized kinship and descent rules, the family unit remains a relatively small one within the context of the larger society. This is most certainly true within the context of the heavily populated complex societies where families are the smallest of all social groupings. In the context of the small-scale and traditional societies, the family group provides the context for undertaking most of the organizational activities of the society, excepting those requiring larger numbers of people to accomplish particular tasks. Where additional groups are found, usually based on rank, sex, age, or special interest, they are generally perceived as simply augmenting the activities and functions of the family.

Without doubt, in the more traditional small-scale society, it is the family or kin group that sets at the heart of social structure and social organization. The family provides the individual with all that they need to know about what is expected of them and what they can expect of others. It organizes all of the activities necessary to meet all the needs of the members of the group and the society at large. In the context of the family, marriages are regulated, political and economic decisions are made, leadership and the succession of leadership are determined, inheritance is handled, social order is established and maintained, and the cultural training of the young is undertaken. Social order comes from the mutual claims and obligations the individuals in these groups have to one another. The family also provides the context and the means for sustaining the culture. Within them, each new generation learns all they need to know as members of the group, where all the necessary economic and political decisions and activities will be accomplished, and where even their spiritual (supernatural) needs can be met. They help to define one's place in the world and role in the universe. In very real terms, this social group becomes the way the people organize themselves to accomplish all those things they must get done, if they and their culture are to survive. Not only does this social group form the basis of the social structure of the society, it becomes the social organization for the entire society as well. From the study of social structure in small-scale societies, where the family accomplished all these necessary things, came the strong belief among anthropologists that understanding the social structure of a society would just naturally lead to understanding its social organization as well. In these earlier studies, there was simply no need to distinguish between social structure and social organization, more often than not, they were the same thing. With the development of larger and more complex societies, new kinds of groups appeared that became part of social structure, groups that would replace family at the center of social structure and relations.

In studies of traditional societies, groups beyond family or kinship that were noted were seen as part of the society's social structure, but little more than groups that brought larger numbers of people together when there was a need to do so. They were seen to reflect no more than special interests, specializations shared by only a few individuals, or they were groups formed out of the shared activities or experiences of their members. Their importance was limited and they were not viewed as very significant in the social structure that focused on family, kinship groups, and the presence or absence of some form of stratification. For example, group distinctions based on sex and age were recognized when the distinctions were important to the society in question, but their significance rested with gender or age role assignments or in the division of labor that might accompany them. In fact, sex and age groupings are evidenced in most cultures. It was recognized that members of these types of groups had no choice in the matter of membership. People became members of them by virtue of their time of birth or because of their biological sex. Membership in these groupings was strictly nonvoluntary. There was no particular thought or conviction that the resulting groups of people would then share ideas and behaviors that would make them a cultural group. Groups were established along many different lines—religious, regional, military, occupational, or other special interests—were seen as voluntary special interest or special purpose groups with only minimal significance to the social structure of the culture or society in most cases. Membership in these particular groups was determined by voluntary choice. They were seen to merely augment or provide an alternative avenue of meeting some particular need(s) of the society, particular individuals within it, particular specialized or skilled groups of people. That they could consist of members who held beliefs and reflected practices that could make them cultural groups in their own right was not considered, nor was the idea that such groups made for cultural diversity even in the small-scale society. In the modern complex nation-states there is little or no question they have to be considered in this light. In the modern complex society, such groups have become significant elements and players in social structure, social organization, in providing part of the individual's identity.

AMERICAN SOCIAL AND CULTURAL GROUPS

In all modern, complex, and fragmented nation-states, circumstances dictate that the social structure will go well beyond just family or some voluntary/nonvoluntary associations. In these kinds of societies, the ability of family or kinship to respond to the core needs of the entire society is limited. In fact, families become isolated in these contexts, lose their central role in organizational activities (except on the level of the household unit), and only partially provide the individual with crucial elements of their identity and only a limited understanding of social relations (their claims and obligations to others within the society at large). In the complex society, the emphasis of social structure shifts away from the family or kin group to other types of groupings. Some of these are social, as with the social categories created by grouping people together based on some overgeneralized and arbitrary criteria such as race (blacks, whites, reds, yellows, browns, etc.), sex or gender (males, females, heterosexuals or homosexuals), perceived ethnicity (be it real or imagined) based on no more than the language spoken or a person's point of origin (American Indians, Hispanics, Asian Americans, and so on), special interest groups tied to the specific organizational interests of society (e.g., politics, economic class, education, etc.), and some related to individual interests or purposes shared with others (e.g., age groups, conservation, the environment, consumer groups, etc.). In the complex society, constituent cultural groups (e.g., African-Americans, Japanese-Americans, and all the other unique cultural groups that developed out of immigration) become part of the social structure. The organization of activities shifts from family, which assumes only a minor role in such things, to these other kinds of groupings that have assumed the primary responsibilities for those core concerns with which the entire society must make provision if the society and its culture are to continue to be viable.

Nation-states, such as the United States, come into being by incorporating already established cultural groups into artificially and consciously created cultures (based on people deciding what they want their cultures to be or based on some arbitrary notions upon which they could agree). In the case of the United States, this meant that groups of people who already had culture awoke one day to find suddenly that they were Americans, as in the case with the aboriginal population. The United States became an assemblage of constituent groups that altogether make up the social fabric of the society and contribute to its culture. Together they became the core of its social structure and the basis of its social relations. Together these constituent groups combine to help define the culture of the nation-state. New social groups appeared that made them multicultural or culturally diverse. Groups were created out of simple differences that appeared in different segments of their population. In America, some groups were created around the physical differences exhibited among its population (racial groups and categories such as black Americans, Asians, Indians, and so on). Some groups were created on the basis of socioeconomic class differences (lower, middle, and upper classes). Some were merely born of the vast complexity and fragmentation of the nation-state, tied to specializations (occupational specialities), and to all manner of special interests (religious, political ideologies, the needs of various physically challenged people, conservation, and so on). Still others came by virtue of immigration as people moved from another one country to the United States, and who managed to maintain some elements of their former cultural patterns in the new areas and cultures of which they were to become a part. With the proliferation of groups, social structure changed considerably. The appearance of all of these groups in America impacted the social structure of the country and its culture. Out of their presence came the need to distinguish social structure from social organization, for many of these groups came into existence for the sole purpose of handling the core organizational activities of the larger society. Existing ideas concerning social groups and cultural groups and how they are formed and function in the complex environments must change. In complex environments, social and cultural groups go well beyond what previous (traditional) research has established. Even stratification has taken on new dimensions as even the characteristics of the stratified groups and there origins have changed considerably. In America, as in all complex societies, kinship alone no longer functions efficiently because of the shear numbers of people involved, the number of occupational specialties, and the fragmentation of the population into social groups by categorization, cultural groupings, the stratifications of these and other special interest groups, and the competition among them. The family in the social context has been replaced by these new groupings. They have become the more efficient, perhaps even necessary, means of handling all the activities and concerns of the large and varied population. Serious problems have arisen that are tied directly to the existence of so many groups brought together under the mantel of a nation-state. The competition and conflicts between them were inevitable.

In the United States, characterized by diversity, complexity, and fragmentation, it will be necessary to distinguish social structure from social organization, for understanding American social structure will not naturally lead to understanding its social organization. While the two are closely interrelated, they are not the same thing as found in the small-scale type of society. While social structure highlights social relations, an important part of any cultural pattern, the social organization of America addresses how the entire society organizes itself to get the things done that must be done for its survival. In the United States, as within other modern societies, the family remains a significant social unit, as important to the individual's identity or providing one's closest relationships as they may be anywhere else. But they are not the means by which the society accomplishes that which it must, nor is it the means by which people obtain the required knowledge of social relations or even their identity. Families alone simply cannot function within the fragmented or complex societies as they do in the small-scale society. Diversity, fragmentation, and stratification have all become quite commonplace within this larger and more complex group. The role and functions of family and kinship are usurped by other groupings that have become part of the social structure of complex society. In America, the family has been isolated within the context of the larger whole. In this nation-state, a diversified assemblage of social and cultural groups, some voluntary and some nonvoluntary, have assumed many of the functions of family. It is now these kinds of groups that address the core concerns of the societies, and family has been relegated to only a minor role in such things.

In their insightful discussion of American culture, Jorgenson and Truzzi (1974) see America as revolving around the social class system, involving both voluntary (special interest) and nonvoluntary groups. This oversimplifies the real complexity of American social structure. While the social makeup of a nation-state includes those same kinds of groupings found nearly anywhere, for example, family and the larger kinship groupings, the complex nation-state society will include many other social groupings and a whole host of constituent cultural groups. This means that while some social groups are established through marriage and descent, as found nearly universally, others appear based on similar interests or purposes, or based on some other shared cultural patterns that distinguish them from other groups within the society at large. Some are no more than a consequence (product or result) of people being grossly categorized together according to some real, imagined, or overgeneralized physical, geographical, or cultural characteristic(s), the distinction is not always clear. The differences between these social groups, social categories, and cultural groupings, all significant parts of the nation-state social structure, need to be understood. A social grouping consists of people tied together by personal relationships, who identity with one another and interact on a regular basis. A family is a social group, but in the complex society, it is not all that important except to the individual who obtains part of his or her identity from it and derives some measure of support from it. In a society that isolates the individual, family provides him or her with the closest relationships to others that they will ever experience. Other groups provide many of these same things to the individual in the complex society, in some cases, even more so than family can provide. Some of these are artificial, but all are real components of the social fabric of America. All of them can potentially become constituent cultural groups in the multicultural and diverse context of the United States.

A constituent cultural group will nearly always be a social group. But groups created out of the practice of categorizing people together for some ulterior motive and based on overgeneralized criteria will not necessarily result in a real group, despite the fact that most people will interact with them as if they were. More often than not, the created group will be made up of people who share little more than the artificial characteristics used in creating the group. Culturally, they can exhibit tremendous differences. Social categories and cultural groupings are parts of the stratified socioeconomic class system, and they play significant roles in the social structure of the nation-state. According to Jorgenson and Truzzi (1974), all of these groups function to produce some objective effect, to exert some control, to maintain their own structures, or to satisfy the psychological needs of their members, the members of other groupings, or the collective society as a whole.

The idea of cultural groups in the complex society is generally reserved for those made up of people with similar cultural backgrounds, such as the ethnicity that comes with immigrant status or being identified as Native American. Ethnicity is not associated with the more homogeneous small-scale and traditional societies where nearly everyone generally shares the same set of beliefs and practices. They are a product of the territorially based states that incorporate already established cultural groups into their more arbitrary, artificial, and consciously created cultural groupings now recognized as nations or countries. Ethnicity is tied to groups of people (migrants) who become constituent groups of these larger complex societies and maintain at least some aspects of the cultures they brought into the new context. In a real sense, the terms ethnic and ethnicity are just alternative words for culture, in this case to designate orand identify a particular kind of cultural grouping within diversity. America certainly has its share of these kinds of groups.

Social categories are simply aggregates of people grouped together by others according to some criteria they select, or who elect to identify themselves as a group if there is a benefit in doing so, for example, to achieve the strength of numbers necessary to successfully compete in a large and diversified context. Categories of people might include all dark or light skinned people, everyone who believes a particular religious doctrine, anyone who comes from a particular geographical region of the world, or even those who may speak a variant of the same language. These categories are not natural social or cultural groups, but imposed groupings for whatever purposes those doing the groupings might have. Members may have little in common, may not even interact. Individuals may not identify themselves as members of such groupings unless they perceive some advantage in doing so, for example, strength of numbers or to increase their political base and influence, or because it is the only way to respond to those who created such groups and assigned (prescribed) their membership into them. These social groupings (categories) are not cultural groups, made up of individuals who all share the same learned beliefs, behaviors, and products. In fact, people prescribed into membership in them can share nothing more than the characteristic(s) used by others to categorize them. America certainly has its share of such categories, and many of them are well on their way to becoming cultural groupings.

Intensified stratification is another product of the complexity and fragmentation of nation-states, tied to both social and cultural groups. Inequality among society's groups is simply broadened to include all the new kinds of groups that appear. The practice of distinguishing groups on the basis of physical characteristics evolved with larger and varying populations. Why they did is not well understood beyond it being a means of distinguishing *them* from *us, we* from *they*. But in the case of the United States, as well as in the minds of most Americans, these racial groupings are also closely tied to socioeconomic class groups and they represent actual cultural groups. All such groups experience prejudice, discrimination, and inequality within the society at large. In addition to the racial groups, out of the fragmentation that accompanies very large populations, many special interest groups only appear to complicate the situation further. Inequality is applied to them as well. Distinctions among all these social and cultural groupings have assumed tremendous importance in this context simply because of the competition among them as constituent groups of the whole. Each of them is concerned with, and competes for recognition, legitimacy, resources, place, power, and importance (prominence). This determines their relationships to one another and guides their interactions. In complex societies, all these social and cultural groups are quite common, although their definitions vary from individual to individual, group to group. In the nation-state context, all of these play significant roles in the social structure and cultural fiber of the larger society.

Memberships in some of these newly established groupings within the modern nation-state do not fit easily into the categories of membership rules as they have been established up until now. Even membership in groups that have been long recognized has assumed different characteristics from what has been generally accepted. Traditionally, membership in social groups beyond kinship or family groups was ascribed (one was born with the necessary criteria), variably ascribed (born with the necessary characteristic, but not everyone born with all that might be required), or it was achieved (membership by doing something required by the group). These categories of group membership were reserved primarily for nonkinship types of groups, also referred to as voluntary/nonvoluntary associations or interest groups. Membership in family and kin groups was simply assumed as it came from marriage or blood descent (real or simply by being recognized by the society at large). Membership in the nonkinship groupings of the modern society (social, cultural, or special interest ones) is no longer simply based on the ascribed, the variably ascribed, or achieved characteristics, nor is it simply voluntary or nonvoluntary. Where voluntary always meant choice, it no longer does. Where nonvoluntary meant membership was automatic, primarily based on age or sex, it no longer does. In complex societies, membership in some social groupings is established for a specific purpose by members of other groups within the society. Membership is prescribed and based on some physical or cultural characteristic(s), real or imagined, that is used to categorize people into the various groups of people that the society has chosen to recognize. Becoming a member of some of these new social groupings is actually prescribed by others who have decided, for whatever reason, to categorize certain people together into a group. Whether the individuals being so grouped share or recognize any affinity with one another is apparently not important. For example, in American society, Black Americans, Hispanics, Native Americans, Asian Americans, Middle East Americans are groupings of this kind. The people incorporated (categorized) into these groups do not necessarily share anything but the characteristic on which the group was created by someone else (based on physical features, a language, geographical origins, etc.). People are categorized together, made into social groupings, but the members may share little or nothing with the other people prescribed into membership. Of course, the others all interact with them as if they do.

Groupings based on ethnicity, religion, race, or even socioeconomic status are not simply based on ascribed status or achieved status. They are nonvoluntary in the sense that an individual is identified as a member whether or not they might choose such affiliation or not, or even if by that assignment, the individual and group are then forced to operate under severely limited (unequal) conditions. Assignment to particular groups has simply been determined by someone else, and the people who are categorized together must face the consequences. Most of the social categories created within complex societies are tied to the stratified system of the society. Because of the origins of such groupings, and the tendency to overgeneralize people into them based on socioeconomic income, ethnicity, race, or religion, they can be powerful forces in the social structure and organization of America. There is no choice for the individual who is incorporated into such social categories by others. If an individual meets the criteria as established by others, he or she is seen as a member of the created social group. Where voluntary membership once meant it was based on choice or achievement, sometimes both, now it has come to mean much more. In the traditional view, individuals achieved membership through his or her own efforts, exhibiting the right characteristics or doing the rights things. Achievement now takes into account more than what an individual might or might not do. Membership by achievement now requires recognition by the group to which someone aspires. Achievement is not an individual thing, but something that lies totally in the hands of the group to acknowledge or withhold. It depends on the group recognizing that the person has done what is necessary or exhibits the right characteristics. Even if a person has done everything required, that person still may not be accepted as part of the group if the group chooses not to recognize him or her. Achievement is never in the hands of the individual. Achievement is always in the hands of the group to recognize or not. If they choose to recognize it, the individual has met (achieved) the criteria. If they choose not to recognize it, the individual simply has not met (achieved) the necessary qualifications, displayed the necessary characteristic(s), nor met the criteria for membership.

There are also groupings that in a sense defy the application of voluntary or nonvoluntary criteria for membership. For example, there are groups formed on the rural-urban continuum and the territorial or regional groupings established on the basis of where one geographically lives. These groupings also have been created in the complex society, reflecting the complex history and development of the nation-state. Actually, characterizing such groupings (e.g., New Yorkers or Easterners, Southerners, Californians, Midwesterners, etc.), the farmer from the city dweller or urbanite, is a favorite American pastime. These groups are based on territorial and geographical proximity, wherein the members reside with or near each other and thereby form a distinct community with special, albeit somewhat vague, boundaries. Sometimes people can choose where they will live, at other times, they simply have no real choice in the matter. Of course, membership in these groups is similar to membership in any cultural group. It will be based on learned and shared patterns of belief and behavior—learning its culture. It can be likened to an individual learning all that it might take to be identified as "one of them."

The kinds of social groups based on kinship groupings or nonkinship groupings based on age, sex, or special interest will be found the United States, as they are in most complex societies. Because of the complexity of this large society, they take a different appearance from that associated with small-scale societies. For example, in America, age and sex groups may even be better characterized as special interest groups, perhaps cultural groups. To understand American social structure, one has to look at the usual kinship groupings, and then all those created by larger and more complex populations. All social groups in America are task-oriented in that they develop strategies to respond to the kinds of circumstances each group has to face in the American context, and they all function to maintain their own structures. Membership is exclusive and members derive a mutual pride in belonging to them.

In a real sense, with the possible exception of one's immediate family, and based on the shared beliefs and behaviors exhibited by all of their members, most of America's social groups, by definition, will be (or are becoming) cultural groups as well. Their members do share beliefs and behaviors (along with the products of these) that will distinguish them from other groups characterized by different beliefs and behaviors. These social groupings take social structure well beyond family or kinship. In this society, members of the culture are socially grouped for a variety of purposes, and it is with these groups that most of the organizational activity of the society will be addressed. They assume many of the activities and functions that in other contexts are assigned to family or kin groups. In American culture, family and kin groups will be found, but these are augmented by a whole range of special interest groupings that combine to produce an exceptionally complicated social structure. The stratification of the society by class adds still more groupings to the social structure of America. Spradley and Rynkiewich (1975) see American social structure as being based on kinship, descent, sex and age, residence, occupation, ethnicity, and social race. They have left off their list a vast number of other group, the special interest groups, that are also part of the social structure of America. As the family tends to be a significant social unit in all societies, it is probably the place to begin the discussion of American social structure, for despite the voluminous verbiage on the "decline of the American family," the family is as important to individual Americans as it has always been. Beliefs, attitudes and practices surrounding sex, mating activities, and marriage are all tied to the creation of the family and how it is structured within American society and culture.

SEX AND MATING PRACTICES

The study of human sex, gender, and human sexuality is a complex subject to say the least. While sex is biological, the topic goes well beyond this to almost every aspect of human culture. Human societies almost always infuse anatomical sex with profound social meaning and use it as a differentiating factor among humans. In America, sex pervades almost every aspect of life, even to the extent that would suggest Americans are primarily focused on, if not preoccupied, with sex. Sexual differences are expressed through dress, hairstyles, body carriage, a person's walk, language, earning power, greetings, laughing, and probably a whole lot more. Sex identity is fundamental to the daily behavior of the average American, while sexual activity actually takes up only a small portion of their actual time. Gender roles are determined and assigned by society or its cultural groups by virtue of biological sex. Assigning gender roles is a cultural universal, but the content can certainly differ from group to group. Gender identity derives from the interaction of the biological and cultural systems. It is something that the individual begins to experience at birth and accelerates into a life-long process, and this is basically a product of cultural perspectives and forces as regards what they are, or rather what they should be. In short, culture determines the appropriate roles for the sexes and then teaches them, both formally and informally, to the group's members.

Most Americans recognize two physical sexes, male and female. Some recognize an "intermediate" sex, one based on inherited genes and hormones that produce an individual who is hard to classify as one or the other. Thus, sex is recognized as a biological thing, while gender is determined by culture. The roles for the recognized sexes are culturally determined and transmitted (consciously and unconsciously) by one's immediate family, later by teachers, political and religious leaders, peers, and through the media. Typically, American males are characterized as aggressive, independent, and objective. American women are generally viewed as nurturing, empathetic, and emotional. Of course, while such characterizations have been changing for years, the typical stereotypes are still being verbalized. In the context of assigned gender roles, sexual activity (mating activity) is regulated and its expression controlled in the United States just as it is nearly everywhere else. Premarital, postmartial, and extramarital mating activities are very much restricted in American society as it is seen as tied to the perpetuation of the group, the culture, or special interests. All known societies regulate sexual activity among their members. Americans are generally strict on this issue because of economic and religious beliefs, but many of them regularly defy the restrictions in their everyday behavior. Even with the constituent cultures of American society, there is significant variation in sexual activity. The incest taboo of America, delineating whom one may have access to as a sexual partner or marriage mate, focuses on the members of one's immediate family—brothers, sisters, mother, and father. Beyond this, there are informal preferential mating patterns (closely tied to marriage patterns) where pressure is exerted on individuals to remain endogamous (stay inside their groups), but there are no laws in the United States as to whom one should marry or mate, excepting for incest applied to the nuclear family members. The selection of sexual or marriage partners among Americans seems to be quite open. But, without doubt, there are restrictions placed on sexual activity in American culture. Beyond the limitations of incest prohibitions applied to individual family members, there are strong pressures from many quarters regarding the way sex should be performed, where, when, and under what kinds of conditions it should occur, and so forth. Even in America there are normal expectations among Americans on the question of sex. Individuals perceived as not conforming to generally accepted practices are judged to be practicing *exotic* or *deviant* sex (both mean not as usually prescribed). While there seems to be no pattern for the time or frequency of actual sexual activity, that it should be done in private is a near universal rule for the American.

According to a 1990s sex survey conducted by Chicago's National Opinion Research Corporation and widely circulated in the popular press, Americans are sexually "circumspect and traditional" as opposed to "permissive and libertine" as often portrayed in Hollywood movies, across the media, and even as reported by some social science scholars . The surveys suggest Americans begin sexual activity at a later age than normally assumed and have fewer partners than has been suggested even in the most recent past. Fidelity seems to be exercised more than generally reported, as is the decreased likelihood of homosexual encounters than has been reported. According to the statistics reported, one in five persons report having no sex partners for the previous year; 1.5 percent of married people report having sex outside of marriage over last year; only 1 percent of Americans report homosexual encounters exclusively; age for first sex encounters is rising among males; and, the use of condoms has increased dramatically. The picture that has emerged from the results suggests a population now concerned about the dangers of AIDS and this is altering sexual behavior substantially.

As pointed out in this same report, in the responses to questions about sexual behavior the survey researchers found that the average American had 1.2 sexual partners in the previous twelve months, and had sex about twice a week or fifty-seven times in the previous twelve months. Men reported sixty-six times, while women reported sex fifty-one times across the same time period. The researchers sensed that men exaggerate and women under-report their sexual behavior. Some 22 percent of the respondents reported having no sex in the previous twelve months. General abstinence from sex is lowest among the married respondents (92%), intermediate among the never married, separated, and divorced (20 to 26%), and highest among the widowed (85.9%). Of all the respondents, between 91 percent and 93 percent indicated they were exclusively heterosexual since age 18, 2 percent sexually inactive since age 18, between 5 percent and 6 percent had been bisexual, while only 1 percent have been strictly homosexual. This seems to contradict earlier studies that estimated that as high as 10 percent of Americans as homosexual. The study also found that the average American reports having 7.15 sexual partners since age 18 (3.01 reported for widowed, currently married [5.72], never married [11.75], divorced [13.3]). Some 70 percent of the males admit to having at least one sexual encounter while married, as opposed to 35 percent of women reporting partners outside of marriage. Among respondents, 6.3 percent of all Americans reporting sexual activities in the previous year are at high risk for AIDS (2.4% had more than five partners, 3.2% had sex with a stranger, while 0.7% had sexual encounters with a homosexual).

In general, most Americans feel very uncomfortable with the topic of sex or their own sexuality. This is a product of the restrictiveness associated with the topic. By comparison to other societies, Americans have placed severe restrictions on the sexual activities among the very young, among those in the premarital age group, and among those in the postmarital group. The restrictiveness even extends to the public discussion of it or as a topic among them individually. Even with the so-called liberalization of Americans, the restrictions on sexual activity or discourse have remained fairly constant, as evidenced in the heated debates on sex education in American schools in different parts of the country. Sex is not seen as a natural part of living because it is considered by so many as a taboo topic—one does (should) not talk about it in public or private for that matter. Americans remain fairly naive about sex until quite late in life, well beyond the onset of puberty and only after (if) they overcome their ignorance and lack of willingness (ability?) to talk about it, even with their marriage partners.

Body ornamentation (believed improvements on the natural body), habits of modesty, the use of cosmetics and jewelry, paints, tattoos, mutilations (pierce ears or other body parts), circumcision, all play a role in American sex. In addition, there are a multitude of spoken and unspoken rules associated with the *dating game* that are directly related to the *mating game* of Americans. Some of these are universal and some are not. Mating is under the influence of the sex drive, which has become a major consideration in the dating game. Both mating and dating are closely related to marriage, thus are strongly influenced (even controlled to a large extent) by the society as a whole which is a response to the need of American society for social order. Directness is not a major element of sexual encounters in the American context. While a certain level of experimentation among Americans is frequently found, the rules must still be observed, and males and females approach the issue quite differently. Men seek sexual experiences and encounters, while women seek long lasting relationships. This has produced a dual standard regarding the sexual activities of males and females throughout history. Clearly, women are expected to remain "pure," while men have been encouraged (even so much as expected) to experiment. A male "playing" around is not nearly as frowned upon as would be a female doing the exact same thing. Americans structure sexual activity among the members of their culture, just as most other societies structure such activities. The ultimate purpose of the dating and mating activity for most Americans is to identify the individual with whom one wants to spend the rest of their life. In fact, it is apparent that a growing number of Americans believe that only within the context of the permanent relationship of a man and women is sex actually okay. In other words, as with most societies, dating ultimately leads to marriage (a universal institution found in all societies), which establishes the minimum social units of any society, the family or household.

Tiersky and Tiersky (1975) suggest that the American feeling of having no roots, their indifference to community welfare, and shallow personal American marriages all go together. For most Americans, the selection of a marriage partner is based on mutual attraction (oftentimes meaning no more than sexual desire) or motivated by such things as class, faith or race, all of which place limits on the possible selection of a mate. Unlike a great many other societies of the world, marriage for Americans is rarely arranged, although an arranged marriage does appear at upper-class levels on occasion. The selection of a marriage partner is simply left up to the individual. In the overwhelming number of cases, the dating game, the mating activities, and the marriage patterns preferred by Americans are based on romance and love, two rather ambiguous ideas that differ substantially in their definitions as one moves from individual to individual and group to group. Love is perhaps the most difficult to define, for it means and encompasses so many different things, prime of which is the belief that sex is only legitimate (good, acceptable, moral, and so on) within this state. Thus, the term is frequently used as a substitute word for sex. Americans speak of "making love," when clearly they mean to engage in sexual activity. Romance is based on images that have evolved historically (or have been created through the media) as to what constitutes the "perfect mate" who measures up to an ideal physical standard, does the "right things," and "sweeps the person off his or her feet." Unfortunately, it is rare that any individual measures up to the composites created in the perfect images people use in evaluating potential mates. Part of this includes sexual expectations that derive in a large measure from the media and are as unreal as the perfect partners individuals seek.

MARRIAGE

For Americans, marriage is a socially approved sexual and economic union between a man and a woman. It involves a complex set of norms that define and control the relations of the mated pair to each other, their offspring, other kin, and the society at large. It defines the rights and obligations of the pair, shapes the form and activities of the family or household as a social unit, and it provides for descent, inheritance, personal security, support, and identity. Throughout the United States, homosexual (same sex) marriages continue to be legally denied primarily because of strongly held Judeo-Christian religious beliefs on marriage and family. Despite such opposition, the attempts to achieve recognition for such relationships are far from over. At the present time, marriage is only recognized between members of the opposite sex and is presumed to be permanent, although, based on the divorce rate in the United States, this might not seem to be true. Regardless of what might be suggested in the high percentage of marriages that fail, people who go into the marriage bond do so with the idea that the relationship will be a life-long one. The rule of monogamy is the national norm. But, by law, polygamy (legally allowed multiple spouses) is allowed and practiced by some individuals and communities across the country. In some of these cases, it is allowed by default—authorities simply refusing to enforce the laws against it. The existence of bigamy statutes (laws which make it a criminal offense if a person has more than one spouse at a time) also attests to the fact that some Americans choose to ignore the rule that limits the individual to a single spouse at a time. As with most other societies, marriage continues to be the socially approved union of man and woman that involves sexual and economic obligations. Most of the economic aspects of marriage in America revolve around the household unit created, as opposed to something such as bride price (payments) or gift exchanges between the families of the marrying couple, as might be found in other societies.

Marriage in the United States can be accomplished through either formal or informal rituals. In some cases, there is no ritual at all save the legal registration of the union. While the normal case is for a couple to participate in either a religious or secular marriage ceremony, common law, group marriages, and cohabitations take on all the characteristics of marriage except for the formal approval of the state. Such unions are recognized de facto in that they are allowed to continue but without the permanency, recognition, or legal benefits of a registered marriage. Descent, inheritance, and social benefits have been denied individuals in such relationships in the past, but this seems to be changing. Cohabitation seems to be on the increase as young people of different sexes choose to live together in what they view as trial marriages without long-term commitments, and older people choose to do the same as a means around social security and tax laws, which tend to penalize married individuals. There appears to be a decrease in the number of people subscribing to the formally approved marriage, as many Americans are simply taking up residence with each other. Many of these cohabitations do become socially approved through common law marriages, where individuals simply register as married couples after meeting specified conditions, such as how long they have lived together or by representing themselves as a married couple. Such laws differ widely from state to state. In group marriages, where several men and women live together and have sexual access to one another (communes), social approval has never been sought or achieved. However, such variations fit into the American pattern, as with most marriages, both sexual and economic obligations are incurred by the participants, and these are usually tied to the American household unit.

For the vast majority of Americans, the selection of one's partner for marriage is based on romance (love), as opposed to economic or alliance value. This tends to limit the relationship of marriage to only the individuals involved and only minimally involves parents or other family members. Marriage is not allowed between persons within one's immediate nuclear family, but such persons are the only ones stipulated in the law. Historically, cousin marriages were preferred in some parts of the country, but not required by law, but this particular preference has fallen out of favor in recent years. Thus, there is a rule as to whom *not* to marry, rather than rules as to whom one should or must marry. While there are no formal laws of exogamy or endogamy, there are strong pressures exerted on individuals as to whom they should seek as a marriage partner. While romantic love lies at the heart of marriage, strong pressures emanate from their families, the social, or cultural groups with which they affiliate to marry someone of the same economic class, educational level, racial classification, ethnic or religious background as themselves. Because of this, most marriages in the United States actually turn out to be homogeneous relationships—involve people who are very much alike. Age can be a significant factor in that the majority of Americans prefer spouses of a similar age to themselves, but this may be changing because of the rapidly aging population of the United States. Religious overtones in marriage are strong, and the Christian belief of Adam and Eve, with the subordination of the female, remains ever popular. In recent years, with the women's movement, this model has come under increasing fire, while the body and soul relationship, the union of souls (a spiritual unit), the union of bodies (carnal union), and marriage for love decreed by most churches remain intact. Marriage is viewed primarily as a transaction, a contract wherein the parties recognize the rights of sexual access to each other, and women become eligible to legitimately bear children. It establishes the family and the economic unit known as the household. Upon marriage, newly married couples set up new households of their own, usually quite apart from the parents or families of either spouse (a neolocal residence pattern). Marriages typically include a secular or religious ceremony, a reception, and a honeymoon. Some marriages now focus on individuality, or "doing one's own thing" without the usual or more common fanfare.

On the reverse side of the marriage question is divorce. In American society, divorce rates are high. Some see it as a consequence of the shallow love base for marriage, others see it as a product of the emancipated woman in America and a consequence of the "battle of the sexes." This probably reflects the changing roles of both women and men in the United States and the constantly changing marriage relationships that obviously have to accompany that. Be that as it may, romance and love combine to provide the basis for rather shallow marriages and the rather high divorce rate among Americans. Recognizing that a mate is not perfect (does not measure up to the ideals) at marriage, both parties immediately go about trying to change their partners. The romance that was part of (determined) dating rules and expectations may no longer be viewed as necessary and quickly disappears. The strong sexual or physical attraction that initially drew the two people together begins to weaken until it is simply not enough to keep two people together in the assumed permanency of the marriage bond. As with marriage, divorce also involves the approval of society. Divorce rates in the United States are exceptionally high, even compared to other nation-states. Lots of reasons have been offered to explain this phenomenon, but it is probably best explained with reference to the flimsy basis for most marriages. As easily as one can fall in love or be sexually attracted to a member of the opposite sex, falling out of love and losing sexual interest is just as quick and easy. There is also an element of conflict built into the system that comes with the American emphasis on the individual. The breakdown of marriage relationships naturally follows where individual gratification is so highly valued, and individuals are brought up to believe they are the "center of the universe." Two self-centered individuals attempting to coexist in the same household are bound to clash, and with one's wishes gaining precedence over the other, the resentments begin to build. Marriage counselors tend to identify sex, money, and lack of communication at the heart of most divorce proceedings. Divorce is controlled just as marriage is controlled. Obtaining a divorce in the United States means a rather long and complex legal process, involving the courts, judges, and lawyers. It is ideally designed to ensure that children are cared for and the parting individuals remain economically stable. In reality, divorce usually ensures the economic stability of lawyers (the ones who probably gain most from such proceedings). While children are usually left in the custody of their mothers, a mother's ability to financially accomplish the task of raising children can be substantially reduced, despite any legal responsibilities of the father to provide financial assistance. Even if made part of the decree, the numbers of fathers failing to live up to the decree are very high. While marriage may not always result in a new family, more often than not, it does. In nearly every case, it results in a new household unit.

AMERICAN FAMILY AND HOUSEHOLD

For all societies, family is a social and a residential kin group unit that represents a means of adaptation, one based on group living. In the United States, with the women's liberation movement, sexual freedom, soaring divorce, the need for two incomes to maintain even the most modest household, and decreased time being spent with children by parents, the functions usually associated with family are constantly questioned. Despite all the statements to the contrary, family is as important to individual Americans as it is to anyone else. It provides individuals with part of his or her identity, it represents the place wherein people begin to learn about their culture, where they learn of the social relationships most significant to themselves, as opposed to total culture transmission, which resides primarily in the hands of the state. Outside of basic social relationships, the family contribution to teaching culture to the young is minimal. Cultural transmission and acquisition are primarily in the hands of the publicly established and funded educational system and its schools. In the United States, even the day care facilities may have more impact on young Americans than the family. But family represents "home" to the individual, a refuge, and the place of the closest relationships an individual will know until they enter adult life. For the normal American, family is highly valued and has never declined in importance. The family is still involved with socialization activities (albeit minimal), still controls sexual relations (among close family members), and is still concerned with the sole care of children (until they reach school age). After that, the family contribution to young family members is minimal, this despite the fact that the law holds that parents are responsible for the actions of children until at least age 18. When people suggest that the family has declined in America, they usually mean that it is not as important as it once was, does not contribute to the organizational activities of society as family might elsewhere, or that it has lost even more of its basic socialization function. Clearly, the homogeneity of traditional societies organized around family is not present in this culture. They also mean that the "decline of the family" is somehow responsible for the moral breakdown among young people, a sense of loss as to what is right and wrong, something said about every new generation since the time of Pericles.

In the United States, both the nuclear and extended forms of family structures will be found to exist. Usually the extended family will be associated with recent immigrants from areas where this type of family structure predominated, or where constituent groups need more support among its members in order to succeed in the American context. For most Americans, the nuclear family is still the ideal pattern, but because of the high divorce rate, the most stable family unit (household) is actually a woman and her children, perhaps with an adult male joined to her by marriage. In point of fact, in American society, both the numbers of single-parent and childless families have increased dramatically in recent years. In the past, Americans have been rather unique in their emphasis on the nuclear family (father, mother, and children), as this form of family seems to be an ideal pattern for the complex society organized around a socioeconomic class system and a market exchange economy. But the nuclear family is neither universal nor common in the world. Its presence in other societies is on a dramatic increase because of its adaptive advantage in a global economy based on the money dominated market exchange system. As hinted previously, this type of family unit has its problems. Husbands and wives are frequently pulled in different directions. Members of the family units can be of unequal backgrounds, which can cause considerable stress. Individualism produces much conflict and the unit can completely break down as members of it approach old age. Be that as it may, most Americans still hold on to the image of the nuclear family as the preferred structure. Americans have even created a whole set of fictive kin so that a constantly shifting group can still be considered as family (e.g., stepfather, stepmother, half-brother, half-sister, and the use of such terms with members of one's cultural groups).

Arensberg and Niehoff (1971) see Americans as focused on the nuclear family, but also see this family structure as changing. These authors note the preference for neolocal residence upon marriage and the creation of a new household (a newly married couple establishes their own residence quite apart from either set of parents). The preference for this informal rule comes from the nuclear family that is also reinforced by it. They also see Americans as highly mobile, which they credit for fluid relationships and a reliance on voluntary associations of common interest, instead of kinship ties, for their various activities. The nuclear family is primarily concerned with child rearing (the same nurturing function as in any other society), and in this, mothers have the greater influence. However, as already noted, some families consciously choose to have no children at all. For the Tierskys (1975), the American family is seen as the result of the marriage bound, typically revolving around one household (most of these existing in the urban environments), with parents and unmarried children. They also recognize that childless families have become more common. This produces the image of the perfect nuclear family with which most Americans identify and which serves as the basic family structure for the culture. Even with the very high incidence of divorce and remarriage, in the reconstitution of the household, the nuclear family ideally seems to remain intact, even where parent and child may be more fictive than real. These family groups tend to live in apartments, low cost houses, or mobile homes (the cheap American Dream). Parents tend to be devoted and permissive with their children, and most tend to rely on the many self-proclaimed experts, the family counselors, writers of guidebooks (e.g., Dr. Spock), or others who appear so willing to offer advice on what they should do as parents, as single parent families or as divorced parents. For the most part, parents focus on providing opportunities for their children, many believing this to be their primary responsibility to their children. This may be a consequence of the changing parental roles tied to the necessity for working parents. In the American family, disagreements over finances are common, as are power struggles, generation gaps, and the need for mobility. The significance of family remains, however, as shown in its re-creation among groups large and small. African-Americans use kinship terms (brother and sister) to refer to each other and as a sign of their close relationships. Frequently, youth gangs use similar kinship terms when referring to each other and the group itself as "the family." Family (real or fictive) represents the place where the need to relate to others is a constant, where one always feels attached to other humans, and where the individual, lost in the "sea of humanity," can identify and be identified.

Other researchers see American family life somewhat differently. While most would agree that the American family is based on the idealized notion of the nuclear family, Americans also identify relatives outside of this structure. Now the father-dominated family is less dominant (maybe never was a reality given the role and functions of females in the family). Now both parents work outside of the home, which has only blurred any division of labor that may have existed in the past. Unmarried couples and blended families (families constructed out of previous marriages) now appear with regularity. Overall, it would seem quite justified to suggest that children do get less attention from their biological parents than ever before. The family does, however, continue to reflect the dominant beliefs, values and assumptions tied to independence, individuality, equality, and informality. The rebellious teenager is merely simply assumed to be in a period of turmoil, while achievement, work, and acquiring material goods are all given significant attention.

Based on what the scholars say, the kinship groupings beyond the family deemed important to Americans appear to be those associated with genealogies (lineages), or relations by marriage and blood as far back as one can determine. Beyond the family, Americans generally recognize kinship lineages, those of their mothers and fathers to whom they can easily relate. Their preoccupation with lineage is probably tied to a general lack of historical roots (essentially without a long history to their culture), but in actual practice, lineage is really quite unimportant. Americans give "lip service" to lineage, but its significance was clerly left behind in Europe or from wherever their ancestors might have come. Some constituent groups (e.g., Native Americans and very recent immigrants) continue to recognize their kinship based on the principles of matrilineality or patrilineality (recognizing descent through only female or male lines). American descent is bilateral and the resulting kinship system is of the Eskimo variety wherein relatives are lumped together (classified) under one term, while siblings are distinguished. In this type of system, cousins are lumped together, aunts and uncles are lumped together by sex (but distinguished from father and mother), and generally the closest relatives are the most important. This seems to fit and flow from the focus on the idea of the nuclear family held and valued by most Americans. The tendency to identify America as a patrilineal (descent through only the male's or father's descent line) society is suggested in the practice of newborn children being given the surname of their father. This is misleading. This does not mean that only the male line is important, rather it is a practice instituted by the state for the purpose of record keeping. While in other societies, larger kin groups provide for various organizational activities, in the United States these things are handled by the state.

NONKINSHIP SOCIAL GROUPS

It is the nonkinship type of group that assumes prominence in American culture and society and provides for most of the society's organizational activities. As in any other society, both sex and age provide the basis for some of this, common interest groups providing for more. As already discussed, membership in social groups is normally characterized as ascribed, variably ascribed, or achieved, thus, most groups are also characterized as voluntary or nonvoluntary associations. But groups in America go well beyond what the term association might embody. In this society and other complex societies, their classification is not so clear-cut because they take on different characteristics. Sex groups exist in America, but rarely are they limited to only one of the sexes. For example, in the United States, women's associations help women in all kinds of social relationships and men belong right alongside women. Rarely are they unisex groups (limited to only one sex) as they are elsewhere. Women and men recognize their affiliation with others of their own sex, and both recognize the physical differences between them. Based on that, generalizations and stereotypes abound about members of the opposite sex and these directly impact their interactions with one another. Age groupings are not as formalized as when they become formal age-grades or age sets that group people throughout their lives and according to formally recognized stages of the lifecycle. Age is used for social groupings in America. They are recognized as groups, but not as organized or formal groups. These groups are determined by chronological ages or changes in the social conditions of the individual. Birth, puberty, marriage, or retirement can be used to denote membership in a particular group, for example, the teenager with the onset of puberty, adult upon marriage irrespective of actual age, retirement, or the onset of menopause with the older generation. On the more formal level, the state determines that young people below the age of eighteen years are not yet adults and must have a parent's permission for most things. Eighteen-year-olds may vote, are eligible to serve in the military to fight for the state, yet most states have determined that they cannot buy or consume alcohol until they are twenty-one. All people must attend school for a minimum number of years or until they reach a certain age. Retirement is likewise set by law (which changes rather frequently), but many people work well beyond the chronological age that has been established by such laws (usually because they have no choice). For most Americans, retirement age is set within the laws that govern when an individual can collect social security benefits, which were created to guarantee security for older Americans.

American Stratification

Human inequality is a universal phenomenon as no two people are alike anywhere in the world. But this does not mean that the inequality of individuals translates into stratification of society. Inequality comes by way of individual differences in skills, abilities, even talents. Stratification comes about as individuals are grouped with others according to some arbitrarily selected criteria, the resulting group being afforded a differential access to power, economic wealth or resources, political or status positions. Stratification involves a structured (institutionalized) system of unequal access to such things simply because of the group(s) to which one identifies or has been assigned. America is not an egalitarian society as might be suggested or reflected in the high value placed on equality (equal opportunity) among Americans. It is simply not the case that everyone has the same access to such things in the United States. Groups of people are systematically restricted in their involvement in the economic and political systems, even in the legal and religious systems. The reality of a social class system based on accumulated wealth precludes the egalitarian concept for Americans. In this society, one can be allowed lesser access to wealth, status, or prestige simply because of membership in a racial grouping, an ethnic grouping or category, or because of the religion, church, political party, or special interest group to which they affiliate and subscribe. The basic form of stratification in the United States is that normally identified as a class system, differentiated from other stratified systems in the potential for one to change their individual status or condition, but in some cases, one simply cannot (e.g., racial groupings).

In America's class system, the individual's class identity comes by virtue of their economic success. While class membership can be associated with one's family, occupation or social group, but most primarily in the United States, it comes with wealth. The lower, middle, and upper classes are generally recognized by everyone. Of course, family and constituent cultural group affiliation can play a major role in one's class membership because of the discrimination (structured inequality) of the society. As with other class systems, at least ideally, one can change their class identity and this possibility of movement distinguishes it from other types of stratified systems (caste, rank, slavery, etc.). While certainly there are possibilities for movement in the class structure, the reality of it is questionable. In the past, education has been viewed as one of the primary means by which the individual can change their social standing, but it generally takes more than that. It takes money. The fact that one can come up with a money producing idea or win something like a lottery, thus providing the person with the wealth necessary to participate in the economic system as a manipulator, is still a possibility. No matter how remote in real life, Americans want to believe in that possibility. In many ways the United States is fast approaching a "have" and "have-not" type of system. More and more of the wealth of America is being monopolized by fewer and fewer people. If one has wealth, one has access to resources and more wealth. If one does not have access to the productive resources, changing one's position in the social order becomes less and less of a realistic possibility.

SOCIAL INTERACTION

Despite the reality of America as a stratified society of structured inequality according to the groups one affiliates with or is assigned to, most Americans like to see themselves as egalitarian (here meaning equal as humans). Althen (1988) identifies informality and egalitarianism in relationships with others and in general behavior for Americans. According to this author, this informality accounts for the remoteness and aura of "untouchableness" in their dealing with those they do not know, or a superficial friendliness, a characteristic noted for members of this culture by people of other cultures. Americans tend to avoid personal commitments, and even their friendships are based on spontaneity and superficiality. Althen uses the expression, rarely very "deep." In addition, the usual style of Americans is toward depersonalizing their interactions with others and is centered on directness and assertiveness—laying one's cards on the table, but there are topics to be avoided (e.g., personal or controversial ones, religion or politics). While Americans prefer to see themselves as open, friendly, and direct, they are mostly unaware of their own communication styles. Saying it straight and keeping to the facts is frequently contradicted by their individual worship of opinion (especially their own). Preferred by members of this culture is "small talk," and the only variations allowed should be based on life situations. In actual personal or speech act interactions, the rule seems to be that no one speaks for too long. Ritual interaction is minimized between Americans and in their dealings with people not of their group. They tend to avoid arguments as much as possible and will disclose little of their "self." Becoming personally involved with others at all seems limited to only a small number of close friends, usually related to each other in terms of roles. Spoken communication is preferred to nonverbal communication, which remains basically an unconscious thing for them. Meaning is emphasized over anything else, as they tend to pay more attention to facts than emotional content. In interaction, courtesy, punctuality, treating males and females with the same respect, and standing at arms' length are all terribly important. Even choice of those with whom they will interact is usually tied to prescribed roles as most clearly seen in gender interactions. Americans need to be "liked" and thus will frequently appear as cooperative despite the competitive nature of their everyday lives and interactions with others. This is directly tied to their belief in the will of the majority with which virtually everyone wants to be associated. In social relations, and despite their many affiliations from which they get their individual identities, Americans may appear lonely, consumed with "self," inner-directed, and paranoid of the idea they may not be fitting in. Jin K. Kim and Janusz Mucha (Althen 1988) present some additional suggestions on American approaches to such things as interaction, manners and cordiality, but with the usual ethnocentrism of people who already know the truth.

Behaviorally, Americans subscribe to courtesy, punctuality, treating everyone (males, females, other races and ethnic groups) the same. Because they subscribe to such notions does not mean that Americans live up to the notions. Parents tend to be devoted and permissive with their children, focus on providing them with educational or learning opportunities. Conflicts between parents and children are much the same as they are for different age groups within the society. In the normal American family, disagreements over finances and sex are quite common, as are the power struggles between fathers and mothers (particularly with regard as to how the children will be brought up). Given the great attention paid to sex within the whole society, it is not surprising that this topic is also the basis of great conflict within the household. George and Louise Spindler (1993) note that most Americans recognize the presence of various ethnic differences among the ranks of the fellow Americans. Ethnic categories are not the same as ethnic groups (Naylor 1996). Overgeneralized categories are based on something such as race, language, and so forth. Conscious recognition of Jewish, European Catholic, European Protestant, African, Hispanic, Asian, Native American (or simply Indian) groups are readily forthcoming when Americans are queried about such things. Ethnicity is usually ascribed to other people or used by specific groups of people for personal identity, social, or political purposes. Along this line, Arens and Montague (1976) provide a good collection of essays on Americans, American culture, and social strategies via the mass media. Their focus is on social strategies or how people adapt and use information to formulate real behavior in various social contexts. Stewart and Bennett (1991) see the social relations of Americans in much the same way as they note Americans tend to see themselves as egalitarian middle class, where equality is based on humanness. Because of this, many Americans tend to avoid any personal commitments, avoid confrontation, like straight talk, and tend to be highly informal. They also believe that American friendships are based on spontaneity and are rarely deep (except with best friends). In most social relations, Americans tend to be depersonalizing in interactions with others. Their need to be liked extends even into their focus on competition ("playing fair"), but in the context of cooperation and a specialization of roles.

Some Do's and Don'ts

With the presence of so many different social groups, many of which are cultural groups with their own sets of beliefs and behaviors, their own established truths, one could expect to find considerable conflict between them, and not just ethnic to ethnic, religious to religious, interest to interest, and so forth. Political correctness is now the "rule of the land." Say nothing that some group might find (or could interpret) as offensive. Unfortunately, given the many different multiple definitions of most English words, almost anything can be viewed as offensive to someone. What is significant therein is not the state of "political correctness," rather what it says about the social interactions of these many social groups, social categories, and cultural groups. Clearly, as each attempts to place his or her social group, category, or culture into a more prominent position on the social ladder of the country, competition is great. More important, from these many social groups, cultures, and categories, and out of their own strategy choices, positions on virtually every major social topic and concern have been generated, positions that put different kinds of groupings into conflict, that put individuals into the position of having to choose which group is more important to them individually. That these are frequently at great odds, sometimes even turning into violent circumstances is obvious. More on the consequences of America's diversity will follow in the next chapter. But it is important to note here that the idea of a social group in complex societies is very different from that formerly associated with cultures and societies that were more homogenous, smaller in numbers, and where the needs of people could be handled quite well within a family context.

Any discussion of social interaction or behavior would be incomplete without some reference to Americans and food. Of course, the world sees the United States at the global center of the "fast food," and there is certainly sufficient evidence to suggest that Americans are more interested in getting this necessary activity over with as opposed to enjoying it. But it would be wrong to assume that they are not concerned with food per se. Hall and Hall (1990) point out that regional foods are quite important to Americans, as are racial and ethnic foods. In the South, southern-fried chicken, grits, and black-eyed peas may dominate, while in the West the beef barbeque and beans will be preferred, or the Tex/Mex food combining those foods of nearby Mexico with the tastes of the Southwesterner. In other regions of the country, ethnic foods are emphasized, as for example Italian foods in the Northeast, the Creole foods of New Orleans, the Chinese and Japanese foods on both east and west coasts, not to mention the Thai, Greek, Polish, Russian, French and just about every other type of cuisine found throughout the world. All the worlds' cuisine will be found in the United States in general, but clearly most Americans will emphasize that most closely associated with the groups with which they identify. Eating for Americans is as important for survival as it is for anyone else. They do tend to want to get it over with, except when it is closely tied to social interactions associated with their own goals or aspirations. They eat most times to survive and this has meant they want it done in the shortest time possible for "wasting time" eating is equated with "wasting time" in general. They do subscribe to the notion of three meals a day, and as many "snacks" as their systems may allow.

While it is impossible for anyone to outline all the things one should and should not do that are part of social structure (social relations), many Americans have come to take such things for granted, and newcomers are often only confused by them. Francisco Ramos (1993:1–10) provides some good discussion of language use, body ritual, leisure activities, and customs for Americans. He points out the need to keep to the right (on sidewalks, on stairs, on the highway, etc.). It is hard to understate the importance of this rule to Americans. Ramos also notes the strong belief among Americans that everyone should "line up but wait their turn." A great deal of confrontation can be avoided by simply following this rule. It is closely tied to an American belief that the first to come should be the first to be served. Woe to those who try to improve their position by cutting in line or who simply do not wait their turn. The author also points out the rules of not blocking traffic or someone else's view. Just about everyone seems to have a commentary on the idiosyncracies of Americans. There is the strong desire to suggest that when walking in the United States, look down (at the sidewalk, or whatever). With this behavior, you do not have to speak to anyone that may be passing. This is tied to the belief that if people cannot see your eyes, they do not see you. It also avoids the necessity of speaking with people you do not see. Another behavior that seems to be widespread among Americans, old and young alike, is the rule of not taking responsibility for your own actions. Always look for someone else to blame, it is always someone else's fault, never assume blame or fault. Another practice of most Americans when they do not know something is to be aggressive and loud. And then there is the reaction to conflict and confrontations. Make the other person feel guilty. To a certain degree, some of these observations are made with "tongue in cheek," but even in satire, there is always a "grain of truth."

SUGGESTED READING

Arens, W. and Montague, S. P. 1976. *The American Dimension: Cultural Myths and Social Realities*. 2nd edition, 1981. Port Washington, NY: Alfred Publishing Co. Contributors to both editions of this book look at some of the social aspects of American culture by way of social strategies as presented in the mass media. The volume presents some interesting perspectives on social realities of American culture.

Jorgenson, J. G. and Truzzi, M. (eds.). 1974. *Anthropology and American Life*. Englewood Cliffs, NJ: Prentice-Hall. This collection of readings covers virtually every aspect of American culture and society, the mainstream and the marginal, albeit somewhat dated.

The volume covers the organization of American society, kinship and family, language and communications, religion and cults, education, work, deviance, leisure patterns, and subcultures.

Schneider, D. M. 1968. *American Kinship: A Cultural Account*. Englewood Cliffs, NJ: Prentice-Hall. American kinship is treated as an example of the kind of kinship found in the modern complex societies. While primarily aimed at theory and analysis, the author does provide an excellent ethnographic treatment of American kinship. For this reason, it can serve as foundational in obtaining an understanding of this aspect of social structure in the United States.

Spradley, J. P. and Rynkiewich, M. A. (eds.). 1975. *The Nacirema: Readings on American Culture*. Boston: Little, Brown and Co. This is one of the earliest collections of readings on American culture, covering enculturation, language and communication, kinship and family, social structure, economic, political, legal and religious topics. Contributions on American values, world view and perceptions on change are also provided.

FIVE

AMERICAN
ORGANIZATIONAL STRUCTURE

As pointed out in the last chapter, in a complex society such as the United States, the social structure, altered with the proliferation of all kinds of social and cultural groups, still focuses primarily on the social relations, claims, and obligations of people (groups) within society. Social organization focuses on how the society organizes itself to get the things done that must be addressed if the group and its culture are to survive. It was suggested that the confusion about social structure and social organization, the use of these terms interchangeably, could be attributed to the fact that in the small-scale society, the distinction between social structure and social organization becomes blurred simply because the organizational activities of the society are basically accomplished within the context of the family or other kinship groupings—the model upon which the perception that they are synonymous is based. In small-scale society, the family provides for most, if not all the concerns of the individual, the family, and by extension, the larger group or society. It is in this group that the problem of social order is addressed and maintained, that the various customs for utilizing available resources to meet the needs of the group are established, and the crucial tasks of cultural transmission (teaching) and acquisition (learning) are accomplished. It can even be the context for meeting the spiritual (supernatural) needs of the group.

In a society as complex and diversified as the United States, neither a family nor a larger kinship group can adequately undertake these necessary activities to meet the needs of the society, except for individual members of the immediate family or household. The problems encountered in meeting the needs of the larger society and so many social and cultural groups, extend well beyond the capabilities of a family or larger kinship group. In this kind of society, additional groups even appear just to handle the core activities or concerns of the society. These new groups become cultural groups in their own right, adding to the already long list of constituent groupings that characterize America and its culture. The organizational structure becomes one in which the multitude of constituent cultural groups that actually make up the larger society must pursue their own special ideas, interests, and goals, frequently (if not always) competing with one another. It is out of the ideas of these competing groups and their interactions that what should be taught and learned by all Americans will be determined, what customs will prevail as to how resources will be utilized to meet the needs of the people, and the complex and difficult problems of social order will be established and maintained. In some cases, it even determines what supernatural beliefs will prevail.

As with the original founding of this nation in response to the needs of a large, diversified, and fragmented population, a significant amount of negotiation between groups with competing interests must nearly always take place. This will revolve around the special circumstances (history, limitations, opportunities) of the groups and individuals, each of whom believes that they know the right way or ways to handle all these crucial matters. The consequence is a social organization that will reflect the diversity and the ideas of these new cultural groupings. Thus, not only is social structure changed in the context of nation-states, social organization is also changed in the process. That organization will reflect the social standings of these groups, their relative power or status in relationship to one another, and it will reflect the relationships among them. In getting anything done, in arriving at any decision with regard to any activities related to the core concerns of America, the specific concerns and beliefs of the varied constituent groups will have to be taken into account and considered. Each group has a significant role to play in the process and its outcomes. Each group has a stake in the ultimate success or failure of the society and its culture to respond to the core concerns of the society at large.

With the great number and variety of constituent cultural groups of the United States and the fragmentations born of the conflicts, competition, and specialization among them, getting Americans together on much of anything is a monumental task. Each social and cultural group has its own agenda to pursue. The consequences of ethnocentrism or each group's belief in its own truth, are substantially magnified. Each group advocates its own truth and attempts to extend (impose) that truth onto everyone else. This will lie at the heart of the difficulties in bringing such a diverse assemblage of cultural groupings together and building some kind of national awareness and unity. Something as limited as a family or other kinship group simply could not do this, nor could it provide for the activities necessary for this wider, more diversified group, to function and survive. The society and culture have to turn to other ways and other kinds of groupings to accomplish the necessary tasks.

For American culture, specific groups form around the core concerns of culture, groups that become additional cultural groups based on those specializations (educators, politicians, economists, etc.). Other groups form around shared ideas or perceptions as to how to approach the problems to be solved. Groups formed around ideas and views held on the right things to be taught in the educational system, the right political philosophy, things that should or should not be part of the legal system, and religious ideas that should be made part of the national thinking. For the culturation process (cultural transmission and acquisition), the culture relies on education, a formalized system and process for ensuring that new members (both the young and newly immigrated) learn all they need to know to become effective members of the national group. But, there are significant differences between groups as to how the system should be constructed, what it should teach, and what the outcomes should be. In dealing with the material needs of the people, a stratified socioeconomic class system has evolved based on money and market exchange that pits class against class. Each one of these socioeconomic classes becomes a cultural grouping with its own specific interests to advocate and pursue. In the economic system itself, an extremely large number of additional cultural groups are created around occupational specialties to ensure the members of the society get the things they desire or require. For establishing and maintaining order and to deal with violators of expected norms of behavior, the society relies on a series of other occupational specialists that form cultural groups made up of people who specialize in law and law enforcement. In response still more groups are created, made up of people who share similar ideas about acceptable behavior, how to establish it, and what should be done with violators of the rules. To handle other necessary concerns (e.g., the supernatural needs of the populace or segments of it), American society relies on a vast number of special interest or purpose groups, nearly all of which are voluntary. These groups also take on all the characteristics of cultural groups.

By comparison to the small-scale society, where a degree of harmony exists in getting things done, the social organization of the United States is, indeed, complex. With all the competing interests of its various constituent groups, conflict and competition are the normal state of affairs. Harmony is not that easy to attain. All of the constituent cultural groups that evolve in response to organizational activities simply add to the diversity of the society and its culture and to the competition and conflict already established with racial and ethnic groupings. Cultures in contact mean cultures in conflict, for truths must compete. Because of the stratification of the society and the unequal status of the social and cultural groups—the presence of a majority (those with the power to effect their own lives) and minorities (groups with limited access to power)—the conflicts are intensified.

CULTURATION PROCESSES

The culturation system refers to how societies handle cultural transmission and acquisition. As with any culture group, if it is to survive, there must be some system (process) of transmitting the culture to each new generation of members. Culture is learned, not inherited. While many Americans believe that the only thing necessary for membership in the culture group is to be born in the United States, being born in the country only gives one the rights of citizenship. This alone does not make an American. To achieve this designation, the individual must learn those beliefs and behaviors that have been established for them as members of the group. They must acquire that knowledge necessary for them to function effectively as members of the group. A culturation process directed at cultural transmission and acquisition is absolutely essential for the continuing survival of any cultural group. Traditionally, anthropologists have spoken of this as the *enculturation* process—the means by which young people are brought into their primary culture. But in the context of complex nation-states, adults also have to be brought into full membership of the group, adults that have already learned a primary culture somewhere else. To speak of bringing these who have immigrated into the nation-state culture from other nation-states (countries) and who have already learned and practiced another cultural pattern, the term *acculturation* process might seem to be more appropriate. Acculturation was originally used to refer to change that came with the close and continuous contact between people representing different cultures. As this is basically what occurs with people moving from nation-state to nation-state in the modern world, the term would seem to distinguish the kind of process to which they are exposed, one significantly different from that used to bring young people into their first or primary culture. The term points to the cultural change that must occur as an individual or group moves from one nation-state society to another, a change essential if the individual is to survive in their new surroundings—as when people have to relearn culture. In the United States, as with all nation-states, the task of cultural transmission and acquisition is assigned to the educational system. This centralized and highly formalized system is given the primary responsibility for bringing both the young and the immigrant into cultural membership, ensuring that they learn all they need to know to function within the context of American culture and society. This is not the only means by which people learn culture. There are other processes by which Americans learn their culture. Most of these occur within more informal contexts.

Most Americans tend to believe that it is in the context of family that they learn their culture. Nothing could be further from the truth. The existence of this widely shared belief does reflect the context where this cultural acquisition is initiated. It is in the family that the young are first introduced to the sociocultural and physical worlds in which they will live out their lives. It is here that one's primary language is acquired. Language is both the means by which culture is acquired and it is part of the culture that is being acquired. It is within language that all the culture is symbolically encoded, where all the rules, ideas, behaviors, and products are categorically organized (at least ideally). From the family, the young will come to understand the basic claims and obligations (expectations) they have to the other members of their family and gradually the other social or cultural groups with whom they will relate to and live among, even the American culture to a limited degree. From family, individuals acquire some of the basic guidelines for behavior, learning what is expected of them at home and outside the home. From family, young people learn some of the most fundamental ideas and knowledge that are shared among Americans and essential to being a member of American culture. But the actual amount of American culture learned in the home and from family is quite limited. For the bulk of this activity, the society depends upon the centralized, formalized, and institutionalized system of education. Education is supposed to ensure that everyone receives the same required, necessary and equal information to be fully functioning members of the group—they learn the "right" things. From this system, the young learn the skills and knowledge necessary for them to live out their lives.

In the United States, the educational system was created just for the purpose of culture transmission and acquisition. Its existence was created and continues to be justified on the belief that a successful democracy depends upon an educated populace. Of course, it was also based on the idea that all the members (citizens) of the nation-state must share (at least to some degree) the same basic ideas and follow (at least to some degree) the behaviors expected for all citizens or members of the group. It also had to provide the individual with the basic knowledge and understanding of the products of culture, the physical (material and technological) and social (political, economic, etc.) systems, with which they will be concerned in their day-to-day living or that will govern their lives. Of course, these same things must be conveyed to immigrants and acquired by them to bring them into full participation in the society and culture. The task is somewhat more complicated in that it involves moving people (the immigrant) away from one culture and their integration into another. This involves the unlearning of older ideas and behaviors (putting assigned an already learned cultural patter), and the learning of an entirely new culture, usually in a different language. This acculturation of immigrants is also within the role, scope and function of the educational system, just as it is formalized in curriculum and even in the places where it must be done. It is because of the actual diversity, complexity, and fragmentation of the United States, as with any complex society, that the need develops for centralizing and formalizing the cultural learning process for aspiring members of the society. This does not only come from one's family as is popularly believed.

The United States had to develop (institutionalize) such a system to have any chance of bringing an otherwise diverse population together into something that can be called American culture and society. To this formalized educational system falls the task of building a sense of unity—nationality and a sense of patriotism—amid the diversity. A culture of the nation-state has to be imposed on top (or in addition to) the many diverse and competing cultures of the nation-state. But learning culture is not limited or restricted to just the formal educational system. Learning culture is also accomplished in the context of the household and family, in churches from religious leaders, from peer groups, on the job, at play, and from the media. These contexts and processes are simply less formal. Given the ideal focus of learning in the educational system, the learning of culture that occurs in these informal contexts is geared more toward real culture. This can even take place within (or in spite of) the formal context of education and the school, such socialization just is not made part of the formal curriculum (Spradley & Rynkiewich 1975). While there are both formal and informal ways of ensuring that people learn what they must know to be members of the American culture and society, it is in the educational system that the primary task of cultural transmission and acquisition of the nation-state culture is accomplished. This represents the primary culturation process of the United States whereby all Americans are created, are brought into full membership, in the nation-state group. But it is not the only way this is done, for a variety of other processes are also used to transmit culture as well. To distinguish between what is transmitted, where, and how, a distinction must be made between education and socialization. Education is probably best used in reference to the institutionalized, formal system of cultural transmission and acquisition, while socialization is best reserved for the informal transmission and acquisition of culture.

Education (The Formal Process)

Education in America is institutionalized in that the place for it (schools), its content (the curriculum), and the roles of the participants in the process (teachers, students, and administrators) are all formalized and established by law. Every aspiring American has to go to school for a required length of time. In the case of young people, this can amount to twelve years or more. In the case of immigrants, they will have to attend class until they can successfully past a test demonstrating their competence and understanding of the American culture. Such things are determined and set by law. Children know that the school is where they will have to go to learn the things they need to know. They know that in the schools will be teachers, those responsible for transmitting what must be learned, and they know they will be students, those who must learn certain things. They know they will be tested to see if they have learned what they are supposed to learn. Few Americans recognize that what will be taught and what must be learned are part of a formal curriculum developed to ensure that everyone learns the same things. The sole purpose of education is to instill (teach the idea, behavior, and product knowledge) the nation-state culture—to make Americans. Immigrants understand this, but very few native-born students, or parents for that matter, recognize this is what the system is designed to accomplish. Virtually no one recognizes that what is taught is an ideal version of American culture—the way things are supposed to be. Few Americans (teachers included) recognize that the goal of the centralized educational system is to make Americans by molding young people (or immigrants) into people who believe and act as Americans are supposed to believe and act.

Standard American English is taught in every school to allow for communication among all members of the American society, regardless of what other languages or dialects many of them can or will actually speak. People will be taught about the American political system, how it functions, and what their responsibilities are in the political process. They will be taught about America's economic system, how it functions and what their role will, or can be, in it. They will be exposed to group worldview, the nature of the universe and world, along with the role of the United States in that. They will learn what serves as explanations for cause and effect in the context of American society and culture. They also will be exposed to many other aspects of the American culture with which they will be concerned throughout their lives, learning the right things to do and the values (ideas) that hold the society together (Ampara 1993). What most fail to understand from this assemblage of topical exposures is that the purpose is to perpetuate the culture by making them into good, functioning, acceptable members of the group who know what they must know (ideas and values of American culture), acquire the skills (to read, write, and undertake simple mathematics), and understand what they will do in terms of acceptable behavior (right and wrong), already established by those already in the know. These things are presented in their most idealized forms and that is the way students will learn them. The educational system teaches the *American* way, and its goal is to produce Americans who can live and work in the American culture and society. Its goal is not to produce international citizens, but Americans.

Americans are unusually proud of their educational system. They value it highly for it is tied to their strong belief in the individual, and it increases their chances of success by providing them with the means (skills and knowledge) to better themselves in the context of the socioeconomic class system. On the other hand, discontent with the system is ever present as the needs of society change, as the system itself constantly changes, and the nation confronts the growing problems and issues of a diverse society. Ideally, education is valued, but in reality, a greater value is placed on money and if education requires that more be spent on it, then education will lose out. This means that most Americans actually place a low value on education once they have completed its program or when providing more money (in the form of increased taxes) conflicts with their personal goals. The low value placed on education is further reflected in the relative status position of teachers as compared to other specialized professionals within the society. Teachers are among the lowest paid of all professionals, sometimes making less than the local garbage collectors, car mechanics, or uneducated construction worker. Athletes and artisans, many times only marginally literate or educated, can command much higher salaries than teachers at any level of education. Legislators, most of whom were taught by teachers, often seem determined to keep teacher salaries the low priority in their budgeting efforts. Among professionals, teachers socially rank at the bottom, this in a society that claims to value education.

Education in the United States has long been viewed as a right (Pinxten 1993). Universally, Americans see the twelve years of schooling (through high school) as an absolute right to which they are entitled. Many would suggest this right of Americans should now include a college education. The public educational system is given primarily responsible for the first twelve years of school. Colleges and universities are assigned the responsibility beyond that. The educational system is often referred to as free "public education" but this is clearly a misnomer. Education is hardly free as it usually consumes the bulk of local and state funds taken from every American in some form of taxation. In essence, everyone pays for "free" education, even long after they or their children are no longer directly involved in it. This idea is probably tied to the notion that the American system (particularly its political system), the system of a free democratic society can only work with an educated populace, indeed, is dependent on an educated populace. In reality, while there is easy access to the educational system, that access is closely tied to social and cultural inequalities. Education is not free in any sense. The system must be supported, and wherever public monies are used to provide educational opportunity regardless of level, it will be centralized and controlled by the national, state and local authorities that determine funding, curriculum, and access.

Education in America is geared to a particular kind of person with an average intelligence (ability to learn). The standard pattern taught throughout the United States is that associated with the white middle-class culture (the mainstream culture). Until recently, it was not designed to meet the needs of the many students who do not fit into that white middle-class cultural grouping, nor designed to meet the needs of either below average or above average students. The idea behind this is that everyone must be taught the same things (given a common ground) in a way that anyone could understand—nobody was left out of the system and everyone would get the required minimum. The awakening of the American populace and educational system to multiculturalism and cultural diversity has begun to change all this. Most Americans are now very much aware that teaching white middle-class standards, values and culture to members of other cultures is not only ethnocentric, it also ensures that members of these cultural groups will fail within the educational system. In place of the standard designed to ensure and reinforce equality among America's people has come the realization of the many inequities that were actually fostered by the system.

That the educational system (faculties and curriculum) is not geared to meeting the needs of non-traditional students—are not white, middle-class, or of European background, has occasioned considerable debate, as have the various standardized tests that take up a considerable portion of the educational experience and are inappropriate for most students. So-called intelligence tests measure the student's ability to succeed in the educational system, again one dominated by the white middle-class standard. Despite repeated efforts to make such tests less culture-bound, all the statistics continue to show that students from other cultural groups (e.g., African-Americans, Mexican-Americans, etc.) do not do very well on them. Students from white, middle-class backgrounds perform well on them and in the educational system in general, while others simply do not. What this says is that basically the educational system is oriented to a single cultural group. In this it is an enculturation process, the means by which the young are brought into full membership in the cultural group. For others, it represents an acculturation process, one aimed at bringing someone who already has acquired a culture into membership of another, for example, Mexicans to white, middle-class Americans. Few, if any teachers will ever face a class made up of a single cultural group. Most will face the multicultural classroom consisting of students from across the spectrum of cultural groupings found in America. Even if one accepted a standardized approach and outcomes as the legitimate goal of education, the system is hardly designed to accomplish it, nor could it ever overcome the fact that even though the students may be exposed to that set of cultural beliefs and behavior while at school, they still return to their other cultural group after school. There is no shortage of issues that accompany the problem; lack of appropriate teachers, the question of the language of instruction (bilingualism and group specific language dialect, etc.), and even subject matter. As pointed out by Stan Green and Steve Perlman (1997), on the issue of diversity in education, the system reflects the diversity dilemma in the society at large.

As suggested by Green and Perlman, there is no shortage of debate on education and the system intended to teach children what they need to know to become fully functioning and productive members of society. The context has been a source of never-ending debate as Americans argue over the skills and knowledge that should be taught in the schools as the needs of the society change. Accountability is now the focus (the buzz word) among legislators who must provide the funds to support the educational system, and among all those groups that feel, in one way or another, that the system is failing. For many, the educational system now appears more concerned with measuring outcomes desired by one or another of the interested groups, not whether students have learned what they are need to learn. A casual glance at America's schools is sufficient to convince anyone that more time is now spent on testing or the preparation for tests than actually learning the skills and knowledge students may need to learn. In recent years it seems as though the system has moved toward more measurement and less learning, evidenced by the numbers of graduates that seem less capable of functioning as contributing adults within society. Teachers readily admit that they teach based on the tests legislatures create to measure the success of both student and teacher, as their livelihoods depend on the results. Students have moved away from the process of learning to an emphasis on obtaining just what they need to know to pass the test—and then promptly forget what they learned, if anything, in the process. Americans also continue to question why students are incapable of identifying problems and looking for the solutions to problems. Americans wonder why graduates of the system lack the minimum skills employers apparently want in their employees.

In many ways, today's students have become the *visual* generation of learners. Many now sincerely believe that all they have to do is to sit and watch, and they will somehow obtain all they may need to know (apparently through some media osmosis). More and more students in the system are convinced that they do not have to do anything but watch and they will learn what they need to know. Students are not expected to do much of anything on their own. The teacher is expected to do it all for them. If they are not taught, or if they do not get the lesson, it is the teacher's fault, the same one that must teach as prescribed by the state, in some cases even as to the number of minutes to be devoted to particular topics each day. The discipline necessary in the learning environment has disappeared as parents and others have taken this away. The student's responsibilities in the learning environment seem to have been lost. Students are told little of their responsibility and role in the process of learning. Learning to learn is disciplining the mind, but in a system where there is no discipline, there can be no learning. Students now expect to get good grades, not information and skills that will assist them later in life. Student evaluations of instruction and instructors, are given more credibility than almost anything else as to quality of teachers and teaching. For legislator and parent alike, the student evaluation has become the best measure or test of good teaching. Teachers are judged on the basis of whether or not they are liked or are entertaining. If they are not or if the teacher forces them to think, they are judged as unfair or poor teachers.

Other debates rage over such things as bilingual education, sex education, representation of cherished ideas of one group or another, on history (particularly what would be taught about diverse groups), whether books used in the instructional program contain the ideas to which they subscribe, whether parents should have more say in the education of their children, whether or not their specific group is represented in the decision-making body, whether education changes to meet the changing times, and so forth. While education and educators have always seemed to favor change, adopting new teaching aids, techniques, or technology on a regular basis, the adoption of the newest technological gadgetry only seems to reinforce the existence of the visual generation. This tendency to accept change is an American characteristic, but not without an inherent paradox. In some ways, education is the most conservative element of society, this conservatism tied to its primary goal of conveying and maintaining American culture, its heritage, its traditions, along with the ideas and behaviors that are such an important part of it and never go out of date. Over the last half century, the educational system of America has moved steadily to the acquisition of the programmed text (learning the answers/learning the programmed recipe to solve all problems) and exposing students to a graduated and well-laid-out schedule of topics. Americans are not taught how to develop solutions to problems, only how to apply the canned responses. When they learn that such programmed solutions do not exactly fit every circumstance, they simply do what everyone else does; they force a fit or simply ignore the parts that do not fit. In the context of changing perceptions of what students are expected to do and the shift to measuring the teacher and not the student, it is now the system or teacher that fails the student, not the student who fails. It is always the fault of someone or something else. The failure to assume responsibility for one's actions is reflected in a nationwide attitude that finds people blaming others for everything that happens to them. It is always someone else's fault. It is interesting that despite the constant criticisms of the educational system, or some part of it, the system does achieve its primary goal to a large degree. Ask Americans about what is expected from them, what is right or wrong, how the economic or political system is structured and functions, or what basic things all Americans believe, and they can and will tell you. It has also produced the most intelligent and skilled generation of Americans yet to assume membership in the culture.

Socialization (The Informal Process)

While education and schools emphasize the ideal culture of America, Americans learn much of their real culture in the informal context. Socialization is the term that best characterizes the more informal context and means for enculturation and acculturation. This begins in the family where a young person learns from other family members, the claims and obligations associated with family and the basic social skills necessary for the interaction with others. These are later broadened to encompass neighborhoods, communities, and, in a sense, the national group. Most of the informal learning of one's culture occurs within the family, later within peer groups, and still later within the groups the individual chooses to affiliate with or with which they are identified. One can argue that while education concentrates on the formal curriculum and ideals of the culture to be learned, in the same school context, and in the social interactions with other participants in the process, they will learn other versions of the culture as well. With this informal learning that occurs right along with the idealized content of the formal process, the actual gaps (paradoxes or contradictions) between ideal and real culture begin to appear. The teacher may speak of the value of equality and equal opportunity, but in their social interactions with students, they may actually reflect, even demonstrate, the reality of inequality and lack of equal opportunity. The students observe that all people are not treated the same, despite any pronouncements (propaganda) to the contrary. While the system is relating rights and wrongs to be learned and practiced, the students may also learn just how far one can deviate and still be acceptable—at least not pay any substantial price for the variance. It does not take students very long to figure out that much of what they are told is "do as I say, not as I do." This is something they have already observed in their parents and other adults. They also can see that the school may not be providing some topical coverages that in their lives will be very important, for example, their own growing sexual awareness. While at school, the topic may not be part of the formal curriculum, it surely can become a significant topic of conversation and part of the normal sharing of information among the students themselves. They know it is something to be learned so they get it via the only route open to them, from their peers and friends.

In a very real way, in the family and among their friends and peers, significant amounts of cultural information are transmitted and acquired as a young person grows older. Not too infrequently, the information being exchanged in these contexts can be at serious odds with the ideals being conveyed in the formal contexts. For example, the students in school learn about being equal and equality of opportunity, but grading designed to indicate progress within the educational effort also demonstrates to them that they are not equal and real opportunities are tied to social categories with which one is identified. At home and among their friends, they learn that everyone is not equal. They may learn of white or black supremacy, or that because of some physical characteristic, one group of people is superior or inferior to another. They learn that one political philosophy is better or at least more correct than another. They learn that one religion is better, more correct, closer to the "real truth," than another. They see that their lifestyles are not the same as other people. From such associational learning, younger people very quickly learn the difference between what is taught them, and what reality (in their everyday lives) is in virtually everything they must learn.

Associations are not the only informal means by which one learns about their American culture(s). Through movies and mass communications (especially the television) they are exposed to more American culture, albeit skewed for a variety of reasons. What they see in the movies reflects what will sell, not necessarily what their culture should be and even actually is all about. The same can be said of the television they watch and things they read. The idea held by Americans that they are a peaceful country is constantly assaulted by what people see on the nightly news or read in the newspaper. What is seen or read emphasizes the violence of the society. That there is right and wrong is constantly challenged by the programming that throws such things into question on a daily basis, for example, the very popular soap operas. Such things are already biased by whether it is marketable, advertising sponsorship, and choices made by media executives who try to influence or limit what people will be exposed to as they attempt to avoid upsetting particular viewers or readers. To understand that such media representations of American culture are nearly always flawed, one only has to ask someone from another country about America, someone whose ideas are based on the media representation. When asked about the America they learn (know) about from the media, it is skewed to say the least, shocking when most Americans hear it. There is also the bias of the messages being sent and received through television and the movies. These are, by virtue of how they are written and presented, frequently the views and attitudes of a single individual. The various media are very powerful conveyors of cultural ideas and behaviors that are assumed by viewers to be real.

People also learn through their church affiliations, in the course of their leisure activities, and from the simple process of watching what goes on around them. Church invariably provides the individual with a particular slant on the culture, a position on what is right and wrong, what the individual must do to satisfy his or her spiritual obligations, and what is "the real truth." Churches can advocate a doctrine that is in direct conflict with national values and this can produce a considerable conflict within the individual. The American ideal of individual equality is directly contradicted by policies of churches that restrict their membership to particular racial/ethnic/socioeconomic groups, or that denies females or representatives of other cultural groups (e.g., homosexuals) the privileges of participation or access to leadership positions. Even the idea of individuality is assaulted by the church insistence on conformity to the beliefs and practices to which it subscribes. Even some religious leaders have gone so far as to epitomize in their own lives the very behaviors they condemn in their followers, for example, illicit sex, theft, lies, etc.

Contradictions even appear in their occupational lives (work) and in their leisure activities. In the free market system that they seem to value, beating the competition is the golden rule. In this arena, things have gotten so bad that a whole new area of business has appeared, business ethics. In their leisure lives, Americans may learn that competition with cooperation is important, but at the same time, they learn that a higher value is placed on winning at all costs, fair or foul (just as in business). They also learn that not everyone is equal in these contexts and this is apparently okay. As individuals simply watch what goes on around them, they learn about their real culture. It is not necessarily what they were taught was wrong or a lie, it simply means that what they were told and taught was ideal culture. They have to live in the real culture, the version of culture in which they as individuals, and given any limitations of their own or imposed on them by someone else, will have to learn to accommodate, live with, or attempt to overcome.

Age is an important element of socialization as already evidenced in some of the previous discussion. Americans tend to see individuals growing over time then declining in their later years. One's chronological age determines such things as schooling, the driver's license, when marriage is possible, when the individual can vote, serve in the military, drink alcoholic beverages, and so on. There is no formal teaching and learning of such things, but there is a general schedule (program expectation) for nearly every stage of one's life, from birth to death. People learn how long (around or until what age) they can be excused from responsibilities. People learn when others expect them to assume the responsibilities of adulthood, get married and settle down. People learn when they are of an age to retire, or have to retire, and what this means—they will be cast aside as no longer capable of productively contributing to society or relevant to a society that emphasizes the young. Chronological measures accompany the individual through all aspects (stages) of his or her life. Naturally, there are significant behavioral implications attached to each age grouping that are infused in all aspects of life. As they move through life, Americans are forever being reminded to "act their age." While there are very formal elements attached to nearly all of these age stages, the individual obtains all this necessary information and behavior informally and through the socialization process.

POLITICAL SYSTEM

Americans place as much value and importance on their political system as they do on their educational system. They are also just as critical and cynical about this organizational system as they are the educational system. The political system found in the United States is a state system in which a central authority integrates many communities, has the power to levy and collect taxes, can draft people for labor, and in which someone, or group, has the sole monopoly on the use of force to ensure that people live by the rules. But asking Americans about their political system produces more responses about democracy and its faults than anything else. The high value they place on the individual is directly tied to their unswerving faith in democracy for their state political organization. This is more than the most correct form for their government. It is a way of life (Tiersky & Tiersky 1975). Garretson (1976) suggests that Americans believe their system of government is rational and moral, and they recognize a sanctity of established government. More precisely, the American state system is not a true democracy, but a representative form of the state. People do not participate in decision making or vote on every single issue. Rather, they leave this in the hands of elected representatives to represent their interests, which in reality they rarely do.

To suggest or contend that Americans are proud of their political system would be an understatement. They actively advocate their kind of political system for the world, for every other nation-state of the world. Americans are convinced their type of political system has advantages over other forms of the state, if for no other reason than they are equally convinced that it protects the individualism they value and guarantees the social equality they also expect. Despite their pride in this political system in which people are free to criticize, perhaps freer than citizens of any other nation-state, Americans as individuals and in groups have a rather negative view of that system much as they have with regard to their educational system. Studies have repeatedly shown their cynicism and distrust of that system. They decry its slowness as inefficiency, yet praise the process as it prohibits the quick decision. What they criticize in it, they also recognize as part of its strength. The division of powers (separation of powers into its three branches of government) that contributes to its slowness and inefficiency also protects the rights of individual or specific minority groups from discriminating actions. Through a complex maze of political parties, branches of government, bureaucracy, special interest groups, campaigning, voting, lobbying, law-making bodies (national, state, and local) the culture does establish policy, establishes order by determining acceptable behavior, maintains social order, deals with disorder (violations of acceptable behavior) and conflict resolution, both at home and abroad in the context of the modern world of international affairs. Of course, the legal system and the political system function for the exact same purposes of establishing social order and dealing with disorder. Americans tend to see their legal system, with all of its adjudication bodies, courts, lawyers, and penal institutions, in the same way they view education and political things—they highly value them while at the same time they strongly criticize them. Finding faults with the legal system is as popular as finding fault with the political system.

Government is an administrative system of specialized personnel which, in the case of the American culture, is part of the political organization. In point of fact, the complexity of the bureaucracy of the government oftentimes seems to reflect the complexity of the nation itself. The United States operates under the state form of political organization and is best seen as a nation-state, a designation that best represents the political unit as well as the political system by which it operates. As with any other state, power is centralized and force allocated to regulate the affairs of the state and its citizens. The authority to use force is delegated by the central authority to the police units within each of the multiple communities integrated in the overall national context and to the military for the purposes of international affairs. It is a centralized system integrating a number of communities and different levels of organization. Unlike other nation-state governments, it does not include religion for the purposes of integrating the people, rather it steadfastly maintains a separation of church and state.

Political organization is primarily concerned with social control, ensuring that people behave in acceptable ways and it defines actions that will be taken if they do not. Part of this involves laws, and the sanctions (both rewards and punishments) used to encourage or force people to follow the rules. The idea of law, formalized in a written code of law in the United States, is designed to define the relationships (claims and obligations) among members of the society—define proper behavior. In the American culture, the system is best characterized as a public law system as opposed to a private law system. This means that a behavioral violation is viewed as a crime against the state not an individual. While there is also the notion of disputes or crimes against the individual (usually referred to as tort law), this too is handled within the public law system focused around courts, judges, juries, and what the codified law might permit. This system provides Americans with the rule of law, compromises to settle disputes, and separates it from other aspects of their lives—at least they think or believe that it does. While they want to believe that the system provides for impartial judgments and laws, it is actually influenced by class status, discrimination, prejudice, religious, and political agendas. Most Americans recognize this reality. Despite the real or imagined weaknesses of the system, Americans tend to believe their system of government (political organization) and law is rational and "morally" right.

Given such a description, one is immediately impressed with constantly rising crime rates and the growing lack of social order in the country. One is constantly bombarded in the news and on television with all sorts of crime on a daily basis. Of course, every American can fix the blame for this—lawyers, judges, racism in the courts, decline of family values, etc. There is also the anomaly of criminals (those who have been judged guilty) getting a light sentence, getting time off for good behavior, and even being let out early because of overcrowding in the nation's prison system. The fact that some of these commit additional crimes, occasions an immediate outcry among the nation's citizens, but usually to no avail. Another impression of the American legal system revolves around the "rights" of the accused, oftentimes appearing that the system is more concerned with the rights of the accused than the person against whom a crime was committed. This is obviously related to the idea of individualism and individual rights. While Americans may be somewhat sympathetic to the victims of crime, in fact, they are more committed to protecting the rights of those accused of crimes—just in case they themselves are wrongly accused of a crime. This same idea lies behind their willingness to let criminals go free from punishment based on technicalities despite obvious guilt. Of course, the question of ultimate ostracism by society—the death penalty—is a hotly debated topic between those arguing for a prominence of societal morality and those arguing prominence of religious morality. In this, the legal system and religious groups can come into serious conflict, and depending upon the relative strength (numbers or simply political influence), the religious groups can inhibit society's efforts to maintain social order by effectively dealing with violators of behavior expectations or rules of social living.

ECONOMIC SYSTEM

All economic systems (customs or patterns) revolve around the resources available for a culture in meeting their desires or needs. Spradley and Rynkiewich (1975) point out the importance of culture in the production, distribution, and consumption of goods and services among Americans. Economic systems consist of sets of customs about who has access to the resources needed to produce those things people want or need. They also consist of customs for transforming the resources into the things wanted or needed, and this usually means technology and labor. Finally, economic patterns include some customs or provision for getting the finished products to the people who may require them. Together, these sets of customs will become what for Americans will be seen as their economic system. As with most nation-states, the particular set of customs that serves as the prime mover for everything else in the system, will revolve around the choice of how to get the finished goods out to the people who need them—the distribution of the finished products and services. This means that the money-dominated market exchange system will have tremendous influence on the customs aimed at who has access to productive resources and which will directly impact the technology and labor customs. The so-called "law of supply and demand" that seems to determine what occurs in the marketplace seems also to dictate events in all other aspects of the economic system. In America, the forces of supply and demand revolve around capitalism, private enterprise, and competition. This goes quite well with the central role of the individual in the thinking of all Americans and the ideas of equal opportunity, equality, work and measures of success. Americans focus on individual or group ownership, and community property, thus, a good case can be made for the suggestion that individualism creates many of the barriers to a sense of community among them (Hoggang Yang 1993). There is an ultimate faith in the prosperity made possible by capitalism and the "plenty for all" myth that goes along with it.

Generally, Americans appear a little confused about their capitalism. Many consider it a political system, while others see it as an economic system. In the vocabulary of today, this is probably a reflection of what is now being referred to as a political economy. The close relationship of its major tenets to the political process is unmistakable. Private enterprise lies at the heart of it, along with competition, and supply and demand. Perhaps this does nothing more than to point clearly to the marketplace where supply and demand forces seem to drive the entire economic system of the United States. In reality, private companies provide for most of the material needs of the people. Social needs generally are not viewed as part of the system. Access to productive resources is limited by class status and the wealth that allows one to gain that access. Those who have wealth have access, those that do not have wealth have no access to the resources, technology, or labor necessary for transforming them into products. The historical trend has been toward large-scale production. Even the production of food now lies predominantly in the hands of corporations and stock markets. Big business and major corporations exert tremendous influence on government, the national welfare, and ultimately all other aspects of this nation-state. The marketplace dominates American life, a place where anything and everything is bought and sold. Credit card economy is rampant, as installment buying allows Americans to have now and pay later (frequently over long periods of time). The "land of plenty" is false in this sense and the "rich American"—the characterization of most Americans by people of other nation-states—is an illusion. This may also be related to the fact that Americans seem to have so much more than people in other countries. Plenty to *pay for* might be a better way to characterize this aspect of America. Both marketplace and credit are tied to an ultimate faith in the individual who knows what is best for him- or herself.

Keeping in concert with other complex nation-state societies, specialization characterizes the nature of work and cooperative work patterns. The extent of this specialization produces individuals who are totally dependent on others doing their job just to meet their basic needs. It also means that Americans must work more and more just to meet such needs. Outside of the household, itself an economic unit in which the primary consumer is the female for the bulk of the day-to-day purchases, labor is organized into cooperative work units by virtue of specialization and business affiliations. Increasingly, even education has become viewed in more economic terms, as students are viewed as consumers, and schools, colleges, and universities as places to go primarily to acquire job skills. This would seem to speak directly counter to the ideal of producing people who are well rounded as is so often heard from the educators and politicians of America. Religion and leisure activities have also become part of the system, driven by the same forces of supply and demand found with the production and sale of computers and paper clips. The costs of leisure activities continually go up and the wages paid to athletes seem to defy reason. Religion is "sold" on television just like beer, beauty products, cars, clothes, or toothpaste.

In American life, the acquisition of money has become the primary preoccupation of people. In many ways it can be said to have replaced even food as the primary survival concern (basic need) of Americans. Without money, obtainable only through the economic system and occupational avenues open to them, they cannot meet any of their other needs—food, shelter, material items necessary for their survival. In the American context, one can earn money by working, inheriting, or winning it, or one can obtain it from the central government in the form of social welfare payments. Whole cultural groups have evolved around each possibility. This circumstance, with which all Americans are all too familiar, is a consequence of the "new age of specialization," wherein every individual must specialize in something, just to earn enough to meet his or her needs. No individual American is self-sufficient, or capable of meeting all his or her own needs. In fact, it can be suggested that outside of their own occupational speciality, Americans are totally dependent on every other American. As each does his or her part within the context of the whole, both the whole and the individual parts of it survive. The American system functions as each individual and group contributes their specialization so that they will survive, and they all survive. The whole system works as each of its parts continue to work. Of course, it is money that lies at the heart of all this and leads most Americans to see this as the driving force in their own personal lives and in American culture.

RELIGION IN AMERICAN LIFE

The United States is one of the few nation-states in the world without a national religion. Because of this, many people in the world tend to see this culture as an irreligious one. Most of the modern nation-states have designated national religions to supernaturally tie its citizens together with its social and political ideologies, to legitimize government, and so forth. While a great many Americans see the United States as a Christian-based society, in fact the country was founded on the idea of religious freedom. The principle of separation of church and state is a fundamental one for most Americans. Althen (1988) points out that Americans tend to separate religion from other aspects of their lives and take pride in their religious freedom. As with any other cultural group, religious cultures tend to believe they have the ultimate "truth" and make every effort to impose that on everyone else. Given the direct involvement of religious groups (cultural groups) in the political process, particularly the Christian ones, there is a tendency to assume that that means America is a Christian culture. The fact that politicians are forever invoking Christ and God to convince people of their positions only strengthens this perception. But the actual diversity of religious belief systems in the United States is extensive, and this goes well beyond the organized or recognized religions and churches. This would also include groups that organized religious groups would identify as *cults*, putting them into as negative a context as possible. While in most things Americans stress individuality and freedom to be different, in this aspect of American life, the tolerance of which most Americans speak is much more myth than reality, even as the separation of church and state, written into the Constitution, is more myth than reality. Religion means different things to different people. For the members of denominational groups, religion means what they believe, their own particular set of beliefs and practices. What others believe and do is characterized as something else, magic, superstition, the occult, paganism, witchcraft, Satanism, and so on. Of course, what members of other groups believe with regard to them as members of their recognized churches and religions is exactly the same thing. For the most part, religion tends to be a personal matter, even as it is obviously a force organized and grouped throughout the culture and society. Americans are more interested in saving their money and improving their present life than in saving their souls and preparing for another life beyond their present one. Religious movements in American society are more socioreligious movements—they tend to be fundamentalist in character. In recent years religious groups have moved increasingly into the sociopolitical arena in an attempt to force their ideology and practices on everybody else.

Religion is as important to Americans as the supernatural is to most everybody else. It provides a real service to a great many people, explains the unexplainable, reduces stress, substitutes for family in providing for social interaction, and of course, it promises they will never "really" die. For a great many of them it becomes a social strategy as well, it helps them up the socioeconomic ladder as they can call upon other members of their group for help when family does not provide much support and help. It certainly provides a sense of rights and wrongs, even if these differ or are in direct conflict with those necessary for the successful continuation of the nation-state. Religious ideas of right and wrong will always be similar to those of the state for both arise out of the needs of any human group. They help others know what to think and do. In this, they are no different from the nation-state. But individuals also obtain their ideas and positions on social questions as well, and these differ from one religious group to another. It also can create conflict for the individual when these differ from those advocated in other groups with which they also identify. For some people it becomes the primary cultural set of beliefs and practices in their lives, the cultural set that takes precedence over and above all other cultural beliefs and practices. Religious culture provides a blueprint for some Americans to get through daily life, to confront the trials of that life, and to understand their reason for being and the ultimate goal of their existence.

In the context of a nation-state with no national religion, but rather a diversity of religions, the setting for serious conflict is automatically set. In the nation-state with a national religion, the religion provides definitions of what is right and what is wrong, what the individual and the state must do, and so on. Everyone knows what is, why it is so, and what their personal relationship to that has to be. People simply learn their "truth" and function with and by it throughout their lives. In diverse nation-states without such a unifying religion, and with many different religious groupings (cultural groups), each of which knows that it has the sole monopoly on "truth," it is inevitable that these different "truths" come into conflict. The never-ending debates abound as to whose truth is the more correct one. The problem of ethnocentrism that naturally accompanies culture is magnified in the religious culture. It is based on belief and directed at things that cannot be verified or proven false. It is ideational, based on ideas of a reality that can never be disproved or proved. Belief is all that is necessary—one must only believe. Of course, judging other beliefs and practices is commonplace, and the competition between them is on. The attempt to dictate that all others adopt similar beliefs and practices is a singular goal of all organized religious groups. Perhaps religion in America is best characterized by pointing out that Americans put the word God on their money. How much more importance can it have? How more can it be valued?

CEREMONIAL CYCLE

The United States is not unlike most other cultures in that it recognizes the usual rites of passage, marking the movement of people through the various stages of life (birth, age grouping changes, marriage, and death). For Americans, such ceremonies tend to be strictly family affairs as opposed to community events. This reflects the compartmentalization of most American life. Ceremonies celebrating the birth of an individual are usually restricted to the immediate or extended family. The event is marked by a birth certificate representing the only notice taken by society at large. The same can be said for the usual transformations through the various stages of life; birth, school graduation, marriage, and death. But once again, the only community involvement is the issuing of a certificate (notice of accomplishment or recognition) representing the community recognition (approval as in the case of marriage) of the events. Some of these rites of passage can be mixes of social and religious life, but they can also be strictly secular. The economic transactions found in many other cultures associated with various stages of life, as with marriage, are more limited among Americans and rarely do they involve more than one or two nuclear families.

Most American ceremonies focus on the recognition of nation-state holidays or religious holidays (Althen 1988). Ritual holidays of the United States reflect both "Americanisms" and the other culturalisms of the many constituent culture groups that make for the American culture. As in most nation-state cultures, ceremonies marking historical events in the development of the nation-state are part of everyday life, basically to constantly reinforce nationalism, patriotism, or national loyalty. This is a necessary function of ceremonies in such states where the culture being celebrated is more artificial or arbitrary, and laid over the top of other cultural understandings people will have as well. Some of the other culturalisms are just state or regional holidays, others may be tied to ethnicity, gender, and sex, or any number of special interest groupings, even based on things for which states might be known or associated (e.g., an agricultural product such as cheese or potatoes). For most Americans, irrespective of their other cultural affiliations, certain rituals or holidays are indeed celebrated by nearly everyone for they reflect major values, orienting ideas of Americans in general, or the foundations for America itself. For example, Labor Day attests to the ideal value Americans have in hard work, the vitality and industrial spirit of America. Columbus Day celebrates the discovery of America. Halloween is a celebration primarily by and for children. Thanksgiving is a day set aside for Americans to give thanks for the blessings of the year, a holiday whose history extends back to the very beginnings of the country. New Year's Day marks the basic premise of Americans, out with the old and in with the new, and reflects the American's belief in the value of change and constant "new starts." President's Day, combining the birthdays of various presidents, is symbolic of the values, ideals, and traits admired by most Americans as reflected in their political heritage and idealized to past presidents. Washington is honored for being the first and for his honesty. Lincoln is honored for his honesty and courage to do what was right. Martin Luther King Jr. Day is set aside as a celebration of the life of a significant figure in the civil rights movement of America. A number of strictly patriotic holidays dot the ritual holiday cycle, for example Memorial Day, Veteran's Day, Flag Day, and Independence Day, and others, all of which celebrate days that are important to the history of the country or the sacrifices of some of its people. Among these, Independence Day (July 4) is the most important, for it marks the independence of Americans from their English rulers and serves as the day when America became free. This is probably the one day of the year when differences are set aside and just being an American is sufficient—best among all the available alternatives. Religious holidays such as Easter, Lent, Palm Sunday, Christmas, Rosh Hashana, Hanukkah, and Ramadan celebrate important events in the religious life of the people and are tied to specific religious groups. In New Orleans, Mardi Gras is an interesting mix of both native and religious celebration. But given the cultural diversity of the country, not everyone sees them in the same way or even as holidays to be celebrated. For many Native Americans, Columbus Day denotes the genocide of the original inhabitants of the United States and as marking the beginning of the end for of native cultures. Reflecting the legacy of the civil war, Abraham Lincoln's birthday was never celebrated in the South as it was in the northern states.

A number of minor holidays (minor in the sense that they are generally not celebrated by all Americans and in all parts of the country) are also observed. Valentine's day is celebrated as a festival of romance and things at the heart of marriage and family. St. Patrick's Day is celebrated by Irish for a beloved Irish religious leader who is credited with miraculous deeds, and this emphasizes the pride the Irish take in their cultural heritage. While the celebration of this day occurs nearly everywhere, it is clearly more important in areas where the Irish immigrants have tended to congregate. Similar ethnic days are celebrated by other groups, Polish-, German-, Chinese-, Japanese-, Mexican-Americans, and so forth, in various parts of the country to varying degrees. April Fool's Day represents a sport holiday aimed at silly, but harmless jokes on family members, friends, and co-workers. Mother's Day is set aside for honoring mothers for all they do, and a Father's Day is set aside to honor fathers and what they do. Other holidays or simply days set aside to honor or bring attention to something, to some category of people, or an event important to some American groups somewhere, will be seen throughout the calendar year. For example, in Texas, there is a Juneteenth to celebrate the freeing of slaves. There also is a day to celebrate the Battle of the Alamo and all this has come to mean for Texans and other Americans. In Wisconsin, a day is set aside to note and celebrate the role and place of cheese in the lives of people living there, and the economy of that state as a whole. In other states, days are set aside to celebrate the role of cotton, potatoes, tobacco, corn, peanuts, and almost everything else that is important in the economy of the state. This same kind of special day recognition will be found in association with every constituent cultural group that can be identified with the American culture, including America's original inhabitants. There are even days that specifically note, honor or recognize, the special days in the lives of families and individuals, for example, anniversaries, birthdays, graduations, as well as others, and even the change of seasons. While Americans generally do not see themselves as having the rituals and ceremonies as do other cultures, there seems to be no lack of them throughout the year.

LEISURE AMERICA

Althen (1988) provides some good insights into leisure America, noting that for Americans, sports and recreation activities devour considerable amounts of time and money. Even to the casual observer, Americans seem to take their leisure activities to extreme levels, even to the point of making sports or other entertainment figures some of their most admired heroes. It would not be too extreme to suggest that because of the highly competitive nature of this society and the constant striving to succeed, Americans work hard and thus play hard because they really do not have much time away from work. But in many ways, leisure activities, especially sports, also reflect the competitive nature of individuals and groups within this society. Americans are both spectators and participants in all manner of sports. American baseball has long been touted as "America's Pastime," having been played first in the United States, but this particular sport has been supplanted in some regions of the country by football, the American version (noting that for many people in the world, football denotes soccer), basketball, or hockey. In the American southwest, football can dominate Friday nights and the entire community as residents empty their homes to take in the local high school game, making it as much a social event as a sports event. In other parts of the country, for example, the Midwest or Northern states, basketball or hockey accomplishes this same thing. Naturally, sports have been commercialized like everything else, made into a commodity for the marketplace, heavily influenced by money, the laws of supply and demand, just as most everything else in this society.

Team sports are viewed by many as vehicles to success in other areas of the culture, for example, business, government, and so forth. Such sports are justified and advocated as "good training grounds" for building leadership skills, teamwork skills, the desire to succeed, competitive attitudes, and of course winning. While Americans do give verbal credit to how one plays the game, there is little doubt that winning is much more important. While praising those people who try even under the most severe conditions, winning is the object and most nonparticipants will only value the winning team record. They support the team only as long as it is winning. This is readily seen in baseball, basketball, and football where the winners have huge followings and losers barely have any support whatsoever. Of course, in the true American fashion, sports represent very big business, with lots of financial success for owners and players who have a record of winning. Owners are encouraged to spend lots of money in securing the most talented players who will give their team that winning edge and thus fan support. Salaries of sports figures are frequently higher than most other occupations. Of course, earning a large salary for an athletic ability is still being successful and for this reason, the figures are made into heroes, they have achieved the American Dream. It is common for a talented athlete to be paid millions of dollars to play his or her game over the course of a season (only a minor portion of the year), despite coming from an underprivileged background or perhaps being unable to read, write, or speak intelligibly. For many Americans, there is nothing worse than a fallen hero, an athlete who displays the same limitations or frailties as mortal humans.

Of course, most Americans are not participants of the team type of sports, for team sports only provide for a very limited number of participants. Most of those who cannot participate in team sports will turn to other sports activities that require fewer skills or can be done individually. Individual sports can still require huge commitments of time and funds. People who enjoy fishing can spend incredible amounts of money getting just the right bass boat and just the right rod and reel. Golfers do likewise in getting just the right clubs, shoes, or other apparel. The bowler spends a considerable amount obtaining just the right ball(s) for the various tasks involved with that sport. Even the hiker or runner must spend considerable amounts of money to obtain just the right boots or running shoes and the other equipment and apparel associated with those individual sports. Of all the leisure activities of Americans, the various sport activities are probably the most important. Next in line to sports in the leisure life of Americans come television, movies, radio, and the CD player.

Hall and Hall (1990) point out that Americans spend about five hours of each day (of the sixteen available to them when not working) with television and the radio. Television monopolizes the most time, and most homes have multiple sets. Radio is used while traveling to and from work, at work in some cases, to and from forms of play, even doing those kinds of activities, thus, enabling the individual to do more than one form of leisure activity at a time. The hiker, the baseball or football fan can be seen listening to radio as they participate as a spectator at games. When not sitting in front of television sets, Americans can be found attending movies, another activity that gobbles up significant time and money. In both the case of television and movies, the primary purpose appears to be escape from the realities of dealing with the stresses and anxieties of their real work-a-day world.

Sometime each year, most Americans will also vacation—usually meaning additional financial expenditures and perhaps travel. All in all, leisure activities among Americans simply reflect other aspects of their lives and cultures, maybe taking on some of those characteristics found in other parts of their lives. They are competitive. It is done with gusto. It nearly always involves heavy commitments of resources. But, at the same time, leisure activities provide Americans with the escape they seek and need from their work-a-day world. In the main, Americans can make leisure activity out of virtually anything they do and in the context of every other part of their lives. Americans find leisure in the context of their occupations, their churches, their families, their friends, their groups, their politics, their ideas, and frequently they will make leisure a significant part of them. In other cases, one's financial commitment to such things, for example, owning a professional sports team or financially backing the performing and visual arts, is a public affirmation of success.

SUGGESTED READINGS

Bellah, R. N., Madsen, R., Sullivan, W. M., Swidler, A., and Tipton, S. M. 1991. *The Good Society*. New York: Random House (Vintage Books). This volume takes a critical look at the institutions of America through historical overview, personal narratives, and proposals for revitalizing our core systems.

Garretson, L. R. 1976. *American Culture: An Anthropological Perspective*. Dubuque, IA: Wm. C. Brown. This is an interesting treatment of the political system, especially the government of the United States. The author observes that most Americans believe their system of government is rational and moral, that they value the sanctity of established government. He also addresses how people learn to be Americans, both formally and informally, and within the family.

Jorgenson, J. G. and Truzzi, M. (eds.). 1974. *Anthropology and American Life*. Englewood Cliffs, NJ: Prentice-Hall. This collection of readings covers virtually every aspect of the American culture and society, the mainstream and the marginal, albeit somewhat dated. The volume covers the organization of American society, kinship and family, language and communications, religion and cults, education, work, deviance, leisure patterns, and subcultures.

Orion, L. 1995. *Never Again the Burning Times: Paganism Revived*. Prospect Heights, IL: Waveland Press. Although the presentation is somewhat biased, the author does provide an excellent ethnography of contemporary witchcraft in America and discusses why some individuals resort to magical beliefs and practices of the occult, especially those of Wicca, what kind of people engage in such movements, and their demographic characteristics. For this reason, it is a good balance to the usual denominational discussions of religion in America.

Spindler, G. (ed.). 1963. *Education and Culture: Anthropological Approaches*. New York: Holt, Rinehart and Winston. While primarily an examination of the application of anthropology to education, a number of readings in this collection deal with various aspects of American culture, particularly its educational system and participants.

Spradley, J. P. and Rynkiewich, M. A. (eds.). 1975. *The Nacirema: Readings on American Culture*. Boston: Little, Brown and Co. This is a collection of readings on American culture, covering such topics as enculturation, language and communication, kinship and family, social structure, values, economic, political, religious topics, worldview and perceptions on change.

———— Six ————
THE DIVERSITY
THAT *IS* AMERICA

AMERICAN CONTEXT OF DIVERSITY

Earlier, it was suggested that the core of American beliefs, values, and ideas is embedded in mainstream culture and in the American Dream. Historically, and despite the often repeated promise (ideal) of America, many people who have come to the United States have found it very difficult to achieve the American Dream, or experience American equality or equal opportunity. Some of this is due to traditions immigrants have brought with them and continue to maintain in some fashion. Some of it is due to unique cultures such people have created in order to cope with the sociocultural environment(s) or context(s) in which they have found themselves. Some of this is based on the social groupings created by others for social, economic, or political purposes. Whatever the cause, the diversity created also is tied to the major social issues and problems that accompany cultural differences. It is also directly related to the problems of prejudice and discrimination that are usually based on overgeneralizations and stereotyping. Americans recognize the differences that have evolved with social groupings, but have little appreciation of the differences between social groupings and cultural groups, nor the consequences of their own stereotyping, ethnocentrism born of the groups with which they affiliate, or the inequality, prejudice and discrimination it produces. Cultural groups are vital in maintaining stability and purpose for many individuals and groups, but nation-state ideals, promises, and aspirations unfulfilled have led to both social group and cultural group competition and conflict—the fragmentations so characteristic of complex societies. Ethnic and racial social groups (categories) in America have seemingly always been recognized (rightly or wrongly) in the diversity of the United States, but real cultural diversity goes well beyond just these groupings. Each category actually includes many distinct cultural groups. A great many other cultural groupings (both self-generated and imposed by others) have been created out of the special interests tied to the social and economic systems, specialization, religion, and any number of other special purpose groupings that accompany the nation-state fragmentation and complexity (Naylor 1997). If nothing else, they are a natural consequence of large numbers of people attempting to live together, the artificiality of the nation-state cultures that brought them together, instigated their creation, and the special problems that evolve in such societies to meet the needs and wants of these groups and the society as a whole.

When the topic of diversity is raised, most Americans immediately conjure up visions of categorized social groups, African-Americans (most often meaning black Americans), Hispanic Americans, Asian Americans, or any one of a large number of ethnic groups with which they have had some contact. Oddly enough, while they can identify such groups as the Hispanic American, Asian American, European American—they speak Spanish, come from Asia, they are white—many fail to recognize the large number of actual cultural groups obscured by the criteria used to categorize them. The existence of cultural groups (also termed ethnic groups), such as the Mexican-Americans, Japanese-Americans, Italian-Americans, and so forth, are lost in the usual tendency to generalize people into such social groupings. Americans do not recognize that these are no more than social categories they have created (e.g., the Hispanics, the Asians, Europeans, etc.), or that they are really composed of many distinct cultural groups, or that the problems of diversity are tied to both social categories and cultural differences. The difficulty apparently comes as Americans fail to differentiate between the social group (categorization) and the actual cultural groupings in which people learn the specific beliefs and behaviors that will actually distinguish them from other groups. Hispanic Americans, Black Americans, Asian Americans, and the like, are not cultural groups, but social categories established according to some simple and overgeneralized criteria. The continued use of social categories such as these is hard to account for and even more difficult to justify because of the real diversity hidden within them.

The practice of using such categories leads Americans to overgeneralize and stereotype across significant numbers of people who actually display significant cultural differences. Each commonly used category consists of a number of distinct cultural groupings that have little more than the single criterion on which they are based, for example, a shared language, common geographic origin, some physical characteristic they share, or religious affiliation, and they share a history that has shaped them. To understand the real cultural differences that exist in the United States requires that people go beyond categories of people to the specific cultural differences that serve to distinguish all the constituent cultural groups that exist. Their histories in the American context can be similar or quite different, while their complex interactions and relationships with other cultural groups within the larger nation-state will nearly always be different. Given the complexity and constantly changing American context, the actual diversity to be found in the United States, it is not easy to identify all the actual culture groups in the United States.

Even to the most casual observer of America and it culture, the many problems accessioned by or associated with such things as race or origins, even common interests, do not go unnoticed. Variations of Black Americans, Hispanic Americans, Asian Americans, and Middle Eastern Americans are classic groupings that also are seen to be racial/ethnic/cultural groups that also represent minority groups within the American context. Even in the 1990s, the idea of a developing white minority is being explored. In exploring ethnic diversity, one can come to recognize the full range of America's ethnic cultures that contribute to the diversity that is America. In addition to the ethnic cultural groups (with significantly different beliefs and behaviors), there are the economic, religious, professional, gender, sex, and other special purpose cultural groupings that also contribute to the diversity of the United States. In most discussions of diversity, the special interest groupings, viable and constituent cultures in their own right that contribute to the diversity of America, are largely ignored. As suggested earlier, the United States is made up of a variety of constituent cultural groups, and ethnic groups, like racial groups, comprise only one area of this total diversity. The total diversity of America is a product of the development of civilization itself, the emergence of the territorially based state, with its urban environments, fragmentations, and occupational specializations, and the needs of large numbers of people attempting to live together. In the United States, as in all other nation-states, these things have produced a wide variety of cultural groups within every nation-state society. With shared beliefs, behaviors, and the products of these things, such groups are distinguished from other groups within the society, and they become part of the American culture. To understand that culture, one has to understand the diversity of groups that contribute as constituent cultures making it up.

In addressing diversity and the many differences between social categories or groupings of America, prejudice, racism, discrimination, and class distinctions need to be clearly understood. In a very large measure, as already noted, they reflect the problems of stereotyping and overgeneralizing across whole categories of people being grouped together. These are the things that can account for many of the paradoxes or contradictions readily recognized by most people. Virtually all ethnic, racial, and special interest cultural groups will experience inequality, prejudice and discrimination at the hands of other groups. Black Americans, African-Americans, Mexican-Americans, Hispanic Americans, women, and homosexuals, and almost all of the special interest groups organized around religion, economic class or any number of other things will experience these things. In general, Americans tend to respond to both social categories and actual cultural groups with culturally learned ideas (the stereotypes and generalizations) they obtained from the groups with which they affiliate. The tendency is to characterize specific cultural groupings, then judge or discriminate against them because the people in the grouping are somehow different. As pointed out a number of times, Americans value difference for themselves and their groups, not necessarily for other groups with which they are not associated.

CULTURE, ETHNICITY, AND RACE

As suggested previously, race is probably the first thing recognized about anyone different from ourselves. The use of race by most Americans to categorize others is quite common. The fact that such categorizations of people have been repeatedly shown as arbitrary and artificial, even within science, does not seem to detract those who would create and use such groupings to combine people into social categories for some purpose. That most people see cultural differences right along with racial differences leads them to attribute (create) cultures for races they create. This only produces more confusion and only makes the problems associated with the practice that much worse. Race, ethnicity, and culture are frequently used synonymously by a great many Americans. Combining race with the use of generalized categories of people to whom others have already attributed culture is based on the widespread belief that most immigrants assimilate to the culture of United States and lose their original ethnicity (culture) in the process. Nothing could be further from the truth.

Spindler and Spindler (1993) have pointed out that the history of the United States has been a history of diversity and constant conflict. More than forty ethnic groups are readily recognized across this history, but there are many more. The diversity of religious groups across American history also is recognized by most Americans. More than 375 different languages were spoken in the United States before its colonization, a diversity only added to by the languages of the people who came to the United States from virtually the entire world. Most Americans also generally recognize the many political, regional, class, and ideological differences among America's population, although not as cultural groups. Most people see them as simply groups of people with some different ideas, with differences of opinion. According to the Spindlers, the white Anglo-Saxon Protestant male domination has always been in direct conflict with children, women, and countless ethnic groups. The Native Americans have been the most forgotten category of America. As aptly demonstrated in Chapter 2, neither the Bureau of the Census nor any other agency of government really addresses the real diversity of America. Rather, they focus on social diversity, meaning they focus on the social categories that have been created for political purposes and the decision-making process. Both race and ethnicity are ascribed to groups of people (in some cases even prescribed) for identification, personal, or political purposes.

Culture, ethnicity, and race are used interchangeably in everyday conversation. Various meanings and assumptions have been attached to them, depending on who is using them. For these reasons, as pointed out by Kimberly Martin (1997), both personal and group-based interactions occur in everyday life, and these vary substantially. Certain assumptions that are made about certain groups influence how people relate and react to their families, neighbors, and friends, as well as to peers, colleagues, co-workers, and the groups with whom they come into contact. They are directly related to community relations, national politics, and how teachers and students function in the academic settings. According to Martin, three diverse orientations affect how we interact in the diverse social context. Our own ideas, behaviors, and even material possessions reflect the culture(s) that we share with others. These things serve to guide our lives and make us predictable—people know what to expect from us. It provides us with guidelines for evaluating others as well, for along with providing us with a measure of our own competency in our culture(s) comes ethnocentrism—the belief that our culture is superior to others and that we should judge them based on the truth or correctness of our culture(s). The natural consequence of learning one's culture is that once learned, it is used to judge the cultures of others who are different. In an unfamiliar cultural setting, not knowing what to expect or how to behave produces frustration, fear, anger, or anxiety. These things cause people to avoid contact with those who are different from themselves in belief or practices. It creates much misunderstanding and antagonism. Resulting behaviors can be threatening or at the very least perceived in a negative way. People representing different cultures represent people in conflict. This produces the social problems, the conflicts, and the struggles among constituent groups in the complex society. In the history of any complex society, the dominant group devalues and discriminates against the subordinate or minority unassimilated groups.

In 1995, the Federal Bureau of Investigation reported that three out of every five hate crimes were motivated by race. Blacks were the primary targets of these crimes in two out of three of the cases reported. During 1995, 7,947 hate crimes were reported, 60.8 percent were racially motivated, 2,988 of these were against Black Americans. Whites were the target in 1,226 cases. But hate crimes are not limited to racial groups. Religious bias accounted for the second largest group (1,227 incidents), and Jews were the most frequent targets (82.9%). Crimes against the homosexual community (1,019 crimes) focused primarily on gay men (72.1%). Ethnicity and national origin accounted for 814 crimes, Hispanics being the primary targets of 63.4 percent of these. While hate crimes far outnumber crimes against property, intimidation was the most frequent (41% of the total). Statistics such as these not only point to the conflicts between cultural groups (racial, cultural, religious, and sexual), they point to the seriousness associated with the social and cultural diversity. People who believe in their own cultural beliefs and behaviors simply do not want to tolerate those of the other groups (even if they create those other groups), and many will go to extremes to defend the truthfulness of their beliefs and to force them on everyone else.

Race

As suggested in the statistics on hate crime and because Black Americans seem to bear the brunt of the prejudice and discrimination in the country, no discussion of American culture would be complete without some discussion of race. It plays such an important role in the thoughts and lives of Americans, this despite whatever cultural groups they affiliate with. This is not to suggest that the prejudice and discrimination experienced by other groups are no less significant or different, but it does reflect the degree of attention given to the Black Americans in the media, press, and by other Americans. Race is a created social category, a grouping of people based on some arbitrary physical, or in other cases, cultural characteristic. Race is a social construction in the United States, a concept based primarily on physical characteristics, "color" first and foremost. But, it can also reflect nothing physical at all. It can be based on nothing more than language spoken, religion, or some cultural practice intertwined with some physical feature. This emphasizes the arbitrary, artificial, and social nature of such groupings. Americans use eye shape to identify a group they refer to as Asian Americans. Skin color or tone is used to determine the African-American (really Black American) from the European American (whites), but not very useful in distinguishing the Pacific Islanders or even some Asian Americans from European Americans (unless the eye and their geographic origin is added on). African-American is used to categorize people who are black (census), but also identifies the African-American cultural group, only one of many cultural groups that actually make up the black race in America. South Asians experience the anomaly of being "white" for the census, black for almost every other experience in America. Children of mixed marriages experience the fate of not knowing what race they are or where they should be listed. The confusion accelerates as not all Black Americans identify with African-Americans, but most people and nearly every government agency does identify them as such.

With the race topic, additional ideas are generated that are directly tied to it. Discrimination focuses on the use of racial criteria to categorize people in order to discriminate either for or against them. Here the word discriminate means to treat differently and can be both good and bad. Differential treatment becomes very significant in the context of political power, where one group exercises control over another. While the main focus in using or creating race(s) is for discrimination, perhaps even racial oppression, it is one of the most powerful and pervasive social concepts in American society. There are, however, other kinds of criteria that are used to categorize people into groups for the purposes of discrimination. While Americans usually think of discrimination just in terms of the racial groups they create, other social groups, categorized along other lines, suffer discrimination as well. Some examples of nonracial groups in the United States would include the youth, women, the elderly, homosexuals, the disadvantaged, the disabled, and any number of groups tied to religious beliefs and practices. Members of these groups experience prejudice, discrimination, and oppression right along with racial groups. They too, have to live and function within the context created by such things. The importance of race or any other kind of social categorization is what people learn about the differences. Of course, these will be defined by the cultural beliefs and values of different groups of people that use them as a basis for interacting with them. Prejudice and discrimination are associated with real or imagined physical differences people think they see, with linguistic, religious, sexual, or gender differences, along with all manner of other cultural differences. It is also interesting to note that most Americans do not distinguish discrimination from prejudice. Discrimination reflects actual practices (actions) of people, while prejudice refers to preconceived attitudes or notions about groups of people, oftentimes based on overgeneralized stereotypes that have been learned. Stereotypes involve negative exaggerations or distortions of individuals or groups in terms of their racial, ethnic, or socially recognized characteristic(s). The history of race, ethnic, and special interest group relations in the United States is a complex one, yet it should be recognized that the cultural beliefs and behaviors, in particular the strategies that have been adopted by these groups (the cultural products), are to a considerable degree the product of a long historical process.

A great many Americans see a race, an ethnic group, and a culture as all basically the same thing. In fact, a great many Americans tend to think that a racial group is an ethnic group, that an ethnic group is easily identifiable on the basis of racial classification. The ethnic group is a cultural group. Race is a social group. Others believe that a race can be attributed to an ethnic group (their categorized social group), and this is a cultural group. For example, Hispanic American is seen as an ethnic group and a culture group when it is neither. Hispanic American, Asian American, European American, Native American, and so on, for all such social groupings are actually composed of a wide variety of specific cultural groups. In the Asian American social group or category, one can identify the Korean-Americans, Japanese-Americans, Chinese-Americans, and a whole host of other cultural groups. Within the category of Native American, one can find the Crow, Apache, Cheyenne, and some 600 other distinct cultural groups. The same can be done with all such ethnic social categories.

The basis of an ethnic category actually comes from a perception of a shared something, language, particular beliefs or some practice. From this belief has developed the tendency to use the terms interchangeably; despite the fact that the practice has repeatedly been shown to be based on many false premises and assumptions and has led to many inaccurate characterizations of different cultural groups. The focus on just ethnicity and race has lead Americans to ignore many other types of cultural groups that altogether constitute the diversity of American culture. Even to the most casual observer of American culture, the time and attention devoted to race and ethnicity is sometimes overwhelming. The tendency for people to categorize others on the basis of race first, or observed physical characteristics, and then attribute social or cultural significance to them—superior or inferior status—is historically well established in American culture. The tendency to grossly group people together in social categories based on imagined ethnicity is also well established in American culture. In both instances, ethnic and racial minority status has been assigned to these social groups, and this has produced some dire consequences for a great many people, not to mention the social problems it has created for the nation-state as a whole.

While all racial classifications have been repeatedly shown to be arbitrary and artificial, there is still a widespread tendency for most Americans to see racial characteristics and groupings almost before anything else. Perhaps this also can account for the widespread practice of using a cultural characteristic to create a racial group as well. Some Americans still hold to the notion of the "pure" races. This tendency is a quite likely a consequence of the government's continued use of race as a means of census categorizations and a continuing focus on racial equalities or inequalities. Racial classifications will always depend on who is looking at what, where they arbitrarily draw the lines, and for what purpose(s). Individuals, groups, government, and religion continue to use the concept with reckless abandon. That physical differences between groups of human do exist is obvious, but no study has ever established any cultural significance to them, yet many Americans continue to believe that some groups are more inferior/superior than others, that cultural or intellectual ability rests on some physical characteristic. In culture groups, people continue to learn that cultural significance can be legitimately implied from physical differences. They then generalize (stereotype) anyone who may come close to the physical descriptions as members of that (those) group(s). Once this is done, the rationalizations and justifications for prejudice, discrimination, and racist doctrines (racial superiority based on the differences) apparently come quite easily despite the fact they started out and remain largely untrue and ill-founded.

In the United States, racial groups are arbitrary and artificial as they are anywhere else. Once created, characterizations and attributes are then credited to them. People then learn what these differences mean or assign meaning to them. It is amazing how many groups have been created by Americans on this basis (anywhere from three to thirty and more) and even more amazing to hear what they learn with regard to each of them. Upon closer examination, there is no doubt that most Americans use color to designate the racial groups. Black and brown are readily seen, evidence in the fact that in some states these are the only two races recognized when it comes to protecting minority rights or allocating resources, as in the state of Texas. The Native American is rarely identified by color, but the "red man" image is still popular. When pushed, most Americans will acknowledge the Indian (American version—the red man), seen as both a race and a cultural group. Asian American as a referent, still basically refers to the "yellow" people, and Hispanics are uniformly thought of as the "brown" people. With regards to the Black Americans, the tendency is to see any black as part of that culture group, in part because so many blacks identify themselves as African-American, reflecting their common origins in Africa. Not all black people come from Africa (unless one goes back to the very beginnings of the entire human group), nor has there ever been a single African culture per se. There are, of course, many cultures to be found on the African continent. This terminological designation is as arbitrary and artificial as is the concept of race. Many existing (and popular) classifications of race can be traced back in history to the seventeenth and eighteenth centuries. In the United States, there has always been a tendency among Americans to equate/identify racial groups and assign them cultural characteristics or cultural capabilities.

Probably the first vision for many Americans when the concept of race comes up is that of the Black Americans (based on physical characteristics) and then the Hispanic Americans (based on their primary language), and then (perhaps) the Asian Americans (based on both cultural and physical characteristics). Rarely, at least initially, will Americans immediately think of the Native American (red man) as the original inhabitants of the United States. The blacks of America have always been viewed as a minority group that has suffered tremendous discrimination and prejudice since being brought to the United States as slaves. Black Americans represent the classic minority group in the American context. As with all minorities, Black Americans have historically been denied access to the power monopolized by the dominant power structure. As the population makeup of America continues to change with the addition of even more minorities into the general population, and as the movement of white urban dwellers out of the cities continues (leaving the others in control of the cities), circumstances may find the white race (whatever that might mean), increasingly becoming minorities in the urban environments and particular regions of America. It is also true that in the 1990s there has been a growing sense of a "white group" becoming a disadvantaged group in America, a minority, and this represents a strange reversal (at least from their point of view) for those who used to be in control. This has produced a growing conservatism among the white population, if not outward hostility and militancy on the part of a growing number of these Americans who see themselves as disadvantaged (as vague as that designation might be). In addition to creating groups on the basis of physical characteristics (races or racial categorization), other groups singled out in America are established on the basis of shared cultural characteristics, sometimes a single trait and sometimes a group of traits.

Ethnic Groups and Ethnicity

The term *ethnic* has changed considerably from its original meaning. As originally conceived, an ethnic group was composed of people who shared a common tribal origin, in essence, shared customs and traditions as well. In its original sense, it could easily be seen as just another world for culture. Ethnic groups were generally identified as groups within larger societies who could be identified on the basis of language or some other distinctive tradition(s) or custom (food, dress, mode of life, etc.). In today's usage of the term, an ethnic group can be a social category or an actual cultural group. More often than not, it is used to refer to those social categories created for some purpose in the complex societies. When used in this way, the ethnic group identification is a prescribed one that overlays the more preferred cultural identity of all those grossly grouped into it. A social group characterization can become a means of self-identity when persons so grouped together perceive there is a value or strength that can come with it, primarily for social interaction (Salamone 1997). There is some justification for suggesting that social groups will ultimately become cultural groups out of necessity in the complex environment, as people come to understand the social or political advantage(s) in it. The social category can then represent political, economic, and social action strategies for people in the group, as a way to cope within the multicultural context. Other scholars suggest that ethnic identities have become the paradox of the times, as globalization of the market exchange systems spreads and populations move, not just to a new nation-state, but, back and forth across national boundaries, maintaining much of the cultural tradition they take with them as they do so. Again, this refers more to a cultural group than an ethnic category. Based on this constant movement, some scholars even suggest that ethnicity now transcends the context of diversity. Others now see it as a segment of a larger community by virtue of shared beliefs, common origin, and shared activities.

There is no dispute with the notion that in today's world, ethnicity means commonality, but there is a growing social importance of ethnicity and this is tied to the issues of cultural diversity, especially the stratification that nearly always accompanies it. Despite the differing views on ethnicity that occasion a great deal of debate among scholars and decision makers alike, for most Americans the idea of an ethnic group continues to persist much as always, it denotes cultural difference and this is part of the diversity they all recognize as characterizing their country. Although ethnic and ethnicity have lost most of their original meanings, as people in greater numbers now move about the world as never before and maintain many of their traditional cultures, the concepts of ethnic and ethnicity still have value in distinguishing at least one category of diversity, the one that is tied to people movement and the tendency to maintain at least part of their original culture. These unique cultures are obscured within the social categories into which Americans put them. But one would be quite wrong in assuming that they maintain the cultures they brought with them. Such groups evolve unique cultures in the new contexts within which they find themselves, cultures unlike any other in the world. This is another reality that goes virtually unnoticed by Americans in the use of social categories. Ethnic cultures are contextualized, the result of the historical experience of groups in the particular social context of America, and they are intricately tied to a self-identification in that context that serves many social, economic, and political purposes. Most ethnic categories are based on some perceived cultural trait(s) (real or imaginary) shared by those being grouped together, or specific customs, foods, dress, and so forth.

As already pointed out, some groups are established on no more than the fact that their people may share a language (at least some variation or dialect of it), as with Spanish being used for all those characterized as Hispanic American, Hispanics, etc. In other cases, groups are formed on the basis of cultural things being combined with physical similarity and a consideration of geographical origin (e.g., African Americans, Asian Americans, Middle Eastern Americans, South Asian Americans, European Americans, etc.). In the case of the aboriginal inhabitants of the United States, all of these things are used to categorize all Native Americans or American Indians into a single grouping. Some categories are created on the basis of religion with only a nominal recognition of geographic origin or physical appearance (e.g., Muslims, Jews, etc.). Unfortunately, the end result of these kinds of categorizations is to obscure more than they clarify. Not only do they obscure the many cultural differences among the peoples overgeneralized into them, they hide the actual diversity that really exists in such groupings and ultimately within the country itself. The practice also leads to more stereotyping, discrimination, and prejudice. In fact, each of these commonly used categories of diversity is made up of a great many specific cultural groups, each with its own beliefs and practices—diversity within diversity as it were. Even within the specific cultural groupings, a significant amount of variation can be noted. This may represent a circumstance where the term *subculture* might even be appropriate. In virtually every case of a social grouping based on ethnicity, and despite the fact people might speak a similar language, may have originated in the same part of the world, share a religion, or physically look alike, they share little or nothing else.

Most Americans tend to view diversity on the level of the social group or category of people, preferring to deal with the diverse group of "Hispanics" rather than all the unique cultural groups that might be generalized into the category. The practice obscures the real cultural differences that do exist. This is not without consequences. Defining or characterizing people in this way glosses over the real cultural differences that exist. The importance of culture to people was discussed in Chapter 1. Stereotyping and generalizing away cultural differences only means that the real cultural groups become that much more defensive of their beliefs and behaviors. One's truth simply becomes even more important to maintain. The group's historical experience and legacy become that much more important to them. Understanding the real American culture becomes that much more difficult.

Minorities

As suggested previously, prejudice and discrimination are directly related to the minority status that characterizes many cultural groups in America, that status is a product of differentiating people into groups in the heavily populated nation-state contexts. In America, both social categories and cultural groupings have been labeled minorities. The designation is recognized by the people within the groups themselves and by members of the dominating category or group. Minority means different things to different people. For most Americans, minority is based on numbers, a particular group is simply not as numerous as another. For example, there are more European Americans than Black Americans living in the United States. But, minority has another meaning as well, it can denote a lack of access to power. In America, women are usually identified as a minority, not because there are numerically fewer of them than men (they are actually the majority), but because they do not have the same access to political or economic power. Tyson Gibbs (1997) makes clear that the ethnic minority is easily distinguished from the majority population by their cultural practices or their customs, religion, dress, food habits, language, and perhaps their group cohesiveness. In the case of an ethnic minority, numbers are important, even more than the shared cultural beliefs and practices that set them apart. Their actual beliefs and practices are not particularly valued by the dominant population. Rather, the beliefs and practices are looked upon negatively, based on the dominant group's own ethnocentrism. Differences are translated as bad when they are compared to the preferred norms of the majority or dominant group. Based on the same criteria, Mexican-Americans also would be considered an ethnic minority in the United States, distinguished by geographical origin, language, food habits, perhaps even their physical appearance. But, the entire social category of Hispanic is seen as a cultural minority simply because people within this category all share the speaking of some version (dialect) of Spanish as opposed to English. More appropriate, this group should be seen as a social minority, owing to the overgeneralization that has occurred.

Since ethnic means cultural, the term cultural minority appears to be the same thing as ethnic minority, used to describe a population that has limited access to power and is distinguishable by prescription or by self-identification. In the case of women, cultural minority may be more appropriate for this majority segment of the American population. The idea of racial minorities promotes the visible skin distinctions between population groups living in the United States. Such distinctions are really developed, formulated, and used by the majority population to maintain distances between groups—distinguishable by their ascribed skin tones—yellow (Asian), black (African), brown (Hispanic), or red (Native American). The assignment of particular groups of people to a minority status directly impacts the interactions and relationships between them and other cultural groups, others minorities and with the majority group. African-Americans generally fit all three categories of minority population—ethnic, cultural, and racial minority.

AFRICAN-AMERICANS

The current label of African-American is a compromise label that is the result of many years of struggle within the Black American group and encompasses much more than the simple identification of a racially based group with a common point of origin in Africa. Concealed in this label is a sense of historical identity, political ideology, group identity, and survival strategy as a minority living in a country whose majority population is of another ethnic and racial category (Gibbs 1997; Hogan-Garcia 1997). Historically, Black Americans have been *slaves, freedmen, colored people, people of color, Negroes, Afro-Americans, African-Americans,* and *blacks.* All of these referential terms can be linked to the ideas of a minority group or population struggling to establish its own identity and finding its place in American society. The Bureau of the Census has not grappled with this problem of labeling all dark-skinned people now living in this country as African-American, despite the fact that their language, customs, and political viewpoints may be quite different from those of African descent who were born in the United States. Furthermore, not all people of African descent born in the United States fully accept other dark-skinned people from other parts of the world. Lumping is the most serious limitation of racial groupings or categorizations based on a single trait such as color. The resulting overgeneralization obscures far more than it clarifies.

Some of the census data on the so-called African-American social category, here meaning primarily Black American and not the African-American cultural grouping presented earlier, bears repeating (Bureau of the Census 1992a, 1992b, 1996). According to the most recent figures, the people of this social group or category are leaving the rural areas for more metropolitan cities, with well over one-half of this population residing in the southern regions of the United States. The median age for Black Americans is 27.3 years, but with a median income 30 percent less than whites. Black males aged 25 to 44, suffer from a 30 percent unemployment rate, compared to approximately 15 percent for white males. In terms of family, the census data indicate that only 53 percent of the Black Americans lived as married couples. The number of single heads of household rose, but so too, has the number of male headed households. In America, not all groups value the nuclear family in the same way. Earlier studies suggested that the Black American household was predominantly headed by females. It would seem that the Black American family structure is crumbling at the central core, if the central core is defined as the nuclear family, consisting of father, mother, and siblings. The black matriarchy and its role in socializing children and marriage stability have always received enormous attention because it was so different from the dominant group family. In addition, black Americans are facing several significant economic issues. The household median income for the period from 1980–1989 for Black Americans was about 55 percent of the white household median income set at $32, 270. Approximately 30 percent of all Black American households live below the poverty level. This group has been termed a permanent underclass with a higher divorce rate than white families, a much higher number of female headed households, a greater percentage of the population deferring marriage, experiencing a substantial decline in jobs in the manufacturing sector.

Many African-Americans (cultural group) are labeled "Uncle-Tom," "Sell-Out," "Handkerchief Head," "Oreo Cookie," by other members of the African-American community when they express work ethics and life goals similar to the majority white population. As more African-Americans achieve significant pieces of the American Dream or join the American middle class, such terms will be heard with even greater frequency. This is becoming a significant problem within this group. African-Americans, indeed, all Black Americans, have a great many problems to face in the American context. First, they must live among a population where the majority is of another race. They face inequality of opportunity in employment and education. They must face constant prejudice and discrimination in job applications, in obtaining loans for beginning small businesses, and in housing. The interaction of blacks and whites remains guarded, one of conflict and ever present suspicion as to motives and behavior. For the African-American, this is tied to America's history of slavery and their experiences with discrimination and prejudice that will not disappear, despite laws and other actions taken to eliminate it. In contemporary America, the Black American social group is a heterogeneous one encompassing all peoples from around the world whose skin tones fit within the color range of brown to black. Persons within this grouping speak many different languages, have a wide variety of customs and habits, believe in a multiple array of religions, and are actually distinguishable, even in skin tones, the classic method for identifying a racial minority. As a social grouping, the Black American has limited access to the political and economic power in America, relegating them to the status of a racial minority. As part of this grouping, African-Americans have experienced these same things. There are wide distinctions between the poor and the middle-class Black Americans and African-Americans. Within the black community, African-American is a label used among people with African heritage, brought to the United States as slaves (or are descendant of slaves), and who developed a unique culture by virtue of their history in this context and the strategies they have developed for surviving within this context.

The identification of African-Americans as an ethnic minority group and the prescription of African-Americans to an ethnic minority group by the majority population, serves to solidify African-Americans and form the group that is also the perfect example of an ethnic, cultural, and racial minority group in America. As with most cultural groups, the African-American population is not one group with a single mind, but displays significant variations within it. There is a range of differing political, economic, and social ideologies within this group that run the gamut of the American belief system and impact routine activities. There are identifiable subcultural groups within this ethnic cultural group. For example, there are Afrocentric, conservative, and liberal African-Americans. There also are many African-Americans who have grown up for generations in America without ever experiencing or knowing poverty and it consequences. Mikel Hogan-Garcia (1997) points out that the terms ethnic and culture are used repeatedly and interchangeably when reference to members of this group. Patterned beliefs and behaviors do set them apart from other groups. In the case of the African-American, it is based on their origin (somewhere in Africa), their particular immigration experience, and the adjustments they have had to make to live and work in the United States. According to Hogan-Garcia, on the individual level, both designations refer to the extent to which individuals feel any sense of belonging and loyalty to the group and share in the way of life being attributed to it. This also can include pride or shame in the association, evidenced by their spending time with other members of the group. Ascription to the African-American cultural group results in economic, educational, social, and political obstacles for the individual. It also means they will experience less than full participation in mainstream American culture and have limited access to the American Dream. African-Americans represent an ethnic cultural group and they are a part of that racial social group better referred to as the Black American, the prescribed membership within which is tied to only a darker skin.

Approximately 30.8 million, or 12 percent of Black Americans live in the South with smaller numbers in the North, Midwestern, Northeastern, and Western regions of the United States. As a group, Black Americans differ widely on issues of education, occupation, religion, generation, gender, region, sexual orientation, and their residence in urban, rural, or suburban areas. Understanding this group involves distinguishing between Black Americans. To understand the cultural group that really is African-American involves developing an awareness of history and some of the specific institutions in the traditions of African-American culture, institutions that provide for mutual assistance, their perspectives on education, and their struggle for equal opportunity. The historical experience of African-Americans has produced the perceptions African-Americans have about themselves and the dominant white group in America. It is within this historical experience that African-Americans developed a sense of group identity, and sense of purpose and desire to confront members of other ethnic or racial groups. Forced immigration, slavery, emancipation, a history of segregation/prejudice/discrimination, urban migration, development of the urban ghetto, and the civil rights movement of the twentieth century have all shaped the ideas and behaviors of this cultural group.

Perhaps the most compelling legacy of the history of the African-American in the United States is associated with their violent removal from Africa and their subsequent life as slaves. This provides the foundation for the formation of African-American culture and many perspectives held by members of this group. Slaves were socially defined as property, not people, with no legal rights, and this led to constant abuse. Families were broken up and owners used all types of physical coercion to maintain control over them. In surviving slavery, African-Americans developed their own family structures and sense of community, both of which enabled them to maintain a sense of group identity and provided them with the means to cope with the oppressive institution in which they found themselves. Even as freedmen, African-Americans had to face the Black Codes and the Fugitive Slave Law that allowed for the return of escaped slaves across state lines, and in some cases, even kidnaping of free blacks. The prejudice and discrimination of the entire black population, free or slave, in both the Northern states and Southern states during the period of slavery, was the context in which the institutional infrastructure of African-American culture and community was created, as was their status as a minority. Even with the signing of the Emancipation Act and the passage of the Thirteenth Amendment to the Constitution (1865), abolishing slavery did not change things dramatically, although the passage of the Thirteenth Amendment does represent the beginning of African-American efforts to obtain the full rights of American citizenship. But, racial segregation and the supremist ideology of the white race were deeply entrenched in America. Despite the establishment of the Freedman's Bureau (1865) to protect and provide for the welfare of the newly freed slaves; political and economic forces, the former slave labor system survived in the development of sharecropping and the crop lien system. The segregation of African-Americans was even legitimized in the decisions of the Supreme Court and legal segregation thus became the law of the land (1896). This legal segregation was to last until overturned by the Supreme Court in 1954.

A significant migration of African-Americans from the Southern to the Northern states occurred at the time of the First World War, and this led to the creation of what is today viewed as the *urban ghetto*. Because northern industry was in great need of unskilled and semiskilled labor, African-Americans were encouraged to relocate in the urban centers of the North. Having done so, the migrants faced poverty and hostility from the white workers who saw them as rivals for their jobs. Competition for housing resulted in riots. In the context of the ghettos that developed, African-Americans faced residential and school segregation and were even denied access to hotels and restaurants, something only associated with the "separate but equal" practices of the South. Restrictions were placed on black men entering the armed services as part of the war effort. Because of the development of the ghetto, African-Americans had to face a revived Ku Klux Klan. With demobilization following the war, they would experience the loss of even more job opportunities. More race riots occurred in 1919. Intragroup conflicts increased within the Black community as older residents blamed the migrants for increased racial restrictions and conflicts. This urbanization of the African-American group played a large role in the civil rights movement of the twentieth century and the equal opportunity legislation of the 1950s and 1960s. It also accounts for the major differences within the community as to the best strategy for achieving equality in America, something yet to be achieved. Some in the African-American community advocated nonviolent demonstrations and legal challenges to achieve African-American goals, others advocated much more militant strategies. From just this brief discussion, it should be clear that history has played an important role in defining the beliefs and behaviors of this cultural group, as well as the strategies that have evolved to cope with living in the American context. There are other things that can help in the development of a better understanding of this cultural group.

African-American Institutions

According to Hogan-Garcia (1997), African-Americans value mutual help, education, and equal opportunity above all other things. Mutual aid begins with the family, an institution with deep African and American roots, and the idea of family extends to other institutions, including their churches. All African-Americans share in the importance of the family. Ideally, the primary family forms include the nuclear family (husband, wife, and children), the single parent households headed by women, and the extended family consisting of a married couple or a single parent and their children, or one consisting of grandparents and their grandchildren, as well as other relatives (nieces, nephews, aunts, uncles, cousins, and so on). Augmented families, similar to the extended family will also be found, but instead of just blood relatives, boarders or friends can co-habit in the household. The extended family is characterized by its flexibility, the support it provides for each individual family member, the pooling of resources, and in its obligation to care for all members of it. This long-standing tradition of a flexible and supportive family has helped the African-American to survive. It continues to be a strength despite the widespread poverty associated with it and the strain it experiences because of high divorce rates and the decrease in two parent families.

African-American churches and mutual benefit institutions have blended together the religious beliefs of Christianity and those of Native Americans to produce a unique hybrid religious belief system. This belief system among African-Americans does not distinguish between secular and sacred activities (all activities are seen as potentially sacred). Religion is a source of social strength and it has played a large role in the formulation of the African-American communities. Black churches are interrelated with community service organizations, providing for both religious and community services. They have become a source of economic cooperation, an arena for political activity, a sponsor of education, and even a place of refuge from a hostile world.

For all the members of the African-American group, education, segregation, and inadequate schools continue to be their most pressing and deserving problems. Even where the African-American might represent the majority group, as in many urban schools, they note a decrease in financial and professional support, and they see this as directly affecting them more so than others. In recent years, there has even developed a split within the African-American community on such issues as equal opportunity and affirmative action, which reflects the fact that this group is far more varied than has been previously assumed. On one hand are those who see a continuation of affirmative action as belittling hard earned accomplishments. This group sees it as inhibiting the equality and acceptance they seek. On the other hand, many support the continuation of affirmative action. They would argue that without affirmative action the entire group will only fall back in times and opportunity, for without it, segregation, prejudice, and discrimination will rise again to wipe out all that has been gained with it. This group believes that only with affirmative action can the injustices of the past be addressed and the equality sought, ensured.

MEXICAN-AMERICANS

According to Alicia Re Cruz (1997), members of this population historically have been referred to as either Chicanos, Mexicanos, Hispanos, Spanish-Americans, or Spanish-speaking people. It seems that Mexican-American is the term used most frequently by members of this group for themselves. Mexican-American is a label devised to distinguish them from the undocumented immigrants of Mexico who, although living in the United States, are not American citizens. Demographically speaking, Hispanic is the term used by the Bureau of the Census to identify a racial/ethnic social group composed of Americans of Spanish heritage or who speak Spanish. However, the term Hispanic American, or simply Hispanic, is another of those categorization terms that masks a broad variety of ethnic, national, and cultural backgrounds within the group established. There is no "Hispanic culture" unless one is speaking directly to the culture of Spain, but there are many different cultural groups generalized into this category as it is used in America. Mexican-American is one of these cultural groups.

As with African-Americans, knowing the history of this particular group helps one to appreciate and understand the ideas, behaviors, and perspectives of Mexican-Americans—their culture. Many Mexican-Americans steadfastly consider the American Southwest part of their original homeland. They steadfastly defend Mexican rights and claim the Mexican heritage as their own. Many even interpret the Anglo presence in the Southwest as an invasion of Mexican territories. The Southwest has been an arena of constant dispute between the Anglo population, who see themselves as the developers of the area, and the people of Mexican origin, who claim their ancestry to be rooted in the Southwest. The debate hinges on the different perceptions of history of both groups, but it also has created the cultural stereotypes used by both to characterize each other and accounts for the terms used to refer to them. For example, today, the popular usage of the adjective *illegal* refers to those who have crossed the border without U.S. authorization, the term signifying for America, the complete and undiscussed sovereignty over all of the territory that the Mexican-Americans claim was originally Mexican. The Mexican-American community uses the description of this group as *undocumented,* which leaves open the question of historical rights to the Southwest. The use of the term undocumented focuses on only the legal status of the individual.

The first influx of Mexican migrants into the Southwest followed the Mexican-American War of the 1840s. As representatives of a culture that was only recently at war with the United States, the idea of the enemy was still entrenched in the basic perceptions the Americans had of the immigrants. Hostility and suspicion led to only very limited acceptance. In addition, they seemed to accept the existing social and economic conditions in which they found themselves which only revitalized and reinforced the old stereotypes of Mexicans as childish, dirty, irresponsible, and dishonest. The stereotypes held by both groups and the conflicts between them would last for many years, constantly revitalized by one world event or another, particularly the two world wars of the twentieth century. Both of these wars created a need for new cheap labor and this fostered additional migrations of people out of Mexico and into the United States. Not only did this revitalize the already bad relations between the Mexican-American and the Anglo society, with each new wave of migrants, the Mexican-American population itself became more varied. Distinguishing lines were drawn between the original Mexican inhabitants of the area, and the more recent immigrants who were simply called *Mexicans*. The economic recession of the United States in the 1930s also produced a number of migrations of Mexicans to the United States and impacted the socioeconomic positions of Mexican-Americans in the United States. In 1929, the U.S. Congress passed legislation that made it a felony for a migrant to illegally cross the border. Deportations of Mexicans became quite common, and the general anxiety being experienced by most Americans simply revitalized the stereotype image Americans held of Mexicans as basically dishonest. At this point, the differentiations and variations between and within various groups of Mexican-Americans began to take on added significance. During World War II, a program was designed by the U.S. government to recruit Mexican laborers and guarantee them a minimum wage (the Bracero Program). More immigrants from Mexico traveled to the United States, this migration only reinforcing the historically based stereotypes that had developed in association with this cultural group. At the same time, young Mexican-Americans promoted their "Americanization," differentiating themselves from their elders who were more attached to their Mexican traditions. These young Mexican-Americans were beginning to feel themselves a part of the American mainstream, but this only contributed to the growing distinction they were making between themselves and Mexican immigrants. In the 1950s, the domestic labor supply in the United States increased and "Operation Wetback" was quickly initiated to stop the flow of illegal immigration into the country. The term *wetbacks* or *mojados* was generated to refer to those who swim the Rio Grande River to enter into the United States. The smuggling of undocumented individuals from Mexico into the United States became a lucrative business—remains so today. The stream of Mexican immigrants, both legal and undocumented, continues to grow at the present time.

The Mexican-American community is a growing element of the ethnically diverse United States. As a consequence of Mexican migration across the years, Spanish has been retained as their primary language because of the supportive nature of their extended families in both the United States and Mexico. It is also tied to their divided sense of community, between residence in the United States and "home" in Mexico. It is also related to the unskilled jobs they tend to fill, most of which do not require English. As with the African-American cultural group, Mexican-American is not a single, homogeneous group—not ethnically, socioeconomically, nor politically. According to the 1990 census, 13.3 million persons of Mexican descent now live in the United States. In terms of the American mainstream, Mexican-

Americans pursue the American Dream like all other Americans, but within the constraints that have been imposed on them as a cultural minority. Over time, most Mexican-Americans become fluent in English. They internalize many of the most important American values, and participate in all the social, political, and economic institutions. Even with their inclusion in the Hispanic American social group, they tend to exhibit characteristics that demonstrate the development of their unique culture that has become so significant a part of American diversity. Mexican-Americans are family oriented and friendly. They develop informal networks for support, distrust impersonality, and strongly adhere to their religious beliefs. They emphasize the role of women and accept males as economic supporters. In the face of hardship they are stoic and prefer privacy and distance in public. They have a very strong sense of responsibility to help relatives and experience severe guilt if they do not (or cannot) live up to their responsibilities and values. Freedom of speech in public is highly valued, as is the notion of equality. For Mexican-Americans, and others of the Spanish-speaking "Hispanic" group, assimilation means an ability to function in the American mainstream culture context, along with a significant reduction in their ability to function in the traditional culture milieu.

NATIVE AMERICANS

American Indians have always presented great problems for Americans. First, the term Indian is also associated with the people of India, the term originating from early explorers who thought that they had reach India when they first touched the shores of the New World. Beyond that, the term has been used to refer to many different things. It has been used as a legal concept, a racial group, and to identify a cultural group in America. To the average American, Native American is a term that refers to simply "Indians," people who also represent a unique ethic grouping of America. They are also seen as a race, with high cheek bones, prominent "eagle-beak" nose, reddish brown skin, and so on. The U.S. government and Bureau of the Census define the Native American as anyone residing on a reservation or whose name appears on a tribal role (tribe here meaning a traditional cultural group of aboriginal Americans as opposed to a kind of political organization the term actually designates). Other state agencies define Native American by the degree of "pure" blood (one-fourth, one-eighth, even less) they must have. Native American is a categorization, a social grouping within the diversity of America. It does not reflect a cultural grouping but a term that becomes the basis for grouping anyone of aboriginal descent together. As with some other groups already discussed, many Americans continue to believe that Native American is either a cultural group or racial group, maybe all three. In actual fact, today, the category is made up of some ten to sixteen million people coming from a wide diversity of actual cultures and groupings. While Americans tend to generalize and stereotype Native Americans, there is no single culture for all the members of this category, not at present or historically. To understand the cultural groups within this category requires an awareness of history just as it did with Mexican-Americans and African-Americans.

In the case of the original inhabitants of American, the history begins with contact. When Europeans first came to the shores of the United States, many saw the natives as little more than primitive savages. The Pilgrims favored the term brutish. In the 1700s and 1800s, both negative and positive perceptions of the natives of the new land existed. Some continued to see them as savages, while others saw them as intelligent, noble, and well formed (a reflection of the "noble savage" idea then current). While both views have created serious problems and different perceptions over time, nearly all the newcomers to America saw the natives as military obstacles to be overcome. This led to the idea of enforced acculturation that has been the mainstay government policy for their interactions with the Native American right up to the present—making them into good, white Americans. Missionary activities focused primarily on getting natives to abandon their traditional ways and accept the Christian ideology, and this left their legacy on the Native American as well. Conquest and reservation placements were also aimed at forcing the Native Americans into the cultural ways of the dominating white European group. The acculturation policy fostered since first contact has been accompanied by conquest, domination, and the concentration of the defeated tribes onto reservations that take on all the characteristics of concentration camps and the enforced impoverishment of large numbers of native people. Prejudice and discrimination characterize the interactions of all native American cultural groups with the white populace and government, regardless of the diverse cultures that will be found within this social group (category) of people. While the society at large celebrates the "discovery of America" by Christopher Columbus, Native Americans view the event as the beginning of the genocide of the Native Americans and the start of "red slavery."

Between the years 1870 and 1928, the federal government adopted mostly coercive policies toward the Native Americans, all basically illegal (as later determined by the U.S. Supreme Court) and in direct violation of the First, Second, Fifth, Tenth, and Fourteenth Amendments. Nevertheless, government policy revolved around Indians as "wards of the government." The idea of a ward of the government had no legal basis within the Constitution. The Fourteenth Amendment specifically says that all persons born or naturalized in the United States are citizens. The designation of ward determined that Native Americans were to always remain ethnic, cultural, and racial minorities in the United States. This significantly contributed to the discrimination and prejudice that has always accompanied that arbitrarily created status. Since the 1980s, the government has focused most its attention on destroying native societies and cultures by attacking their religions, putting all the wards under the control of the Bureau of Indian Affairs, adopting a paternalistic attitude toward their "childlike" wards, individualizing the native, and engaging in gunpoint culture change. Even the Indian New Deal of the 1930s, represented only a temporary change in federal policy toward Native Americans. Congress passed the Indian Reorganization Act, giving Native Americans approval power over their own assets, resources, and so on, only to end the new policy in the 1950s, despite its successes. The policy then reverted to enforced acculturation, although this time, new ways were tried, the relocation of Natives into the urban centers of the United States and termination of the status of ward. This particular effort to acculturate the Native was no more successful that the earlier ones as the vast majority of relocated Natives returned to their traditional homes and ways. Through the 1950s and 1960s there were continuing assaults on Native religions in an attempt to change Native Americans into simply Americans. The government went so far as to "terminate" entire tribal groups and reservations. This effort was so disastrous that most tribes and reservations terminated under the policy have now been reinstated. Since the 1960s, the major efforts have been toward making Native Americans into equal, self-sufficient and participating citizens of the United States, as acculturation has remained the consistent goal. This is an interesting twist in a country that has always prided itself on valuing diversity and defending everyone's right to be different. Apparently this idea applies to everyone but Native Americans.

In many ways, the American Indians are the forgotten minority (Cambridge 1997). According to Charles Cambridge, himself a Navaho, the history of American Indians is a confusing maze of different opinions and perceptions. Americans do not really view American Indians as people with their own cultural reality, but instead view and measure them categorically and with long-held stereotypic images that grossly group all Native Americans cultures into a single (albeit false) culture. Indian cultures are unique in America and many have continued to maintain a great many of their traditional ways. Others have lost their cultures and communities. A continuously burning issue is the claim that the "history" of tribal people in the Western Hemisphere did not begin until Europeans discovered the Americas. Europeans have argued that Indian people did not have a written language and therefore no history. Civilizing and christianizing the native peoples came with the idea they were little more than animals and this came out of the fact that they were not mentioned in the Christian literature. The "discovery" of the Americas rocked the foundation of European Christianity and created the need to ensure that the newly discovered Indians actually became civilized Christian people. This religious ideology underlies the long-lasting approach to Indian policy. Today at the highest level of government, the United States reflects the religious association. The Indian eventually became known as the "White Man's Burden," and death awaited those who resisted.

The United States had more than six hundred different tribes at the time of its "discovery." Each tribe had its own culture, sovereignty, territory, government, religion, and language. Often overlooked is the fact that without the help of some of these tribes, many of the early European settlers would not have survived. Despite this, as the population of Europeans increased and their settlements grew in number, the demand for more Indian land also increased. Many conflicts and wars resulted. Following the American Revolution, the newly formed government quickly concluded that Indian people were a threat to their continual existence. They were the occupiers and owners of the land that needed to be transferred through treaties and purchases. While this recognized the sovereignty of Indian tribes, the complete removal of the eastern Indian tribes to the West was undertaken (Indian Removal Act of 1830), and most of the eastern tribes lost their lands. As Americans continued their westward movement, tribes were forced to move again, this time into Oklahoma, which became known as the Indian Territoιy. For most

Native Americans, one of the most important realities has been the continual loss of land and life across centuries of treaties and wars with the Americans.

The Indian treaty period ended in 1871, when the U.S. Congress decided to no longer recognize Indian tribes as independent nations. No longer a military threat, the government policy turned to the problem of managing the conquered Indians. The Indian relationship with the federal government became paternalistic and a succession of federal legislation all aimed at solving the "Indian problem." The Dawes Act of 1887 (General Allotment Act) established the framework under which large tracts of Indian land were declared surplus properties and reverted to the United States. Indians were made citizens of the Untied States by the American Citizenship Act (1924) whether they wanted it or not. Massive changes in so-called Indian policy were to follow, in particular the Indian Reorganization Act of 1934 (IRA), which slowed the policy of assimilating the Indians into American society. Tribes began to enlarge their reservations, the constant loss of land was slowed, and tribal governments were encouraged. In the 1953, the United States attempted to get out of the Indian business as Congress began to terminate federal programs and control over several Indian tribes by virtue of House Concurrent Resolution 108, otherwise known as the Termination Act.

The Termination Act ended a tribe's legal existence as a sovereign entity, the Indian status as ward was ended, and tribal members were given American citizenship. More than one hundred tribes were selected for termination. Under termination, the tribe's resources were sold, their land was divided and sold to outsiders, and they ceased to exist. Tribal members no longer were considered "Indians." Since most were not standing in line to become Americans, forced assimilation became the answer, with Indian boarding schools and education the means of destroying tribal culture (Civilization Fund and Indian Educational Division) under the direction of Christian organizations. The basic idea was to civilize Indian people by taking their children away from their homes and tribes. Indian kids were taken usually by force and sent to boarding schools far from their home. The schools seemed more like military installments or even prisons instead of schools for the education of children. Some children ran away only to be identified as absence without leave (AWOLs). The school staff then would hunt the AWOLs like escaped convicts. The most appalling and unjust of all of these boarding schools was the Bureau of Indian Affairs' (BIA) Chilocco Indian School in Chilocco, Oklahoma, where children expelled from other BIA schools were located. At this school, young children were often handcuffed and flogged, even placed in solitary confinement. Within the boarding schools, Indians were forbidden to speak their tribal languages. They were taught that their native language was vulgar and only English was proper.

It is hard for most Americans to talk about Native Americans because of the level of guilt most of them carry with regard to this social grouping that was so much a part of their history. Nearly every value Americans hold has been ignored when it comes to these groups of people who have maintained so much of their original cultures right up to the present. Most Americans have little real understanding of the many cultural groups that actually make up the category, or the nature of these cultures. Perhaps this is due to television and the movies out of Hollywood. No other social group or category has been so misrepresented, overgeneralized, stereotyped, and exploited as this one that existed well before an America, a United States, was even imagined.

SPECIAL INTEREST CULTURAL GROUPINGS

Although most people immediately think of racial and ethnic groupings whenever the topic of cultural diversity arises, there are a great many other cultural groupings that make up the actual cultural diversity of the United States. Dealing with these other kinds of diversity is a little more difficult and complicated than when the groupings can be identified on the basis of ethnicity. These other kinds of cultural groupings combine with the ethnic cultures and racially based social groupings to complete the diversity of American culture. These groups come with specializations and the pursuit of all of those special interests that accompanied the development of the complex society. Such groups are easily identified on the basis of their very special beliefs and behaviors that set them apart from other groups. It is also the case that many of these cultural groupings are frequently in direct competition with one another, or in the extreme cases, in direct conflict with one another. No discussion of diversity would be complete without taking these cultural groupings into account.

Some special interest cultural groupings are related to social and ethnic groups already identified. Some are better viewed as subcultures of some of the cultural groups already discussed, or better viewed as cultural scenes. Both are cultural groups created as a consequence of the complexity of the modern nation-state. Cultural scenes bring people from all kinds of other cultural backgrounds together for specific purposes or in pursuit of specific goals. Subcultural groups identify the variations even within well-defined cultural groups. As reiterated a number of times, cultures and cultural groupings are based on learned and shared beliefs, behaviors, and the products of these. They are distinguished from other groups based on such things. In this sense, cultural scenes are cultural groups, made up of people who share very specific information and behavior primarily tied to social situations. Cultural scenes are usually bounded in time and space, which can mean they appear, exist, or function only at regularized intervals, they are active at only certain times and in certain places, or they function only sporadically and for limited periods of time. It can also mean that members may recognize their affiliation with the group while not interacting with other recognized members of the group. Socioeconomic classes represent a case in point. People who relate to the middle socioeconomic class in America, recognize they have beliefs, behaviors, and products they have learned as part of that class. They know they share such things with others. But, it is also the case that as a cultural scene, they will likely never come together. While it can be argued whether or not such groupings fit the classical definitions of culture or cultural groupings, the fact remains that they are culture groups by definition, represent constituent groups in the makeup of nation-states, and they are significant elements of diversity in the United States—or anywhere else for that matter. More recently, a number of special interest cultures or culture scenes have even become internationalized or transnational, transcending national groupings, or the specific cultural groupings that make them up.

Covering all of the cultural groupings that might be included within this kind of diversity would be difficult, to say the least. Nearly every category of the cultural experience as it has evolved in the modern nation-state has spawned cultural groups of this kind. But as with the ethnic categories, already shown to be made up of many different specific cultural groupings, special interest categories also are actually composed of more specific groups. The special interest categories most readily recognized are those associated with age, sex and gender differences, politics, economics, religion and churches, businesses, and occupation. In addition to these, there are a whole host of other more specific interest groups associated with such things as education, conservation, animal and human rights, leisure activities, the physically challenged, handicapped, disabled, and so on. The list is almost endless, but nonetheless significant for one trying to understand the culture of America. It is from such associations that individuals obtain most of their ideas and behaviors, and assume their position on the many social issues that seem to divide America. Some of these categories (and examples of the specific groups that comprise them) simply could not be ignored. Among all the groupings that naturally fall into under the guise of American diversity, women's culture, the homosexual community, drug cultures, religious cultures, those of the physically challenged (disabilities cultures), and organizational groups are among the most significant.

Women's Culture

The very idea of women's culture implies that there is something cultural that defines and binds women, some basic set of things that women from all cultural contexts share, and which are based on the social definitions of the gender woman. While sex is biologically inherited, gender roles are cultural. In the context of culture, the members of the group determine the acceptable roles for both men and women. Groups within the nation-state cultural grouping add to the appropriateness of certain roles for both males and females. Together, these are then passed on to aspiring members of the group along with other traditions, beliefs, and practices. The acquisition of gender identity is deeply embedded in an extremely varied, complicated, and overlapping series of life experiences. The development of the gender identity of women consists of subtle and effective influences (Starrett 1997). For example, while men learn one kind of communication—to be direct, almost confrontational and personally challenged—women generally tend to avoid conflict. On even the topic of sex itself, the sexes respond differently. Men find the topic stimulating. Women find it threatening. On sex, men emphasize behavior, while women take the words seriously. Men expect women to defend themselves. Women, in trying to avoid conflict choose to ignore it, hoping it will go away.

But, neither women nor men can be grouped into a single culture because there are infinite ways for any one person to be grouped and even to differ within these groups. In many ways, the generalized category of woman or man is very similar to the social categories already discussed whereby overgeneralized criteria are used to lump people together, in this case by sex. But just as other kinds of cultural groupings exhibit substantial variations within them, so too, can sex cultures be further broken down into additional cultural groupings or variations. There is no doubt that both men and women do learn beliefs and behaviors according to their sex. Because of this, they can be seen as cultural groupings. But the beliefs and behaviors of women do vary substantially, and women do group with others who share the same beliefs and practices to which they subscribe. In responding to the gender roles assigned, women do break apart into subgroupings with their own and more specific beliefs and behaviors they deem important. They may differ on the strategy of changing such role assignments, or they can differ on which of the roles they accept and which they deem as particularly unacceptable or unfair in a society that idealizes equality, and so forth. Subgroupings also can reform from cross-group similarities.

For example, within the women's cultural grouping, there are feminists, militant feminists, conservatives, traditionalists, and many other specific groupings. Women who do not subscribe to the beliefs and practices of militant feminists would not identify with them, may even resent being grouped with them, or having all women of the society stereotyped according to the characteristics of that particular group. They would argue that the militant feminists do not represent the beliefs of women in America with whom they might personally agree, identify, or associate. They may choose not to affiliate with those who advocate a militant position, or who display the militant feminism approach to resolving women's issues in the context of the nation-state (even across the world). In general, American women are viewed as somewhat unique in the world. Based on women's movements throughout American history, women in America have achieved far more equality, status, and power than women almost anywhere else in the world, especially in comparison to newly created Muslim nation-states. Despite this, women are still struggling to achieve parity with men in the workplace and political arena where they continue to lag far behind. They are the focus of discrimination, prejudice, even segregation just as are the groups that have already been discussed. For women to achieve the American Dream and all the equality and equal opportunity promised in the ideal culture of America there must be an almost never ending struggle because of the significant variations within this group. As pointed out by Starrett (1997), women's culture holds together in a very fragile but reinforcing way.

Gays and Lesbians (Homosexual Community)

The homosexual community (the social category), actually consisting of the gay, lesbian, bisexual, and transgendered cultures, creates important issues for the United States, just as do other cultural groups (Rogers 1997). The difficulty in identifying lesbians and gays, because homosexuality crosses all cultural lines, as well as the emphasis on the sexual aspect of homosexuality, has led to a narrow perception of what defines lesbian and gay cultures. These groups, as with any other minorities, are threatened with both institutional and social discrimination and prejudice. History has been an important factor in shaping their cultural identity.

The history of lesbians and gays in the United States is tied to some significant aspects of the development of Western culture, its beliefs, philosophies, norms, and values, particularly those associated with Christianity. Christianity has provided the philosophical foundation for the social and institutionalized beliefs regarding homosexuality. Ideas about appropriate sex and gender behavior have evolved (and been justified) through the manipulation and interpretation of the Christian Bible. At different times, and for different reasons throughout the course of Western civilization, the Bible has been called upon to evidence the heterosexual's position on the topics of gender and sex. Gender is the assignment of behavioral norms and expectations to the sexes. The roots of Western ideology about such behavior stretch back in history as far as Aristotle, who argued that nature had dictated the roles of men and women by virtue of their biological makeup—males were naturally viewed as superior and females were viewed as inferior. Males were dominant and females were submissive. The Age of Discovery produced a threat to Christian doctrine, exacerbated the hard-line approach to the "appropriate and inappropriate" behavior of individuals, and this consequently affected the rigidity of social norms about gender behavior. The Industrial Revolution intensified the tension between females and males and produced the need to stabilize the sex roles, which in turn increased intolerance toward deviance in sexual behavior. The evolution of Western ideology explains the foundation for many attitudes concerning homosexuals and helps to explain the persecution, prosecution, prejudice, and rejection experienced by homosexuals. Not only does homosexual behavior threaten the society by not conforming to expected ranges of gender behavior, it also defies the scientific beliefs about sexuality that are born of this ideology.

Understanding contemporary lesbian and gay cultures in America requires at least a cursory understanding of the history of homosexuals in the United States, where they have been viewed as outcasts and have had to face more difficult obstacles than other minorities easily identified by color or language. Homosexuals always have had to face the problems of legitimacy and identity. Religion, psychiatry, the emergence of the gay civil rights movement, and the AIDS crisis—all have contributed to the development of a homosexual sensibility and a cohesive cultural identity. The prejudice and discrimination that homosexuals in the United States have faced since colonial times has been the result of religious ideology, political expediency, and a set of Western values and norms defining appropriate gender and sex behavior that were brought from Europe and translated through the dominant Puritan ethic. Outlawing of homosexual acts was common in almost all of the states up through the 1940s, even perceived as a national threat. This resulted in not only a legal response against homosexuality, but exacerbated a rapidly growing social malevolence toward homosexuals. Institutionalized condemnation of homosexual activity has been used to legitimize the condemnation of same-sex activity in cases of spouse benefits, child custody, housing, employment, and so on. The political manipulation of "family" and family values has only further undermined the status of lesbians and gays in America, used to justify withholding marriage, equal rights, and equal opportunity under the law.

Religion in America has played a vital role in both institutionalized and covert acts of discrimination against gays. The Judeo-Christian community has always viewed homosexuality as a sin against nature and a sickness of the soul. Because religious ideology so often reflects social attitudes, it should come as no surprise that religious positions are reflected in the political scene where homosexuals have been identified and treated as outcasts. The homosexual response to their expulsion from the mainstream churches and the religious community was to establish their own churches (e.g., the United Fellowship of Metropolitan Community Churches [UFMCC] in Los Angeles, California), to provide for the religious and spiritual needs of lesbians and gays that organized churches had taken away from them.

A lesbian and gay civil rights movement in the United States emerged during the 1950s when the appearance of the Mattachine Society and the Daughters of Bilitus, both organized to actively pursue equal rights for gays and lesbians and protection under the law. Both of these groups sought to show that lesbians and gays were fundamentally the same as everyone else. Increasing solidarity and organization now characterize the entire gay civil rights movement, which focuses on the unique qualities of lesbian and gay cultures and their unwillingness to accept heterosexual assertions that their homosexuality is a sin or a sickness. Since the late 1960s, many efforts to seek equal rights and protection from discrimination have been focused on the legal system, in the form of lawsuits against the military services, and against heterosexist discrimination in employment, spouse benefits, and housing. Gay newspapers, neighborhood organizations, tavern associations, and organizations at work and church have created a solid movement that resists any violence from the state and gives the gay civil rights movement an ethnically based quality.

Homosexuals are not identifiable because of their color, ethnic background, socioeconomic status, age, gender, language, or any other factors that have been used to distinguish members of other culture groups within the American context. Homosexuality exists on all strata of American society and with all of its other cultural groupings. Homosexuality refers to sexual orientation and erotosexuality. However, the terms "lesbian" and "gay" are peculiar to specific culture groups. One may be homosexual in orientation without acting upon it sexually, or one may be sexually active with same-sex partners but not have contact with the larger gay context, thereby not being culturally lesbian or gay. Once identified as homosexual, both gays and lesbians begin to learn the norms, language, history, and values of lesbian or gay culture. The language and cultural symbols used by the homosexual community serve to distinguish it, which is referred to as gay speak. Beyond language, there are other symbols that gays have appropriated and transformed into positive identifiers, in much the same way that the Christians appropriated the cross as a positive symbol. The pink triangle has emerged as a symbol of the gay rights movement and now is considered a positive symbol of pride, one that is used throughout homosexual representations. Another symbol that has emerged is the rainbow flag, which is used to symbolically represent the diversity of the lesbian and gay cultures, as have certain colors such as pink and lavender. Networking is also important to members of the lesbian or gay cultures. Networking enables various organizations in the community to reach out to individuals and groups to accomplish group goals or to provide aid. In the more formal networking spheres, there are now newspapers, political and social organizations, bars, churches, and businesses that frequently advertise homosexual-oriented activities and resources.

Representing a threat to the dominant ideology, homosexuals have been placed in an adversarial position in their struggle for tolerance and legitimacy. To finally accept homosexuals as a normal facet of contemporary American life will require a dramatic change in the historically based Western ideas of appropriate behavior and norms, as well as an expansion of the gender concept. In the current political and social environment in which other minority groups such as Jews, immigrants, and welfare mothers are being attacked and assigned the role of scapegoat, there is little likelihood that this change will occur. The focus on "family values," a return to traditional morals, and the assertion of dominant heterosexual white male power in this country likely will worsen homosexual problems associated with cultural diversity. Lesbians and gays will be rejected right along with other minority groups, perhaps even more so. It is from this circumstance that an approach to cultural diversity that is actualized in education and community becomes increasingly important. The pain of ostracism and ridicule is all too common for homosexuals who express their identities, and ostracism threatens their ability to be healthy and functional not only within lesbian and gay culture, but in the American culture at large.

Drug Culture(s)

The popular interpretation of *drug culture* generates a narrow, restricted image of people unlike ourselves who engage in illegal and immoral activity. An adequate characterization of drug culture depends on an awareness of the use of medicinal and psychoactive substances. It must be based on the fact that virtually every culture has its own complex system of substance utilization. In America, various scenarios can demonstrate the wide variation in beliefs and behaviors that are in competition, are culturally patterned and that have specific meaning within the cultural context. Meanings are conceived in both the idealized value system of the culture, and as they are operationalized in the reality of daily existence. Historically, humans have used pharmacologically active substances because of their healing properties, to affect health and well-being. Generally speaking, humans have been using various substances for medicinal, spiritual, and recreational purposes for thousands of years.

The most basic psychoactive pharmacopeia that traditionally has been available to various cultures in different regions of the world consists of alcoholic beverages, tobacco products, opium, coca, marijuana, and hallucinogenic plants. No culture utilizes all of these substances, but almost all cultures permit or encourage the use of at least one of them. Alcohol receives the blessing of the American culture as a legally approved, highly psychoactive, and recreational drug. Most Americans drink some form of an alcoholic beverage. The ceremonial and social importance of participation in alcohol consumption as part of the leisure life of American culture can be observed at bars, restaurants, business meetings, and Super Bowl parties. Hallucinogenic substances were first introduced to many Americans in the 1960s (mushrooms, peyote, LSD-25) and a lot of young Americans were bombarded by suggestions to "turn on, tune in, and drop out." This particular message was totally unacceptable to mainstream culture and the government quickly outlawed all of these substances. Tobacco was first used by Native Americans as a hallucinogenic, smoked, chewed, and administered as an enema because of its quick and efficient absorption into the bloodstream. For Americans, tobacco use is perfectly legal and, although attitudes toward it are changing, it is almost universally condoned in this culture. Synthetic drugs, such as the barbiturates and depressants, amphetamines, and other central nervous system stimulants, seem to have a similar history.

The over-the-counter drug industry is one area that does not actually provide many drugs for recreational use, but in the day-to-day reality of the drug business, the over-the-counter industry has an enormous impact on what Americans believe drugs are all about. The idealized cultural value concerning the over-the-counter and prescription medicines is one that is consistent with the most basic meaning of all drug use, namely, that these substances can heal us or improve our state of being. The reality of the legal drug business is that people increasingly believe that it is some substance or drug they need to make them feel better. Almost all Americans are members of the over-the-counter and the prescription drug cultures. Doctors prescribe and most responsible people participate in this culture based on their belief it positively affects their health and well-being. They buy these drugs in the belief that they are ill, that they need them, and that they will be healed by them. Economically it is big money, and politically it is viewed as correct in comparison to those drug cultures identified as illegal.

Illegal drug culture includes both the medically and legally unauthorized use of prescription drugs, as well as the use of substances that are prohibited by law. The common thread in this culture is the illicit nature of the use, but this group is also widely diverse. Marijuana smokers, pill poppers, cocaine snorters, heroin shooters, speed freaks, and vision seekers all believe that their state of well-being will be meaningfully affected in some way as a result of their drug use. Members of this particular drug culture are in quite belligerent competition with nonmembers. This competition has resulted in disagreements over the meaning of drugs and the incarceration of thousands of individuals. These drugs are used recreationally and also as self-prescribed medicines. Heroin addicts frequently may refer to the drug as "my medicine." Economically, it is big business; politically, it is dangerous; legally, it is prohibited; socially, it's rejected; morally, it's wrong.

Religious Cultures

Diversity also comes with the supernatural realm, in the form of groupings based on religions, churches (temples, etc.), and the many new groupings that appear from time to time in America. The most commonly heard distinctions, when discussing religions are those among *denominations*, *sects*, and *cults*. Denominations are major religious groups that have established themselves as acceptable to a society and have become part of its civil religion. A civil religion shapes the worldview of the members of a society by embodying a belief system that incorporates that which comes out of the denominational faiths. In many ways, members of such cultural groupings are the most ethnocentric of all groups simply because religion is based entirely on faith and all associated belief systems are the "ultimate truth." Religion results in a totality of values, ideals, and beliefs based on things people feel strongly about. An adherence to these shared understandings about the proper ways of behaving sets American culture apart from other cultures. This provides identity for both its culture and society. Compared to other societies, America exhibits a variety of denominations. This religious pluralism is primarily a result of the separation of church and state combined with ethnic diversity from immigration.

Splinter groups eventually tend to break away from denominations and form smaller groups called sects. Each sect's doctrines and behaviors depart in some ways from the denomination from which they came, but they continue to retain many of its characteristics. When beliefs go against the fundamentalist doctrine of the larger denomination, a group will be forced to separate and form their own sect. The sect might become sufficiently organized with a well-established doctrine of its own to attract a strong committed membership and become considered a new denomination. Or, it might not be able to establish an organization that can attract and retain members and eventually disperse. Its members also eventually could be reunited with the original denomination since sects, by definition, do not exhibit a significantly different cultural content from that of the established denomination.

The cult is an often heard word in the context of religion for Americans. To the scholars, a culture is another word for revitalization movements. Culture is not fixed, changeless, and universally accepted within any society. Cults play a prominent role as independent movements of culture change. They syncretize, or blend, elements drawn from a variety of sources, both internal and external to the society, religious and secular, and also often create new doctrine not previously known. Cults are characterized by precarious doctrines, a minimal organization, and loose relationships among their members. Yet cults, like sects, also may or may eventually become established denominations. The Church of Latter-Day Saints, or Mormons, initially were considered a cult because their doctrine, while including major Christian beliefs, also contained new, dramatically different precepts. It is now the fastest growing denomination in the world, characterized by its extremely well-organized, large, committed membership.

Cults have deep roots in American history, with a particularly strong increase in numbers since the 1960s, out of the loss of a sense of community and increased secularization within the major denominations. While most explanations are based on assumptions of alienation or deviation, there are positive conditions that allow for the formation of these new innovative groups as well. They introduce vitality into American culture, as the name revitalization implies. Cults whose participants form intentional communities become sufficiently different to warrant calling them separate constituent cultures. Members attempt to transform their physical, social, and psychological environment through alternative lifestyles, exhibiting innovative values and beliefs. This cultural grouping becomes their key source of social-psychological attachment and begins to have more influence on the participants' behavior than does the larger society. Members develop ideas of "in group" versus "out group," and tend to judge others by their standards and values. Depending on the degree to which they are able to separate themselves through such behaviors as a tendency to marry within the group, distinguishing traits such as distinctive dress and vocabulary may develop. It results in further increasing their identity as a cultural grouping.

Intentional religious communities in America vary from one another in beliefs. They may be looked at on a continuum with most falling somewhere in between. On one end, a group may adhere to traditional, authoritarian moral absolutism. In other words, it may sharply distinguish between good and evil, tend toward the politically conservative, and have rigorous expectations regarding social conduct. On the other end, a group may envision an alternative social order, often drawing from Eastern religions and psychotherapy. It may evaluate morality relativistically, be concerned with the importance of individual consciousness, and hope to re-create loving relationships as an extended family. Behaviors generally reflect where a group stands on this belief continuum. Cults usually are perceived negatively regardless of how much Americans voice acceptance of religious pluralism in their society. The public has developed preconceived notions, or stereotypes, of what a cult is that causes them to expect their members to behave in a deviant way. The public's prejudicial attitudes, or derogatory beliefs, toward what they think are cults, often is expressed through discriminatory acts against them. Public fears have forced both state and federal levels of government to consider anticult legislation at one time or another.

Disabilities Cultures

Various cultural groups that are generalized into the disabled culture are significant constituent cultures of American culture and society as well—they suffer the same prejudice and discrimination as do other groups that are somehow different from the power groups. Deaf people, visually impaired, and all those impaired with some other physical condition as is combined within the generalized category represent unique and powerful cultural units within America. That they also have had to face prejudice and discrimination from other groups is attested to in the passage of the American Disabilities Act in the 1990s. Katherine Christensen (1997) demonstrates how deaf people are characterized in the United States and the accommodations they have to make in beliefs, behaviors, and products. Visually impaired individuals can also be characterized as a unique cultural group as well. They are unique because their worldview is, by necessity, visual in nature. Other groups formed by categorizing people together based on some disability are also made up of unique cultural groupings. The tendency to simply categorize all such people in one social group does a disservice to the unique circumstances of the real groupings that have simply been collapsed into the disabilities category. All of them are powerful because of their vehement refusal to allow the discrimination.

Cultural Scenes

Within the category of special interest groups are others termed cultural scenes. These kinds of groupings reflect special interests, but unlike the special groups evolving around the organizational interests of America that reflect a permanency, they function on a limited or recurrent time basis, are somewhat unbounded, and help people define aspects of their experience (Spradley & McCurdy 1972). While these authors saw cultural scenes simply as a reflection of the many subgroups of the complex society, and as an indication of the multiculturalism of individuals within these societies, cultural scenes are just another form of cultural grouping in the complexity of modern society. They involve shared beliefs, behaviors, and products as do the other groupings already discussed. Perhaps the real distinction of these groups lies in the bounded nature of them. They function sporadically, for specified lengths of time, and sometimes in space as well. There are hundreds of such groupings in the complex society, but the most prominent are those associated with the age groupings (e.g., generational, teenager, college student, retired, etc.), economic groupings (e.g., the lower, middle and upper classes, the homeless, so-called culture of poverty, etc.), groups formed around health questions (e.g., AIDS, cancer, heart problems, etc.), musical taste, and many more. The particular interests and purposes of such groups frequently compete with those of the other groupings previously discussed. For that reason alone, and the fact that they do represent still more complexity in the diversity of modern nation-states, they cannot be left out of the discussion.

The biggest difficulties associated with these kinds of cultural groups come with their fluid membership and that they are time limited. For the age groupings, an individual's membership is prescribed and comes to an end when the individual no longer fits within the age designations. While classified in the group, the individual shares beliefs with others of the same age and engage in the behaviors determined (albeit informally) acceptable to peers. In the case of something like generational groups, a philosophy of life, style of living, making a statement might be involved. Except in the case of Generation X, the Yuppies Generation, an association of retired persons, the individual may simply perceive themselves as part of a group, be seen as part of the group, but may not actively participate in activities involving many others also associated with it. Homeless people learn beliefs and behaviors tied to their survival on the street from older members of this group, just as culture is taught within other cultural groupings. The middle class is distinguished from the upper class by the beliefs and behaviors exemplified with the socioeconomic class. Movement from one level to another is possible and the individual's association is not considered a permanent. Everyone in America is aware of the major differences in attitudes and behaviors of the various class groupings. The many cultural groups organized around people with similar health conditions are well known. While considered a member of the group by virtue of their particular condition(s), they frequently must learn very specific beliefs and behaviors as part of the effort to overcome it. A great many special interest groups have evolved as support groups for these particular cultural scenes.

Cultural scenes are constituent cultural groups that contribute to the cultural diversity of America. They exist for the same reasons other cultural groups exist, to pursue their own particular interests or purposes, and their members share beliefs and behaviors that distinguish them from others. They also learn their truths and thus they provide another element of complexity and conflict in the modern society. Generations are always in conflict. The socioeconomic classes are always in conflict. Groups tied to health issues are always in conflict by virtue of competing for recognition and funds. One of the most interesting things about cultural scenes is that their characteristics can change as their turnover of membership is a constant phenomenon, the primary justification for distinguishing them from the special interest groups tied to organizational activities. Those groups change, but display a permanency that seems to elude the cultural scene.

SUGGESTED READINGS

Naylor, L. L. (ed.). 1997. *Cultural Diversity in the United States*. Westport, CT: Bergin & Garvey. This collection of readings represents one of the first efforts to cover the cultural diversity of the United States, covering examples of all those racial, ethnic, and special interest cultures that combine to make up the multicultural context of American culture. Many of the articles referred to in this chapter will be found among the contributors to this introduction into the real cultural diversity of America.

Spindler, G. and Spindler, L. 1993. *The American Cultural Dialogue and Its Transmission*. Bristol, PA: Falmer Press. The authors emphasize values of individuality, freedom, community, equality, and success being as at the center of the American mainstream to which all groups in the United States aspire. They also present the viewpoints of black and Chicano racial groups on this mainstream and good treatment of how groups not part of the dominant cultural group scene attempt to adapt to it.

Tiersky, E. and Tiersky, M. 1975. *The U.S.A.—Customs and Institutions: A Survey of American Culture and Traditions*. New York: Regents Publishing Company. This is an advanced reader primarily designed for non-Americans needing to understand the ways of Americans. The authors discuss many different aspects of American culture and life, emphasizing the role of immigrant groups in American life. Good introduction to the patterns and attitudes of Americans. This volume is particularly good for helping people understand the various ceremonies of America, their dietary habits, educational system, religious attributes, and leisure activities.

POSTSCRIPT

Throughout this volume, the point has been made that there is something that can be called American culture. It exists in the beliefs, practices, and products (both material and social) that all Americans share regardless of other cultural affiliations they recognize for themselves. All Americans share the same orienting ideas on which the country was founded and they all must adhere to behavioral expectations (prerequisite behaviors and a single law), and they all share the same institutional structures and organizational systems for meeting their needs and wants. Americans share the same set of orienting ideas as laid out in their founding documents and embodied in the American Dream. Members of all cultural groups subscribe to this embodiment and pursue it for themselves and their groups. The American dream is not a fixed thing, but a fluid standard that allows for gradations and provides that no level of achievement of the Dream is ever enough. But every American and every constituent group that combines to make up the whole of American society subscribes to it and pursues it. Every immigrant to the shores of the United States comes for it and enters its pursuit. The dream revolves around, and focuses on, freedom and individuality, diversity and conformity, all at the same time. More important, it is used to measure the individual's success in this world. It accounts for the intense competition among individuals, it accounts for the competitiveness among constituent groups of Americans, it accounts for the paradoxes in the culture (differences in the ideal and real cultural form) with which they have to live, and the conflicts between them as individuals and groups.

That Americans do not share all the same beliefs and behaviors is obvious. This is a product of the complexity, fragmentation, and specialization of the complex nation-state. As the human population grew larger, and these things took on greater importance, the unity of belief and practice that characterized the traditional society and cultural group had to give way to differences in perspectives, opinions, beliefs, and behaviors. The large and diversified populations, with differing interests, goals and purposes goals, were bound to conflict. Social stratification among the many constituent groups that characterize such states was inevitable as the developing groups found themselves competing for place and prominence. Even more cultural groups evolved through which the needs of the individual, the many groups and the society at large were to be met. Each of these groups is convinced of the rightness of their beliefs. Each has unquestioned faith in their truth. Each attempts to impose that truth on others. While Americans believe in diversity for themselves, they deny it for others. While Americans are motivated by the demand for individualism, they quickly group everyone else into social categories and then prescribe inequality onto them. To that end, Americans have created racial, ethnic, social, and cultural groups by categorizing people, generalizing them into artificial groups based on certain characteristics or attributes (physical or cultural) whether the people being grouped actually share anything at all, represent an interacting group of people or not. The groups created are then viewed as something less desirable than the groups to which they affiliate and institutionalized inequality then emerges that touches and affects all groups.

A significant start toward a better understanding and awareness of the real cultural diversity that exists in America comes with recognizing the difference between social groupings (minorities, races, ethnic categories) and actual cultural groupings. The diversity of American culture comes with all the various groupings that together make up the whole of it and this diversity is generally recognized by Americans and non-Americans alike. Diversity lies at the heart of its social and organizational structures. The tendency of Americans to categorize all people into various social groupings, assign them a fictive culture, and a place in American society is widespread. This tendency only hides the real cultural differences that make for a diverse society such as the United States. Everyone recognizes diversity as a significant part of what characterizes American culture, but to really understand all the actual diversity that characterizes this culture and the conflicts among the many constituent cultural groups that together make for it, will not be easy.

The social problems and conflicts that accompany diversity reflect the conflicts between the many constituent cultural groups that make up the American scene. The vocabulary that accompanies diversity (discrimination, prejudice, racism, sexism, social inequities), is more than just words, it characterizes the relations among the many groups in that diversity. Cultural groups exist whenever human groupings learn ways of belief and behavior that distinguish them. The United States is a cultural group because of the shared ideas, behaviors, and products that distinguish it from other nation-states. At the same time, there are serious differences born of the various constituent cultural groupings of the United States.

Throughout this volume, you have been taken through only a small portion of American (U.S.) culture. By now you must recognize that this discussion hardly represents all of the American story, particularly in regards to the total diversity that characterizes it. What has been presented within these pages represents little more than a beginning that can serve as a catalyst for discussion. But that has been the goal of this volume—to help people begin the process of learning more about this culture and the diversity that is its chief characteristic, its strength, and its greatest challenge. Understanding the American culture means understanding its historical foundations, context, and the multitude of ethnic, racial, and special interest groups that evolved to make America such a multicultural society. The greatest challenge to America and Americans is to accommodate to its social and cultural diversity. Appreciation for this culture will come when its people accept the legitimacy of all cultural groupings and recognize that the very diversity that characterizes it must be separated from the dilemma of who has power and who does not. This will be accomplished when people of various cultural groups accept one another as equal constituents of the whole, interact with people representing other groups, as they learn to listen to each other and try to perceive things from the point of view of the other. It will be accomplished when people come to realize that everyone is alike and different at the same time. People are not necessarily wrong or bad because of it—just different. People need to recognize and understand that their particular perspectives and opinions reflect the ethnocentrisms they obtain from the groups with which they associate. Judging others based on that leads to the many problems still to be resolved in this land and among its peoples. Education can begin this process, but it is the individual who must carry it through by making it a pervasive element in their lives. The individual must experience all that is America.

Cultures in contact produce conflicts. Culture is truth. It is what humans know, and once learned, it will be strongly believed, defended, and the measure of all other cultures. There is an American culture, indeed, perhaps it is the epitome of the nation-state structure that now dominates the modern world as it moves into the twenty-first century. Understanding this culture may help us understand others and provide us with better skills in interacting with them. The diversity experienced in America is not unlike that found in every nation-state where social categories are created out of a single trait, a common physical characteristic, a common language, or a particular belief or practice (real or imaginary). Such groups do not represent the real diversity of America or the world, but they are part of it. The real diversity comes with specific cultural groupings of people who learn and share beliefs, practices, and the products. Cultural diversity is based more on cultural differences, differences between groups that learn different things that then distinguish them from others. Many of the arbitrarily created social (categorized) groups become cultural groups in the context of the state. Although such differences have probably always been with us since the development of civilization, the importance and significance of them have probably never been greater than it is now, nor has it ever posed such a threat. The complexity of modern nations has left us with this legacy and it will be with us for generations to come. The question is not whether such diversity exists, but whether our inability to come to terms with it might somehow lead to our demise as a species, as Americans, as humans, or as individuals. The greatest threat to humanity comes with ethnocentrism, the belief that only our truth as learned in our own cultural groupings should be allowed. It comes with our individual and group convictions that our truth should be for everyone, imposed on them if need be, that our truth should be everyone's truth.

As the globalization of the planet continues, modern nations will grow even more complex, and the number of cultural groups, with their differences and contacts with one another, the conflicts among them them, will intensify. But it is also important to remind ourselves of the achievements of our distant ancestors and the richness of what has come to pass because of them. One would like to think that cultural difference does not have to mean conflict. At this point in time it does because cultural groups who exercise their truth, beliefs, and practices keep trying to impose them on everybody else. If we de-emphasize the differences and reemphasize the similarities among all humans, perhaps even Americans will reach their ideal goal of equality and opportunity. Despite someone's physical appearance, despite his or her preferences in religion, despite different customs, particular beliefs, or specific interests, people are all alike. One on one, perhaps we can learn that from each other.

BIBLIOGRAPHY

Althen, G. 1988. *American Ways: A Guide for Foreigners in the United States*. Yarmouth MA: Intercultural Press.

Arens, W. and Montague, S. P. 1976. *The American Dimension: Cultural Myths and Social Realities*. Port Washington, NY: Alfred Publishing Co.

Arensberg, C. M. and Niehoff, A. H. 1971. American cultural values. In *Introducing Culture Change*. Chicago: Aldine.

Barrett, R. A. 1984. *Culture and Conduct*. 2d edition. Belmont, CA: Wadsworth Publishing.

Bellah, R. N., Madsen, R., Sullivan, W. M., Swidler, A., and Tipton, S. M. 1991. *The Good Society*. New York: Random House (Vintage Books).

Bureau of the Census. 1992a. *1990 Census of Population. General Population Characteristics United States*. Washington, D.C.: Government Printing Office.

———. 1992b. *1990 Census of Population and Housing Summary. Social, Economic, and Housing Characteristics United States*. Washington, D.C.: Government Printing Office.

———. 1996. *Total Abstract of the United States*. May 1995. Internet: www.census.gov.

Cambridge, C. 1997. American Indians: The forgotten minority. In *Cultural Diversity in the United States*. Naylor, L. L. (ed.). Westport, CT: Bergin & Garvey, pp. 195–209.

Carneiro, R. L. 1970. "A Theory of the Origin of the State." *Science*, August 21, 1970: 733.

Cerroni-Long, E. L. 1993. Life and cultures: The test of real participant observation. In *Distant Mirrors: America as a Foreign Culture*. DeVita, P. R. and Armstrong, J. D. (eds.). Belmont, CA: Wadsworth Publishing, pp. 77–92.

Christensen, K. M. 1997. Deaf American culture: Notes from the periphery. In *Cultural Diversity in the United States*. Naylor, L. L. (ed.). Westport: Bergin & Garvey, pp. 271–277.

Clay, J. W. 1990. "What's a Nation?" *Mother Jones* 15(7):28.

Crunden, R. M. 1994. *A Brief History of American Culture*. New York: Paragon House.

DeVita, P. R. and Armstrong, J. D. (eds.). 1993. *Distant Mirrors: America as a Foreign Culture*. Belmont, CA: Wadsworth Publishing.

Downs, J. F. 1975. *Cultures in Crisis*. 2d edition. Beverly Hills, CA: Glencoe Press.

Drechsel, E. J. 1993. A European anthropologist's impression of the United States. In *Distant Mirrors: America as a Foreign Culture*. DeVita, P. R. and Armstrong, J. D. (eds.). Belmont, CA: Wadsworth Publishing, pp. 120–145.

Dundes, A. 1975. Seeing is believing. In *The Nacirema: Readings on American Culture*. Spradley, J. P. and Rynkiewich, M. A. (eds.). Boston: Little, Brown and Co., pp. 14–19.

Dussart, F. 1993. First impressions: Diary of a French Anthropologist in New York City. In *Distant Mirrors: America as a Foreign Culture*. DeVita, P. R. and Armstrong, J. D. (eds.). Belmont, CA: Wadsworth Publishing, pp. 66–76.

Fagan, B. M. 1991. *Ancient North America: The Archaeology of a Continent*. New York: Thames and Hudson.

Freilich, M. (ed.). 1972. *The Meaning of Culture*. Lexington: Xerox College Publishing.

Gamst, F. C. and Norbeck, E. 1976. *Ideas of Culture: Sources and Uses*. New York: Holt, Rinehart and Winston.

Garretson, L. R. 1976. *American Culture: An Anthropological Perspective*. Dubuque, IA: Wm. C. Brown.

Gibbs, T. 1997. Portrait of a minority. In *Cultural Diversity in the United States*. Naylor, L. L. (ed.). Westport, CT: Bergin & Garvey, pp. 91–102.

Green, S. W. and Perlman, S. M. 1997. Education, diversity, and American culture. In *Cultural Diversity in the United States*. Naylor, L. L. (ed.). Westport, CT: Bergin & Garvey, pp. 317–328.

Hall, E. T. and Hall, M. R. 1990. *Understanding Cultural Differences*. Garden City, NY: Intercultural Press.

Haviland, W. A. 1997. *Anthropology*. 8th edition. Fort Worth, TX: Harcourt Brace College Publishers.

Henry, J. 1974. A theory for an anthropological analysis of American culture. In *Anthropology and American Life*. Jorgensen, J. G. and Truzzi, M. (eds.). Englewood Cliffs, NJ: Prentice-Hall, pp. 6–22.

Higley, S. R. 1995. *Power, Privilege and Place: Geography of the American Upper Class*. Roman and Littlefield (Univ. Press of America).

Hogan-Garcia, M. 1997. African-Americans as a cultural group. In *Cultural Diversity in the United States*. Naylor, L. L. (ed.). Westport, CT: Bergin & Garvey, pp. 145–158.

Hsu, F. 1972. American core value and national character. In *Psychological Anthropology*. Cambridge, MA: Schenkman, pp. 241–262.

Jorgenson, J. G. and Truzzi, M. (eds.). 1974. *Anthropology and American Life*. Englewood Cliffs, NJ: Prentice-Hall.

Kim, J. K. 1991. American graffiti: Curious derivatives of individualism. In *Distant Mirrors: America as a Foreign Culture*. DeVita, P. R. and Armstrong, J. D. (eds.) Belmont: Wadsworth, pp. 11–20.

Kroeber, A. and Kluckhohn, C. 1952. *Culture: A Critical Review of Concepts and Definitions*. Papers of the Peabody Museum of American Archaeology and Ethnology, Vol. 1. Cambridge: Harvard University Press.

Leacock, E. and Lurie, N. 1971. *North American Indians in Historical Perspective*. New York: Random House.

Martin, K. P. 1997. Diversity orientations: Culture, ethnicity, and race. In *Cultural Diversity in the United States*. Naylor, L. L. (ed.). Westport, CT: Bergin & Garvey, pp. 75–89.

Montague, S. P. and Arens, W. 1981. *The American Dimension: Cultural Myths and Social Realities*. 2d edition. Sherman Oaks, CA: Alfred Publishing.

Mucha, J. L. 1991. An outsider's view of American culture. In *Distant Mirrors: America as a Foreign Culture*. DeVita, P. R. and Armstrong, J. D. (eds.). Belmont, CA: Wadsworth Publishing, pp. 21–28.

Mufwene, S. S. 1993. Forms of address: How their social functions may vary. In *Distant Mirrors: America as a Foreign Culture*. DeVita, P. R. and Armstrong, J. D. (eds.). Belmont, CA: Wadsworth Publishing, pp. 60–65.

Nash, D. 1993. *A Little Anthropology*. 2d edition. Englewood Cliffs, NJ: Prentice-Hall.

Natadecha-Sponsel, P. 1991. The young, the rich, and the famous: Individualism as an American cultural value. In *Distant Mirrors: America as a Foreign Culture*. DeVita, P. R. and Armstrong, J. D. (eds.). Belmont, CA: Wadsworth Publishing, pp. 46–53.

Naylor, L. L. 1996. *Culture and Change: An Introduction*. Westport, CT: Bergin & Garvey.

————(ed.). 1997. *Cultural Diversity in the United States*. Westport, CT: Bergin & Garvey.

Ojeda, A. B. 1993. Growing up American: Doing the right thing. In *Distant Mirrors: America as a Foreign Culture*. DeVita, P. R. and Armstrong, J. D. (eds.). Belmont, CA: Wadsworth Publishing, pp. 54–59.

Orion, L. 1995. *Never Again the Burning Times: Paganism Revisited*. Prospect Heights, IL: Waveland Press.

Pinxten, R. 1993. America for Americans. In *Distant Mirrors: America as a Foreign Culture*. DeVita, P. R. and Armstrong, J. D. (eds.). Belmont, CA: Wadsworth Publishing, pp. 93–102.

Potter, D. 1993. In *The American Cultural Dialogue and its Transmission*. Spindler, G. and Spindler, L. (eds.). Bristol, PA: Falmer Press.

Ramos, F. M. 1991. My American glasses. In *Distant Mirrors: America as a Foreign Culture*. DeVita, P. R. and Armstrong, J. D. (eds.). Belmont, CA: Wadsworth Publishing, pp. 1–10.

Re Cruz, A. 1997. The Mexican-American community in the United States. In *Cultural Diversity in the United States*. Naylor, L. L. (ed.). Westport, CT: Bergin & Garvey, pp. 159–175.

Roberts, S. 1995. *Who We Are: A Portrait of America Today Based on the Latest U.S. Census*. New York: Random House.

Rogers, T. 1997. Of prejudice and pride. In *Cultural Diversity in the United States*. Naylor, L. L. (ed.). Westport, CT: Bergin & Garvey, pp. 229–243.

Salamone, F. 1997. The illusion of ethnic identity: An introduction to ethnicity and its uses. In *Cultural Diversity in the Unites States*. Naylor, L. L. (ed.). Westport, CT: Bergin & Garvey, pp. 117–126.

Schneider, D. M. 1968. *American Kinship: A Cultural Account*. Englewood Cliffs, NJ: Prentice-Hall.

Seidman, S. 1994. *Contested Knowledge*. Oxford: Basil Blackwell.

Shu-min, H. 1991. A cross-cultural experience: A Chinese anthropologist in the United States. In *Distant Mirrors: America as a Foreign Culture*. DeVita, P. R. and Armstrong, J. D. (eds.). Belmont, CA: Wadsworth Publishing, pp. 39–45.

Siegler, G. 1997. New religous movements. In *Cultural Diversity in the United States*. Naylor, L. L. (ed.). Westport, CT: Bergin & Garvey, pp. 259–270.

Spindler, G. (ed.). 1963. *Education and Culture: Anthropological Approaches*. New York: Holt, Rinehart and Winston.

Spindler, G. and Spindler, L. 1993. *The American Cultural Dialogue and Its Transmission*. Bristol, PA: Falmer Press.

Spradley, J. P. and McCurdy, D. 1972. *The Cultural Experience*. Prospect Heights, IL: Waveland Press.

Spradley, J. P. and Rynkiewich, M. A. (eds.). 1975. *The Nacirema: Readings on American Culture*. Boston: Little, Brown and Co.

Starrett, S. N. 1997. Gender identity: Unity through diversity. In *Cultural Diversity in the United States*. Naylor, L. L. (ed.). Westport, CT: Bergin & Garvey, pp. 215–228.

158 Bibliography

Stewart, E. C. and Bennett, M. J. 1991. *American Cultural Patterns: A Cross-Cultural Perspective*. Revised edition. Yarmouth, MA: Intercultural Press.

Tiersky, E. and Tiersky, M. 1975. *The U.S.A.—Customs and Institutions: A Survey of American Culture and Traditions*. New York: Regents Publishing Company.

United States Department of Commerce. 1995. *Statistical Abstract of the United States:* Washington, D.C.: U.S. Printing Office.

Varene, H. 1993. America and I. In *Distant Mirrors: America as a Foreign Culture*. DeVita, P. R. and Armstrong, J. D. (eds.). Belmont, CA: Wadsworth Publishing, pp. 29–38.

Wasserfall, R. 1993. Gender encounters in America: An outsider's view of continuity and ambivalence. In *Distant Mirrors: America as a Foreign Culture*. DeVita, P. R. and Armstrong, J. D. (eds.). Belmont, CT: Wadsworth, Publishing, pp. 103–111.

White, L. 1959. The Concept of Culture. *American Anthropologist,* 61(2): 227–251.

Wilcox, D. M. 1997. Drug culture: Everybody uses something. In *Cultural Diversity in the United States*. Naylor, L. L. (ed.). Westport, CT: Bergin & Garvey, pp. 245–258.

Williams, N. 1997. Multiculturalism: Issues for the twenty-first century. In *Cultural Diversity in the United States*. Naylor, L. L. (ed.). Westport, CT: Bergin & Garvey, pp. 25–33.

Yang, H. 1993. Neighborly strangers. In *Distant Mirrors: America as a Foreign Culture*. DeVita, P. R. and Armstrong, J. D. (eds.). Belmont, CA: Wadsworth Publishing, pp. 112–119.

INDEX

About the Author

LARRY L. NAYLOR is a professor of anthropology, Institute of Anthropology, University of North Texas. He is the author of *Culture and Change: An Introduction* (Bergin & Garvey, 1996) and editor of *Cultural Diversity in the United States* (Bergin & Garvey, 1997).